Kingston Frontenac PL/ARPs

100 Y
100 M

EARS
MENTS

A CENTENNIAL OF NHL HOCKEY

1917 NHL 2017

SCOTT MORRISON

McCLELLAND & STEWART

Copyright © 2017 by NHL Enterprises, L.P.
Text copyright © 2017 Morrison Media Inc.

NHL, the NHL Shield and the word mark and image of the
Stanley Cup are registered trademarks and the NHL Centennial
Season logo is a trademark of the National Hockey League. All
NHL logos and marks and NHL team logos and marks depicted
herein are the property of the NHL and the respective teams and
may not be reproduced without the prior written consent of NHL
Enterprises, L.P. © NHL 2017. All rights reserved.
Hardcover edition published 2017

McClelland & Stewart and colophon are
registered trademarks of McClelland & Stewart

All rights reserved. The use of any part of this publication
reproduced, transmitted in any form or by any means, electronic,
mechanical, photocopying, recording, or otherwise, or stored in a
retrieval system, without the prior written consent of the
publisher—or, in case of photocopying or other reprographic
copying, a licence from the Canadian Copyright Licensing
Agency—is an infringement of the copyright law.

Library and Archives Canada Cataloguing in Publication is
available upon request

Published simultaneously in the United States of America
by McClelland & Stewart, a division of Penguin Random House
LLC, a Penguin Random House Company

Library of Congress Control Number is available
upon request

ISBN: 978-0-7710-5121-0
ebook ISBN: 978-0-7710-5122-7

Edited by Craig Pyette
Book design by Jennifer Lum
Typeset in Adobe Caslon Pro by M&S, Toronto
Printed and bound in the USA

McClelland & Stewart,
a division of Penguin Random House Canada Limited,
a Penguin Random House Company
www.penguinrandomhouse.ca

1 2 3 4 5   21 20 19 18 17

Penguin
Random House
McCLELLAND & STEWART

CONTENTS

INTRODUCTION

A century of the National Hockey League is a lot of hockey.

A lot of great moments and memories, innovation and evolution. For all the ways players and coaches have reimagined taking the puck on a stick, skating it down a sheet of ice, and shooting it into a net, some things about the game never change.

The elegance, the ferocity, the speed: NHL hockey has left indelible memories with generations of hockey fans in North America and, increasingly, around the world. Over the past 100 years, the NHL has had so many of those "where were you?" moments and performances, some that are deeply enshrined in the fans' collective consciousness.

While other moments were quieter, their impact perhaps less notable at the time, they nonetheless played a significant role in the shaping of the game.

The NHL has grown from four teams in its beginning in 1917, to 31 as it closes its centenary and enters its 101st year, each club in determined pursuit of one of the oldest and toughest trophies to win in all of professional sports—the Stanley Cup.

No single volume could capture every significant memory from a century of hockey, but we have collected here 100 of the best, focusing on the top moments, developments, players, executives, coaches, teams, arenas, trades—you name it—that impacted the league's history.

We have tried to explain the changes that occurred in the game as it developed and grew over the years, from the early years through to the Original Six, several expansions, dynasties, and the onset of parity.

You'll read about some of the greatest players who ever played the game and their marvellous feats—the likes of Gordie Howe and Wayne Gretzky, Bobby Orr and Mario Lemieux, King Clancy and Maurice (Rocket) Richard, Sidney Crosby and the young players now trying to live up to the standards set by him and all of these great athletes before him.

Hockey means different things to different people. In the United States, especially in northern cities like Boston and Detroit, love for the game runs deep, and fans' passion for their team has become a part of those people's identities. You'll read about the spread of that passion, from cities like

New York and Chicago, across the northern states and deep into the South, where hockey has taken root in the most southern locales, inspiring kids to learn how to chase a puck and dream of one day playing in the NHL (maybe even scoring a record number of goals in their big-league debut).

In Canada, fans take that passion one step further. From Vancouver to Winnipeg, Montreal to Toronto, hockey seems inseparable from the identity of an entire nation. But no matter where you are, in North America or the many nations in Europe and abroad where the NHL's heroes grew up and learned to play, passion for the game has endured over a century and still runs strong.

You'll understand exactly where that passion comes from—if you don't already—once you've read about the extraordinary moments that define these one hundred remarkable years of the NHL.

A project like this book is a major undertaking, of course. As such, there are major thank-yous due to so many people, starting with my all-star team—Lance Hornby, Tim Wharnsby, and John Whaley. All three have been colleagues at various stages of our careers. Hornby and Wharnsby are two of the top

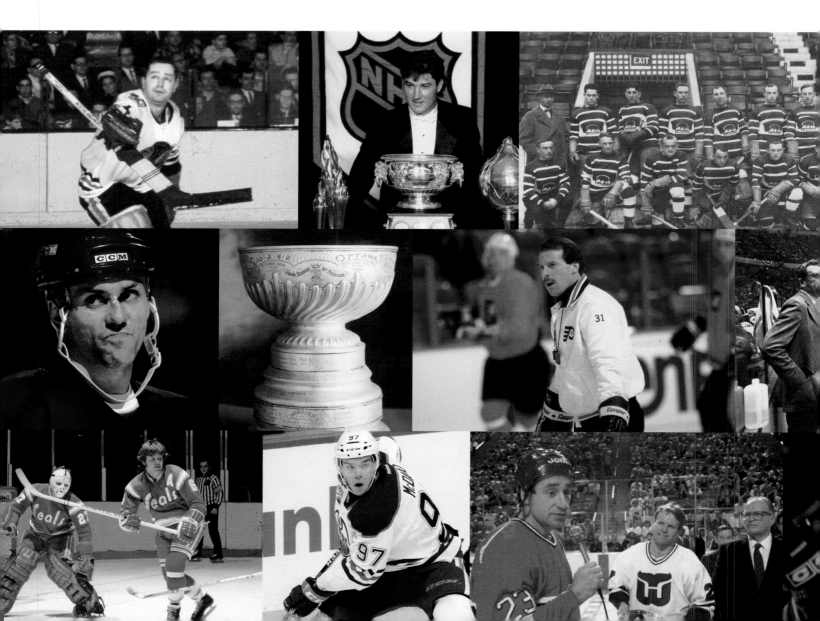

hockey journalists anywhere. Whaley is gifted producer and writer. All three played a major role in assembling this book.

Thanks also to the publishing team, starting with Craig Pyette, the patient and meticulous guiding hand, who saw the project through from the beginning. Lloyd Davis added polish, a big dose of his own passion for the game, and a keen eye for historical detail. Kimberlee Hesas kept the whole operation on track. Joe Lee helped ably whenever needed. Jennifer Lum provided the design. Craig Campbell and Steve Poirier of the Hockey Hall of Fame were a great help with the photos.

A special thanks to the good folks at the NHL, starting with Jennifer Kallas, Manager, Consumer Products Licencing; Mark Jacobson, who helped shape the list of 100 moments; and Stuart McComish, who was a tremendous help with his knowledge, research, and historical files.

It took a long time to make these many memories. I hope you enjoy them.

Scott Morrison

1

THE DONATION OF THE STANLEY CUP

The ancestry of hockey's greatest prize begins a long way from its current home in the Hockey Hall of Fame in Toronto.

Frederick Arthur Stanley was born in 1841 in London, England, the second son of Edward Stanley, 14th Earl of Derby and three times the prime minister of the United Kingdom.

Frederick was raised amid the privilege one would expect of British nobility, educated at the best schools, and steered toward a life of power and wealth. It was a life completely different from the ones lived by the rough-and-tumble farm boys and labourers who were learning to play a new game across the Atlantic Ocean, in Britain's Canadian colonies.

After a varied career in the British military and House of Commons, Stanley was offered the post of Governor General of Canada in 1888, and along with his wife, Constance, and family of eight sons and two daughters, he jumped at the chance, settling in Ottawa.

The Stanleys fell in love with the burgeoning country, and two of his sons became enchanted with the game of hockey, forming a team called the Rideau Rebels after the

governor general's official residence. One of the sons, Arthur, went even further, eventually helping to found the Ontario Hockey Association in 1890, the first organization that would govern the game and declare a champion.

Frederick Stanley could hardly ignore his sons' interest in hockey, and in 1892 he donated a trophy to be presented to "the championship hockey club of the Dominion of Canada." It was purchased from a silversmith in London, England, for 10 guineas, about $1,200 in today's dollars. On one side was engraved DOMINION HOCKEY CHALLENGE CUP, and on the other, FROM STANLEY OF PRESTON.

The first champion, in 1893, was the Montreal Hockey Club, affiliated with the Montreal Amateur Athletic Association. The team earned the trophy after compiling the best record in the Amateur Hockey Association of Canada, a small circuit of teams based in Montreal, Ottawa, and Quebec City. The first challenge came two years later, from Queen's University, who failed to wrest the Cup away, and in 1896 the Winnipeg Victorias became the first challengers to win it.

Lord Stanley's vision had come to fruition, and as the years passed, with teams from Victoria, British Columbia,

Lord Stanley of Preston donated the Dominion Hockey Challenge
Cup in 1892 while serving as the Governor General of Canada from
1888 to 1893. (Hockey Hall of Fame)

and Dawson City, Yukon Territory, issuing challenges, the pursuit of his Cup became truly national.

Back then, it was only a bowl, about eight inches tall and made of silver. The ensuing 125 years have seen it grow in stature, both physically and in mystique.

Today's Stanley Cup is nearly three feet tall and weighs 34½ pounds. The bowl—a replica, as the original has been retired and resides in the Hockey Hall of Fame—sits atop tiers of silver-plated bands engraved with the names of every player to have ever won the Cup. The oldest bands are replaced when another needs to be added.

And fittingly for a trophy named for a British earl, the Cup has its traditions. It is presented on the ice, in front of the fans, and, since 1950 to the captain of the winning team— not a team owner, as is the case with North America's other major sports. It is paraded around the arena, held aloft, passed from one player to the next, in an order of significance determined by the players.

And before they leave the ice, teams now gather around it, in their uniforms, still dripping with sweat, for a picture to capture the moment.

Over the summer, championship-winning players each get to spend a day with the Cup, to share it with family and friends in any manner they choose. It has held newborn babies in its bowl, been paraded around cities all over the world, and been carried to the tops of mountains.

Demanding 16 playoff victories in as many as 28 playoff games to claim it, the Stanley Cup is not only the oldest trophy in professional sports, but arguably the toughest to win.

The Stanley Cup trophy as it appeared in the 1926-27 NHL season—the first time that only NHL teams competed for the cup. (Hockey Hall of Fame)

2

THE FOUNDING OF THE NHL

In large part, the National Hockey League was founded because of a series of disputes and battles between the owners in its predecessor, the National Hockey Association (NHA).

One in particular, Eddie Livingstone, who owned the Toronto Blueshirts, was widely despised by the other five owners in the league.

In the 1916–17 season, the NHA consisted of the Montreal Wanderers, Montreal Canadiens, Ottawa Senators, Quebec Bulldogs, the Blueshirts, and a second Toronto team composed of enlisted men in the 228th Battalion of the Canadian Expeditionary Force. That season, and throughout the following summer, Livingstone was at the centre of several controversies and lawsuits, at one point threatened to start his own league, and even had his team dropped from the league.

Finally, in early November 1917, rumours began to surface that the NHA owners were considering starting a new league, effectively to distance themselves from Livingstone. After a meeting on November 10, the NHA owners decided to suspend operations.

They claimed World War I had depleted the league of too many quality players to continue. However, at a meeting in Montreal on November 22, called at the suggestion of the Quebec Hockey Club, they gathered to "ascertain if some steps could not be taken to perpetuate the game of hockey." Livingstone, and not the war, had been the owners' real concern.

Four days later, on November 26, 1917, the owners of the Wanderers, Canadiens, Senators, and Bulldogs announced after a meeting at the Windsor Hotel in Montreal that they were going to "unite to compose the National Hockey League," with a fifth team awarded to new ownership in Toronto. Ironically, Quebec announced that it would not ice a team during the inaugural season, so with the new Toronto franchise, operated by the owners of that city's Arena Gardens, the NHL was born as a four-team league.

By launching the NHL, the owners had parted ways with Livingstone, whose threats of starting his own league proved hollow, though more legal action followed.

When Toronto joined the NHL, Quebec allowed its players to be taken over by the league at a cost of $700 and divided among the remaining teams. Frank Calder was elected president and secretary-treasurer at an annual salary of $800.

Frank Calder, elected as the first National Hockey League president in 1917–18 through 1941–42, taken at the NHL office in Montreal, Quebec. (Le Studio du Hockey/Hockey Hall of Fame)

On December 19, 1917, the first two games in NHL history were played, with the Wanderers beating Toronto, 10–9, in a game played at the Montreal Arena, while the Canadiens defeated the Senators, 7–4. In that game, Joe Malone, whom the Canadiens had obtained after Quebec suspended operations, scored five goals. He went on to score an incredible 44 goals in 20 games that season. Malone would play just a handful of games in 1918–19 because he landed a job that offered more security and made him more money than playing in the NHL.

The 1917–18 season was also notable because the Wanderers, who were managed and coached by Art Ross, played just four games—losing three in a row after the opening-night win against Toronto—before a fire on January 2, 1918 destroyed the Montreal Arena, which the Wanderers and Canadiens shared.

The NHL board of governors convened for a meeting on January 3, during which the Wanderers withdrew their franchise. Owner Sam Lichtenhein claimed he was losing too much money. A few days later, the Wanderers' membership in the league was officially terminated, after the club failed to "present its team at Toronto on January 5 to meet the Arena Gardens team," and a schedule for a three-team league was adopted for the balance of the season.

The Canadiens, meanwhile, were able to borrow new equipment and moved to the Jubilee Arena.

Back then, the NHL champion played the champion of the rival Pacific Coast Hockey Association (PCHA), run by Frank and Lester Patrick, for the Stanley Cup. That first season, the Toronto Arenas won the NHL title and went on to beat the Vancouver Millionaires in the best-of-five Stanley Cup final.

Joe Malone played for the Montreal Canadiens in one of the first two NHL games, held on December 19, 1917. (Hockey Hall of Fame)

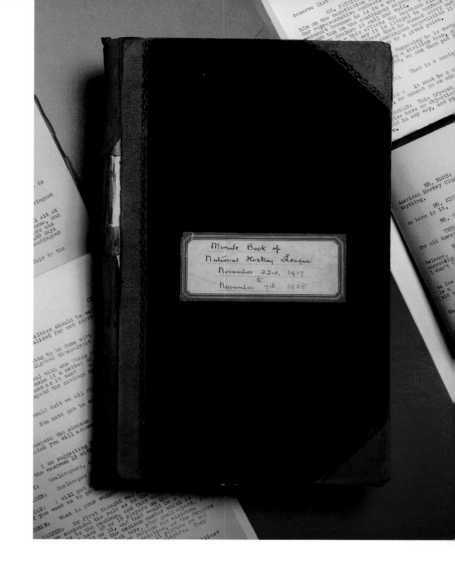

The original record book of NHL business.
(Matthew Manor/Hockey Hall of Fame)

With the war raging on, the league still found it difficult to find talented players, and as a result, attendance was sluggish.

The game itself was wildly different from what it became in the modern era. Forward passing was not allowed, and there were no zones on the ice. Minor penalties were three minutes in duration but substitutes could take the place of penalized players. There were no backup goalies, and if a goalie took a penalty he had to serve it, replaced in net by a teammate.

Goalies, in fact, were not allowed to leave their feet to stop the puck, although on January 9, 1918, Calder announced that the rule had been changed. According to one report, he was quoted as saying, "As far as I'm concerned they can stand on their head if they choose to." Does that phrase sound familiar?

The NHL played with six players on the ice, the position of rover having been eliminated in the early days of the NHA. The PCHA, and later the Western Canada Hockey League, would continue to play seven-man hockey until 1921.

In time, the NHL adopted the forward pass, blue lines to divide the ice into zones, and the requirement that teams play shorthanded when a player took a penalty, all adopted from the PCHA.

Future coaching legend Jack Adams was on the Toronto Arena
Hockey Club roster in their 1917–18 Stanley Cup Championship
season. He was inducted into the Hockey Hall of Fame in 1959.
(Le Studio du Hockey/Hockey Hall of Fame)

3

THE FIRST TWO NHL GAMES

The first two NHL games were played on December 19, 1917, and to say that first night was eventful is an understatement.

The highlights included two five-goal performances and the first "labour" disruption.

In Ottawa, the Montreal Canadiens defeated the Senators, 7–4, with Joe Malone, who had been obtained when the Quebec franchise folded, scoring five goals. Georges "The Chicoutimi Cucumber" Vezina was excellent in net, while Vezina's counterpart, Clint Benedict, was criticized for allowing seven.

According to a report in the Toronto *Globe*, "the ice was sticky and it helped the heavier Canadiens," who took a 3–0 lead. "The only time Ottawa were dangerous was in the second when they scored two and drew within a couple of goals of the champions . . . they had a chance to pull it out in the third period but failed to do so as the Canadiens' defence was too strong and the visitors played an extra man back."

The Senators actually played part of the game without two of their better players, Jack Darragh and Hamby Shore, who were deemed to have gone on "strike."

"There was some trouble over the contracts of Darragh and Shore and the players refused to go on until the directors had been brought into a conference," reported the *Globe*. "Shore and Darragh both got into the game in the second period, but it was then too late to repair the damage . . . [the] Canadiens were in great fettle and they appeared to have it over Ottawa in every department."

Although there were concerns at the time about the quality of play, with so many players headed off to war and low salaries making it hard to recruit the top amateurs, the Canadian Press reported "between five and six thousand people turned out to attend the local game . . . the hockey dished up was, under the circumstances, surprisingly good . . . in the early stages it looked as though the Canadiens would make a runaway of it but Ottawa rallied and displayed some brilliant flashes of aggressiveness in the second and third periods . . . had the Ottawas started out with their regular team they might have landed the match."

In the other game, the host Montreal Wanderers got their one and only NHL win, defeating the Toronto Blueshirts, 10–9. The Wanderers went on to lose their next three games and disbanded after their arena was destroyed by fire. The Blueshirts later became the Arenas.

"The whole trouble was bad goaltending," reported the *Toronto Star*, further quoting one eyewitness who said, "Sammy Hebert couldn't stop a flock of balloons . . . [Arthur]

Brooks and Hebert were bad enough to let in 10 goals but [Bert] Lindsay wasn't any better for he let nine get by."

Harry Hyland was one of the stars of the game for the Wanderers, scoring five times, although Dave Ritchie, who had two goals and two assists, was described as being "the best man on the ice." Meanwhile, Reg Noble had four goals for Toronto.

Montreal led 5–3 after one period, and despite Toronto battling back to tie, they were ahead 9–6 after two and up by four in the third. The final Toronto rally fell just short.

"Wanderers beat the Toronto Blue Shirts 10 to 9 . . . but if there had been a few more minutes to go the result might easily have read the other way about for Wanderers were fading toward the end while the Blue Shirts with youth in their favour were smashing through the defences in a last effort to snatch victory out of defeat," reported the *Star*. "Torontos showed plenty of speed and dash on the attack but were weak on the defence . . . Sammy Hebert started in nets but gave a mediocre display in the opening frame . . . Brooks was very little improvement."

The reports said the game was "ragged at times" and "pretty rough in spots."

Although Wanderers president Sammy Lichtenhein had invited returning soldiers to be the team's guests at the game, the reported attendance was only about 700.

"The game set a couple of records," reported the *Star*. "One was in small attendance, a very small number turning out . . . the other was in penalties, no less than 20 minors and two majors being handed out. The game wasn't rough but the players were irritable."

The *Star* added that the NHL "is always introducing new whistles of a unique brand so that spectators cannot stop the play by using whistles the same as the officials . . . this year president Calder has new whistles, which have been brought all the way from England . . . they are built like a pipe organ only they have but two pipes . . . when blown into from the centre their sound resembles something between the roaring of an infuriated bull and the summer night lullaby of the latter's amphibious namesake, the bullfrog . . . one of these days he will wake up and give his officials bells like the OHA referees have used for the last five years."

That first season, which consisted of 22 games (14 in the first half and eight in the second), Malone was the league's leading scorer with 48 points, including 44 goals, in 20 games. Ottawa's Cy Denneny was second with 46 points, Noble third with 40.

According to *The Hockey News*, "Bad" Joe Hall led the league with 100 penalty minutes in 21 games, while Vezina and Benedict had the only two shutouts.

The play of that first season was a far cry from the high-velocity athletics of today's hockey, and the league and its rotating cast of teams were still an uncertain group. But on that December night in 1917, the NHL established a new standard for competitiveness and entertainment in the game.

> Malone was the league's leading scorer with 48 points in 20 games. Forty-four of his points were goals.

Opposite: A Toronto Arena Hockey Club program from their season in the inaugural year of the NHL. (Hockey Hall of Fame)

OFFICIAL.

Hockey Programme . . .

ARENA GARDENS

TORONTO

Season 1917-18

4

THE FIRST AMERICAN TEAM

The first American team in the NHL almost began its existence as the Brooklyn Bruins.

Let's back up for a moment. By 1924 the NHL was eager to expand. The league had just four teams—the Montreal Canadiens, Ottawa Senators, Toronto St. Pats, and Hamilton Tigers— and President Frank Calder and the owners were concerned a rival league might emerge, one that would control key American markets and hinder the NHL's growth. Seven years into the league's existence, the spectre of war had dissipated, the best players had returned from overseas, and minor hockey was flourishing. There were suddenly more quality hockey players than NHL teams to employ them. Furthermore, rule changes such as the creation of two blue lines and the permitting of forward passes between the blue lines had made the game more exciting for fans. Inspired by what they were seeing on the ice, fabulous young players were emerging all across Canada and the northeastern United States.

Enter Charles Francis Adams. The Vermont native was a force to be reckoned with in the United States, both on and

The Boston owner staged a contest to name the team.

He was looking for a moniker that represented a wild animal, something that signified brains and brawn.

off the ice. He ran one of the largest grocery store chains in America and was also a sportsman of note. Adams sponsored a team in the American Amateur Hockey League, but soured on the venture when he discovered players were giving less than stellar efforts in a bid to extend exhibition series and therefore increase box office revenues.

"The gate receipts influenced the result of an amateur hockey game," Adams wrote to Calder on April 2, 1924. "These are conditions I am fighting hard to improve."

If Adams was going to pay for players, he was determined to pay for the best. Boston became the NHL's first American-based team when he purchased his franchise on November 1, 1924, for $15,000. At the same time, Montreal was awarded a second team, soon to be called the Maroons. The regular season was expanded from 24 regular-season games to 30, to accommodate the new six-team league.

One major obstacle stood in his way. Tom Duggan and Colonel John Hammond held options to expand the NHL into Boston and also New York, where a new arena called

Madison Square Garden was under construction to house a team for the 1925–26 season. But Calder told Adams that any deal he worked out with the pair of businessmen for the rights to Boston would be fine with the league. Adams thought he had just such an arrangement, one that would see his new Boston entry split its revenues from the 1924–25 season with Duggan and Hammond. After that season, Adams believed the franchise would be his alone.

A resulting dispute led to litigation, but was eventually resolved. The Boston Bruins would play their first game on December 1, 1924, and defeat the Montreal Maroons, 2–1. The choice of team colours was easy: brown and yellow, just like Adams's grocery stores. The Boston owner staged a contest to name the team. He was looking for a moniker that represented a wild animal, something that signified brains and brawn. According to hockey lore, after he rejected dozens of suggestions, his secretary suggested "Bruins."

A new arena in Boston was under construction, but Adams still needed a home for his team's first NHL campaign. He received permission from the league to have his Bruins play their first season in Brooklyn until the new facility was ready, but Duggan and Hammond, who owned territorial rights in New York, vetoed the proposal. So the Bruins had to play their first few seasons in the cozy Boston Arena.

Adams had the foresight to hire a future Hall of Famer to build the organization. Art Ross was born in Naughton, Ontario (now part of Greater Sudbury), and was an offensive defenceman who won Stanley Cups with the 1907 Kenora Thistles and the 1908 Montreal Wanderers.

Now all Adams needed were the players. The Bruins won only 6 of 30 contests in their inaugural season, but the fortunes of the team began to change when Adams acquired a number of players from the failing Western Hockey League in 1926, especially the team's first superstar, Eddie Shore. Boston won its first Stanley Cup three years later, in 1929.

Adams successfully fronted the construction of Boston Garden in 1928 and played a key role in the growth of the league. He vetted prospective owners on behalf of the NHL, and the success of his Bruins helped pave the way for more American teams to join. The Hamilton Tigers were sold in 1925, and the players were transferred to New York to become the Americans. The Pittsburgh Pirates also joined that season, while the New York Rangers, Chicago Blackhawks, and Detroit Cougars were added for the 1926–27 campaign.

It took 91 years, but the Bruins did eventually play in Brooklyn. They visited the New York Islanders for a regular-season game in 2015, after the Islanders relocated to the borough's Barclays Center.

The 1925-26 Boston Bruins, pictured here, were one of three American teams in the NHL that year. Back row (left to right): Charles Adams (president), Gerry Geran, Lionel Hitchman, Stan Jackson, Jimmy Herbert, Billy Stuart, Herb Mitchell, Art Ross (manager); front row (left to right): Thomas Murray (trainer), John Brackenborough, Norm Shay, Charles Stewart, Carson Cooper, George Redding. (Le Studio du Hockey/Hockey Hall of Fame)

5

THE STASTNY BROTHERS DEFECT

Before the arrival of Peter and Anton Stastny—and later, their older brother Marian—to the NHL from communist Czechoslovakia, North American hockey had welcomed Vaclav Nedomansky and Richard Farda.

Nedomansky and Farda won the bronze medal with the Czechoslovakian national team at the 1972 Olympics in Sapporo, Japan. Two years later, in 1974–75, they were teammates with the Toronto Toros of the World Hockey Association after they defected to Canada.

However it was the Stastnys, who snuck through the proverbial Iron Curtain on August 24, 1980, whose daring and dramatic escape to the West to join the Quebec Nordiques opened the door for more Europeans, whether they came from behind the Iron Curtain or not.

It wasn't long before Finland's Jari Kurri took his place on Wayne Gretzky's right flank with the Edmonton Oilers, and Sweden's Mats Naslund and Thomas Steen became popular players with the Montreal Canadiens and Winnipeg Jets, respectively. From Czechoslovakia came Miroslav Frycer, Peter and Miroslav Ihnacak, Jan Ludvig, Petr Svoboda, Petr Klima, Frantisek Musil, Petr Nedved, and others.

Peter and Anton Stastny first pondered a plan to bolt

"The Iron Curtain wasn't called the Iron Curtain for nothing."

for the NHL at the 1980 Olympics in Lake Placid, New York. But security was too tight and they needed more time to devise a strategy.

The timing was right six months later. Their hometown club in the Czechoslovak Extraliga, HC Slovan Bratislava, was to compete in the European Cup final in Innsbruck, Austria, against CSKA Moscow; Tappara of Tampere, Finland; and Modo from Ornskoldsvik, Sweden.

Anton was 21 and had been taken in the fourth round of the 1979 NHL draft by the Nordiques. Peter was less than a month away from his 24th birthday. The older Stastny was a free agent, but the brothers figured the Nordiques would want both to play for them.

Just after supper one evening in Innsbruck, they took a pocketful of Austrian schillings to a phone booth. They had scribbled down the Nordiques' phone number from an old media guide, and around 2 p.m. local time in Quebec City they persuaded a receptionist to put them through to owner Marcel Aubut.

The Nordiques owner didn't waste a second. He and his trusted director of player personnel, Gilles Leger, immediately flew to Europe in the hopes of returning home with the Stastnys.

Previous page: (left to right) Marian, Peter, and Anton Stastny sit on their home bench at Le Colisée in Quebec City. (Paul Bereswill/ Hockey Hall of Fame)

Right: Peter Stastny, Feburary 22, 1981, during his rookie season with the Quebec Nordiques. (O-Pee-Chee/Hockey Hall of Fame)

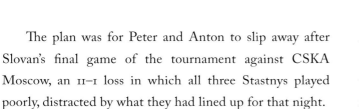

The plan was for Peter and Anton to slip away after Slovan's final game of the tournament against CSKA Moscow, an 11–1 loss in which all three Stastnys played poorly, distracted by what they had lined up for that night.

The team returned to their hotel, a Holiday Inn, in downtown Innsbruck, for a postgame dinner before boarding a midnight bus for the nine-hour ride home to Bratislava.

Peter and Anton Stastny did not get on the bus. Instead, they were in a red Mercedes with Aubut and Leger, speeding toward the Canadian embassy in Vienna, with Czechoslovakian authorities in pursuit. Peter's wife, Darina, was also in the car.

Darina had been informed of the plan previously, in Bratislava. Eight months pregnant with daughter Katarina, Darina had boarded a fan bus from Bratislava to Innsbruck so that she could accompany her husband to Canada.

With the help of Vienna police, Canadian defence minister Gilles Lamontagne, immigration minister Lloyd Axworthy, and Douglas Fisher of Hockey Canada, the Stastnys made it to Vienna Airport in time to board a plane to Amsterdam. The group eventually arrived safe and sound in Quebec City after connecting through Montreal.

Anton had not told his girlfriend Galina of the plan. But she later made her way to Canada and married him.

"The Iron Curtain wasn't called the Iron Curtain for nothing," Peter said at his Hockey Hall of Fame induction ceremony in 1998. "[The Czech government] kept people in concentration camps, and only the privileged could leave, and they made assurances that you came back.

"We used a small opportunity with my brother and wife to leave in 1980 to Innsbruck and never looked back."

Meanwhile, their brother Marian decided to stay behind. Three years older, he had a wife and three children back in Bratislava. The brothers worried that if his family had travelled to Innsbruck, too, it would have tipped off Czechoslovakian officials.

Marian felt it best to go through proper channels. He

Peter Stastny was awarded the Calder Trophy in the 1980-81 season, scoring 39 goals and 109 points for the Nordiques. (Miles Nadal/Hockey Hall of Fame)

later applied to leave Czechoslovakia and move his family to Canada, but he was rebuffed by a communist government too upset at what his brothers had done.

In fact, government officials watched Marian closely. He was suspended from playing for Slovan and the Czechslovakian national team, and prohibited from practising law, his profession. His last act as a barrister, in an unofficial capacity, had been to sign off on the six-year contracts Aubut presented his new players with in Innsbruck. Marian had a similar deal waiting for him.

Ultimately, Marian joined his brothers in Quebec City. But in order to disguise his plan, he renovated his house to give the impression he planned to stay put. He and his family also took a few trips to a spa in Hungary frequently visited by Czechs, but always returned home.

Then, in the spring of 1981, while on a trip to Hungary, he and his family slipped into Yugoslavia and the Austrian embassy in Zagreb. Again, Aubut used his political friends within the Canadian government to make sure Marian and his family safely reached their destination, Quebec City.

Peter would win the 1980–81 Calder Trophy with a 39-goal, 109-point season. Anton also scored 39 goals in his rookie year. In game 62 in late February, the visiting Nordiques defeated the Washington Capitals, 11–7, with Anton and Peter collecting eight points each.

With Marian aboard the following year, the Stastnys became the third trio of brothers to play for the same team. Max, Doug, and Reg Bentley had played for the Chicago Blackhawks in the 1940s, while Barclay, Bob, and Bill Plager suited up for the St. Louis Blues in the 1970s.

The three Stastnys played together in Quebec City for four dominant seasons until Marian was traded to the Toronto Maple Leafs.

Peter was inducted into the Hockey Hall of Fame in 1998, and his son Paul plays for the St. Louis Blues. They weren't the first Europeans to play in the NHL, but from the moment Peter and Anton first stepped onto North American ice, they were arguably the most important.

6

GORDIE HOWE SCORES 1,000 POINTS

Howie Glover only scored 30 times in his 155 NHL career regular-season and playoff games. But during his lone full season with the Detroit Red Wings, 1960–61, the goal he scored late in the first period of a 2–0 win at the Detroit Olympia on November 27, 1960, was a monumental marker.

Gordie Howe registered the second assist on Glover's goal, and it turned out to be his 1,000th point, making him the first NHL player to reach the milestone.

"I honestly can't remember if he scored or I scored," Glover said. "But I do remember we didn't know it was a historic point until someone mentioned it in the dressing room after the game."

Howe and Glover, both right wingers, played on different lines that season. But when Detroit had the power play, Howe would often play the point with Glover and his linemates.

On his historic 1,000th point, Howe fed a pass along the blue line to Red Wings defenceman Warren Godfrey, who managed to fire a shot on Toronto goalie Johnny Bower just as a tripping penalty to Maple Leafs forward Dick Duff expired.

Glover skated out of the corner in time to redirect Godfrey's shot for the game's first goal, six minutes and 36 seconds into the first period.

How did Howe react after the game?

"Like he usually did, he just shrugged his shoulders," Godfrey said. "Gordie was very quiet. Nothing he did or accomplished seemed a big deal to him."

The *Detroit Free Press* didn't even make a big deal about the milestone in the game report the following day. Instead, the focus was on Terry Sawchuk's shutout and the fact that Howe's second assist in the game, on Norm Ullman's goal late in the second period, enabled Howe to tie Maurice "Rocket" Richard's record for combined regular-season and playoff points, with 1,091.

After 18 seasons with the Montreal Canadiens, Richard had retired earlier in 1960, at age 38, with 965 points in 1,111 regular-season and playoff games.

Howe was in his 15th season, and had only required 1,083 regular-season and playoff games to match Richard's point total.

"What can I say about Gordie?" Glover said. "He was the best player I saw or played with, and he did everything well. But I will always remember his toughness."

Glover's older brother Fred, a centre, was briefly a junior teammate of Howe's with the Galt Red Wings, in Ontario, although Howe only played one game for Galt because of a snafu around his transfer. Mr. Hockey wound up turning pro with the Omaha Knights the following season, 1945–46.

Fred Glover and Howe were reunited in Detroit over parts of three seasons. So when Howie was promoted to the Red Wings, Fred warned his little brother to be aware of Howe's elbows in practice.

"Sure enough, in one of my first practices in Detroit, he hit me right in the head," Howie remembered. "I said to myself, 'Oh yeah, there they are.'"

The Red Wings defeated the Maple Leafs in a five-game semifinal in the 1961 playoffs, but fell to the Chicago Blackhawks in a six-game final. These would be the only 11 Stanley Cup playoff games of Howie Glover's career.

After playing 39 games for Detroit the following season, he was back in the minors with the Pittsburgh Hornets in 1962–63. The Red Wings traded Glover to the New York Rangers in the summer of 1963.

But for one night, the younger Glover was part of NHL history with the great Gordie Howe.

Gordie Howe at Maple Leaf Gardens in Toronto.
(Imperial Oil–Turofsky/Hockey Hall of Fame)

7

WAYNE GRETZKY IS TRADED TO LOS ANGELES

The aftershocks created by a big trade can often last for years. But rarely in sports does a deal reverberate for decades.

Such is the case so many years after the shocking news of August 9, 1988, that Wayne Gretzky, the face of hockey in Canada and superstar centre of the Edmonton Oilers, was donning sunglasses and beginning a new life in Hollywood.

Gretzky, along with bodyguard defenceman Marty McSorley and forward Mike Krushelnyski, went to the Los Angeles Kings for forwards Jimmy Carson, Martin Gelinas, $15 million in U.S. funds, and the Kings' first-round draft picks in 1989, '91, and '93. The magnitude of talent and money in the stunning deal, and the element of surprise—it happened during the usually quiet days of summer—made that morning's news bulletins all the more numbing.

The bold move was a necessity for the two owners who engineered it: Peter Pocklington in Edmonton was strapped for cash, and the Kings' Bruce McNall needed a crown jewel to help put his newly purchased team on the sporting landscape in L.A.

Gretzky would later insist that he was sold, not traded. Informed right after Edmonton won its fourth Stanley Cup that Pocklington was shopping him to L.A., Detroit, and Vancouver, Gretzky at first refused to go along with the scheme. But McNall called while Gretzky was on his honeymoon with bride Janet Jones, and not only sold him on the merits of hockey life in L.A., but shrewdly turned the Great One against Pocklington. As long as his preferred teammates were coming, too, Gretzky would agree to the deal—and the charade of asking Pocklington for a trade to save the owner's skin from bitter Oilers fans.

Jones would be scorned in public for supposedly abetting Gretzky's move to L.A. to further her acting career, but Gretzky later said his father, Walter, was the one who advised him to accept the move and pick the Kings. Janet had actually preferred a deal to Detroit, closer to her roots in the U.S. Midwest and the team Gretzky had adored as a kid.

Few sports fans would recall that, on the same evening as The Trade, the Chicago Cubs won the first-ever nighttime baseball game played at Wrigley Field. Most only remember the tears Gretzky shed at his farewell press conference. Every major newspaper in North America covered the story.

The Trade was one of those "I remember where I was at the time" moments.

Gretzky made the Kings and their new black-and-silver uniforms into a familiar brand, and by 1993 they were Stanley Cup finalists. The Kings became a hot ticket on the

Gretzky speaks at the press conference for the announcement of his trade to the L.A. Kings on August 9, 1988. (David E. Klutho/Hockey Hall of Fame)

L.A. sporting scene, with Hollywood stars jumping on the bandwagon.

But the real winner would be the NHL, which would ride No. 99's wave of popularity in the U.S. and grow the game, particularly in California, the Sunbelt, and the southeast. The league would gain new franchises in Anaheim and San Jose on the West Coast, as well as Tampa Bay and Miami (the Florida Panthers). The Quebec Nordiques relocated to Denver, while the Winnipeg Jets moved to Phoenix and the Hartford Whalers to Raleigh, North Carolina. A subsequent wave of expansion placed teams in Atlanta, Minneapolis-St. Paul, Nashville, and Columbus.

In 2016, California-born, Arizona-raised teenager Auston Matthews was drafted No. 1 overall by the Toronto Maple Leafs, and in 2017 hockey will be played in Las Vegas.

All of these developments are courtesy of Gretzky's move to Los Angeles, a trade that spawned the saying, "If Gretzky can be traded, anyone can be traded."

The fates of the key figures in the trade were mixed. Pocklington and McNall both ran into serious legal problems and lost their teams. The Oilers, with help from Gelinas, won one more Cup without Gretzky, but then fell on hard times on the ice. Only one Canadian-based team has won a Cup since: the Montreal Canadiens who beat Gretzky and his Kings in 1993.

Gretzky broke Gordie Howe's points record while in L.A. He briefly went to St. Louis before retiring in 1999, fittingly, after a few seasons with another marquee club, the New York Rangers.

The Kings eventually won the Cup in 2012 and 2014—long after Gretzky departed. He has now come full circle: in 2016 the Edmonton Oilers hired him as an executive.

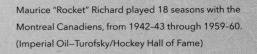
Maurice "Rocket" Richard played 18 seasons with the
Montreal Canadiens, from 1942-43 through 1959-60.
(Imperial Oil–Turofsky/Hockey Hall of Fame)

8

MAURICE RICHARD SCORES 50 GOALS IN 50 GAMES

Before the 1944–45 season, Montreal Canadiens general manager Tommy Gorman approved a clause in Maurice Richard's contract, entitling him to a bonus if he scored 30 goals. It was a reachable objective, seeing as he had just scored 32 in his first full NHL season.

To spice things up, Gorman added an even larger incentive if Richard scored 50—a milestone widely thought to be unattainable in the NHL's 50-game schedule. No one had even reached 40 since Cooney Weiland of the Bruins scored 43 in 1929–30.

But on March 18, 1945, late in the third period of a game in Boston, Richard beat Harvey Bennett of the Bruins and Gorman got out his chequebook.

When he'd joined the NHL a couple of seasons earlier, the newcomer from the Habs' own backyard was playing the left side and wearing No. 15. After suffering through a string of injuries and bad luck in 1942–43, he asked coach Dick Irvin if he could change. And it was after the birth of his daughter, Huguette, who weighed nine pounds when she was born in 1943, that he switched to No. 9.

By the 1944–45 season, Richard had also switched

wings, and was already being hailed with a string of nicknames. With his blazing dark eyes, the "Rocket" was the moniker that stuck, but his fellow forwards on the Punch Line—centre Elmer Lach and Toe Blake—were helping him light up the league.

Just after Christmas, Irvin let his 12-year-old son Dick Jr. sit on the end of the Canadiens bench for a game at the Forum against Detroit. The future broadcaster was mesmerized as Richard scored five goals and eight points in a 9–1 win. Fans started talking about his chances for 50 in 50. And in the Habs' 30th match, in mid-January, Richard scored a hat trick that put him ahead of a goal-a-game pace.

While some killjoys pointed out that the league was watered down by wartime roster absences, Richard's march toward 50 remained compelling for fans. He tied Weiland's "modern" record of 43 on February 10, in another win over Detroit at home, sparking a two-minute ovation from proud hometown fans. And a few days later, with Toronto visiting, Richard was poised to pass Joe Malone's all-time mark of 44, scored in the league's inaugural season.

> As the schedule wound down, rival clubs were resorting to everything in the book, including some nefarious tricks outside the rules, to blanket Richard.

As the schedule wound down, rival clubs were resorting to everything in the book, including some nefarious tricks outside the rules, to blanket Richard. The Rangers tried to intimidate him by putting roughhouse forward Bob Dill on his tail, but in a pair of fights at MSG—one on the ice and one in the penalty box—Richard triumphed.

Against the Leafs, checking specialists Nick Metz and Bob Davidson were deployed to cover Richard and prevent him from getting 45 on their watch. Toronto shut him down as the final minutes ticked off the clock, but at the expense of allowing Blake and Lach to beat them. Just when it looked as though Irvin would hold Richard out of the rough affair, the exhausted star summoned the strength to come back out and score his 45th.

"There are goals and then there are Richard goals," became a popular saying.

Some drama remained in the final games as Richard played the last regular-season home date at the Forum and was blanked by Chicago, leaving him at 49. But in Boston, with 1:42 to go in the last game before the playoffs, Richard scored on Bennett.

Richard did not win the league scoring title, as Lach's 54 assists gave him 80 points, seven more than the Rocket. And the playoffs would end on a sour note for Montreal as the Leafs bounced the Habs in six games during the semi-finals, despite Richard scoring six goals.

But his magical season would be the talk of the league until the early '60s, when a 50-goal season became a more frequent feat, albeit within a longer schedule.

Back row (left to right): Leo Lamoureux, Bill Durnan, and Glen Harmon; front row (left to right): Maurice Richard, Elmer Lach, and Toe Blake, at the Montreal Forum. (Imperial Oil–Turofsky/Hockey Hall of Fame)

9

WILLIE O'REE BREAKS
THE COLOUR BARRIER

Willie O'Ree was in familiar surroundings when he broke the NHL's colour barrier on January 18, 1958.

After turning heads with his play in his hometown of Fredericton, New Brunswick, O'Ree left home in 1954 to play junior with the Quebec Frontenacs, rivals to the Junior Canadiens in Montreal. He then spent a season with the junior Kitchener-Waterloo Canucks before returning to Quebec City to play for the Aces in the minor-pro Quebec Hockey League, which meant frequent tilts with the minor-pro Montreal Royals. Halfway through his second season with the Aces, the Boston Bruins promoted the 22-year-old O'Ree to play in a home-and-home series on successive evenings against the Canadiens.

By the time of his NHL debut, O'Ree was well accustomed to the city of Montreal and its famed Forum. He said he didn't experience any racism that first game, and he didn't even feel anything special about becoming the first black player to play in the NHL.

"I felt I was just No. 22 playing for the Boston Bruins," O'Ree told the *Courier-Post* in Camden, New Jersey, in 2016 when he was asked if he had been subjected to racial taunts from opposing players and fans.

"It wasn't rough until I played in the United States.

I was the only black player and I was exposed to racial remarks and slurs. But I let it go in one ear and out the other."

So focused was O'Ree on his job that night in Montreal, having realized his dream of performing in the NHL, that he wasn't aware he had become the Jackie Robinson of hockey until he read the newspaper the following morning. Near the bottom of a Canadian Press story appeared the words, "The game, before a crowd of 13,712, marked the debut of Willie O'Ree, the first Negro to play in the league."

O'Ree was held off the scoresheet in both his debut—a 3–0 Bruins win in Montreal—and the next night in Boston, when the Canadiens won, 6–2. He was then sent back to the Aces, but he did see his career take a promising turn several weeks later, when he was promoted to play the final six games of the season with the Bruins' top farm club in Springfield, Massachusetts.

Stick-to-itiveness was part of O'Ree's disposition. He was raised in a family of 13—two siblings died in infancy. His older brother Richard was his role model. He often counselled Willie to keep his head down, work hard, and not allow the name-calling to get to him.

O'Ree had to wait almost three years before he received another shot with the Bruins. This stint, which lasted more than half of the 1960–61 season, found him playing mainly

Willie O'Ree with the Boston Bruins, 1960-61.
(Imperial Oil–Turofsky/Hockey Hall of Fame)

Willie O'Ree faces Lorne "Gump" Worsley and Irv Spencer in a game against the
New York Rangers on February 5, 1961 at Madison Square Garden, New York.
The Rangers beat the Bruins, 5–2. (Le Studio du Hockey/Hockey Hall of Fame)

on the left side on a line with centre Don McKenney and right wing Jerry Toppazzini.

On New Year's Day 1961, O'Ree made history by scoring his first goal. He took a pass from Bruins defenceman Leo Boivin, and raced past Montreal defenders Tom Johnson and Jean-Guy Talbot to fire a shot behind Canadiens goalie Charlie Hodge. In 43 games with Boston that season, O'Ree would score four goals, including two game-winners, and 14 points.

He thought he was on his way, until the Bruins traded him to the Canadiens for Terry Gray and Cliff Pennington in the off-season. The Canadiens were the class of the league, having won five Stanley Cups in a row from 1956 to 1960. Beginning in 1964–65, they would win it four more times in five seasons to close out the decade. Facing so much talent on the Habs' NHL roster, O'Ree worried he would be trapped in the minors.

He was right, because the Canadiens eventually sold O'Ree's rights to the Los Angeles Blades of the Western Hockey League (WHL).

When the league expanded to 12 teams in 1967, there was hope that maybe one of the new franchises would sign O'Ree. But by then the word was out that he couldn't see out of his right eye and he would never pass a vision test.

O'Ree had tried to keep it a secret, but back in his junior season in Kitchener-Waterloo, an errant puck had hit him in the face and taken 95 percent of the vision in his right eye. He somehow persevered and earned that pair of promotions to the Bruins. But his eyesight hindered his play.

In the WHL, Blades coach Alf Pike switched O'Ree from left wing to right to compensate for his vision problems, and O'Ree wound up winning a pair of scoring titles before retiring from the San Diego Gulls at age 43.

There wouldn't be another black player in the NHL until Mike Marson of Scarborough, Ontario, made the Washington Capitals roster in 1974.

It took time for others to follow the path O'Ree had carved, but by 2016–17 more than 75 black players had suited up in the NHL, including San Jose Sharks forward Joel Ward, who wears No. 42 in honour of Jackie Robinson, who broke Major League Baseball's colour barrier in 1947.

O'Ree, who once was invited to try out for the Milwaukee Braves of baseball's National League, actually met Robinson twice. The first time was a chance meeting on the streets of New York after a 14-year-old O'Ree and his minor hockey teammates won a tournament and the first prize was a trip to see the sights in Manhattan.

"I shook hands with him after and told him that I not only played baseball, but I played hockey," O'Ree said. "He said, 'Oh, I didn't know there were any black kids playing hockey.'"

The second time was at an NAACP luncheon to honour the Brooklyn Dodgers slugger 13 years later, just after O'Ree's two stints with the Bruins and his trade to the Montreal organization: "'Willie O'Ree,' Robinson said after he was introduced to the hockey player. "Aren't you the young fella I met in Brooklyn?'

"This was from 1949 to 1962. So that made a big impact, a big impact."

It took time for others to follow the path O'Ree had carved, but by 2016–17 more than 75 black players had suited up in the NHL.

February 7, 1976 was an unforgettable night for Toronto fans, and for rookie goalie Dave Reece of the visiting Boston Bruins. (Bob Shaver/Hockey Hall of Fame)

10

DARRYL SITTLER'S 10-POINT NIGHT

Toronto Maple Leafs captain Darryl Sittler felt he had better games than his remarkable 10-point record performance against the Boston Bruins on February 7, 1976, but there was magic in the air that evening at Maple Leaf Gardens.

Everything he touched resulted in a point, and it was the beginning of an enormous 10-month ride.

"You know what happened after [that night]?" queried Sittler, who was inducted into the Hockey Hall of Fame in 1989. "I scored [a record] five goals against the Philadelphia Flyers in a playoff game and the overtime winner for Canada against Czechoslovakia to win the [1976] Canada Cup. I guess it was the year of Darryl Sittler."

A clash between the Maple Leafs and Bruins never required extra hype, but because the Bruins had been playing so well at the time there was a little extra excitement surrounding the game.

Sittler remembered wishing he had extra time in the hours leading up to the game. He was running some errands, and as a result he was worried there wasn't enough time for his usual pregame meal of pasta and either chicken or steak.

His wife, Wendy, was eight months pregnant with their second of three children, Meaghan, who was born five weeks later. So instead of his wife's cooking, Sittler stopped at a Swiss Chalet restaurant for a takeout chicken dinner with fries. He "wolfed" down the meal in his car on his way home.

"I tried it, but it never worked like that time," Sittler said when asked if Swiss Chalet became a ritual.

Sittler had his own reason to play well that night. There had been a story in a local newspaper in which Harold Ballard, the colourful owner of the Toronto Maple Leafs, said he wished his team could find a centre to play between Lanny McDonald and Errol Thompson.

"It was a shot at me," Sittler said.

Three nights earlier, coach Red Kelly had put together the line of Sittler, McDonald, and Thompson, who replaced Dave "Tiger" Williams. The new line scored twice in a 4–4 tie at home against the Washington Capitals.

But at practice a couple of days later, Kelly informed the new trio it was going to be split up.

"Red told us he didn't want to put all his eggs in one basket," McDonald said. "Errol, Darryl, and I went in to see Red after practice and begged him to give us a week."

The line stayed together for more than two years, until Thompson was traded to the Detroit Red Wings on March 13, 1978.

"That line was so explosive, especially when [defencemen] Borje Salming and Ian Turnbull were out there with them," Toronto goalie Wayne Thomas said.

Sittler agreed. "Playing with Borje and Ian was like having an extra forward because one of them often jumped up into the play," he said.

If the excitement before the game was memorable, the scene inside the Maple Leafs' dressing room after two periods was pure giddiness.

"There was such a buzz in the dressing room in the second intermission, especially after [team official] Stan Obodiac came in and told Darryl that he was one point shy of tying Rocket Richard's record [of eight points in a game]," McDonald recalled.

Richard had set the NHL single-game record when he had five goals and three assists for eight points in the Montreal Canadiens' 9–1 victory against the Detroit Red Wings on December 28, 1944. Montreal's Bert Olmstead also had eight points (four goals, four assists) in a 12–1 win against the Chicago Blackhawks on January 9, 1954.

Sittler joined them when he soared past the Boston Bruins' defence 44 seconds into the third period at Maple Leaf Gardens to score his fourth goal and eighth point of the game.

"He was off-balance on one skate; he slams up against the boards," McDonald said. "He had an ear-to-ear grin and held his arms high. It was unbelievable."

Sittler didn't need much longer to break the record. He earned his ninth point when he cut across the top of the slot and beat rookie goalie Dave Reece with a wrist shot at 9:27. The Maple Leafs captain scored his sixth goal and 10th point at 16:35 when he tried to pass to Thompson, in front of the net, only to have the puck hit the right leg of Boston defenceman Brad Park and deflect past Reece to complete an 11–4 win.

Reece had performed well leading up to the game. No. 1 goalie Gilles Gilbert was injured and Reece had helped the Bruins extend their winning streak to seven games by making 20 saves in a 5–1 victory against the Pittsburgh Penguins two

nights earlier. But the rookie knew his days were numbered when the Bruins brought back Gerry Cheevers after a hiatus in the World Hockey Association of nearly four years. In his first game since rejoining Boston, Cheevers was sitting at the end of bench as Reece's backup.

Bruins coach Don Cherry seldom pulled goalies during a game because he didn't want them looking to the bench after allowing a few goals. But Cherry did glance Cheevers's way after one of Sittler's three goals in the second period.

"He put a towel over his head as if to say, 'I don't want any part of this,'" Cherry said. "But I wanted to save [Cheevers] for the next night because we were back at home and it was a homecoming for him.

"I know I took a lot of slings and arrows for keeping Davey in there. But I always felt you sometimes had to lose a battle to win the war."

Cheevers and the Bruins defeated the Detroit Red Wings, 7–0, at Boston Garden the next night to begin a four-game winning streak. Boston finished first in the Adams Division and Cherry won the Jack Adams Award as the NHL's top coach.

However, Reece never played another NHL game. He was demoted to the minors following that night, left pro hockey after one more season, and went on to a successful career as a high school guidance counsellor.

Reece has accepted his role in Sittler's big night. He joined Sittler for a television special to commemorate the 30th anniversary of the game in 2006 and attended a ceremony marking the 40th anniversary at Air Canada Centre in Toronto.

"Every year that goes by, the magnitude of the 10 points gets bigger and means more to me," Sittler said.

Ten players have scored eight points in a game since Sittler's remarkable night, including Wayne Gretzky twice and Mario Lemieux three times. For them and every other player with an eye on the Leaf captain's record, its magnitude remains daunting.

Left: A ticket stub from Sittler's 10-point game at Maple Leaf Gardens, where he led the Leafs to an 11–4 victory over the Boston Bruins. (Hockey Hall of Fame)

Below: Sittler celebrates victory over the Bruins and his historic night with teammate Dave "Tiger" Williams in the Maple Leafs dressing room. (Le Studio de Hockey/Hockey Hall of Fame)

WAYNE GRETZKY SCORES NUMBER 802

By the time the legendary Gordie Howe had scored his final regular-season NHL goal, no. 801 to be precise, hockey fans had already seen enough of the first-year brilliance of Edmonton Oilers phenom Wayne Gretzky to predict he was destined to one day break all of Howe's scoring records.

Gretzky's first goal arrived on October 14, 1979, against Vancouver Canucks goaltender Glen Hanlon, who jokingly said years later, "I created a monster."

Howe, who was 52 years old, playing in his 32nd pro season and fifth decade of hockey, had played a total of 83 games in the 1979–80 season, scoring 15 goals, giving him 801 in total. He had expressed an interest in coming back yet again as a player/coach with the Hartford Whalers to ease into retirement, but instead retired from the NHL for a second and final time.

The chase was on for Gretzky, already off to a fine start with 43 goals in his rookie year. That would be his lowest goal total for the next eight years, until an injury in 1987–88 limited him to 40 in 64 games.

Howe had briefly been introduced to Gretzky when the latter was an 11-year-old minor scoring machine growing up in Brantford, Ontario. Howe told the star-struck kid to work on his backhand if he wanted to become a complete player, the first of many tips from Mr. Hockey that Gretzky ate up. At the 1979 WHA all-star game, when No. 99 was briefly an Indianapolis Racer, he again met Howe, who was then a New England Whaler. The next year when the Oilers and Whalers were merged into the NHL, the two played in the NHL All-Star Game.

Soon they were fast friends, doing promotional appearances, commercials and banquets together. In 1989, when Gretzky reached 1,851 points to surpass Howe as the NHL's all-time points leader, the latter had been part of the entourage following his progress, which in true Gretzky fashion— with a flair for the dramatic—ended with him breaking that record at his old home, Edmonton's Northlands Coliseum.

So when Gretzky was closing in on 801 goals, as a member of the Los Angeles Kings in March 1994, Howe was once more travelling with him to be there when it happened. Gretzky admitted to feeling he was letting Howe down as the games rolled on and they went from city to city without

> Fans had already seen enough of the first-year brilliance of Edmonton Oilers' phenom Wayne Gretzky to predict he was destined to one day break all of Howe's scoring records.

No. 99 scores his 802nd NHL goal, against the Vancouver Canucks on March 23, 1994 at the Great Western Forum in Inglewood, California, breaking Gordie Howe's long-standing record. (Robert Beck/Getty Images)

yet reaching 802. When he tied Howe at 801, the next game was March 23 at home against Vancouver. Howe had been watching for two weeks at that point, but enjoying his time with Gretzky.

"One of the greatest parts of 802 was I got to spend a lot of time with Gordie and his wife Colleen," Gretzky told NHL.com. "A lot of times when you meet your idol, you're somewhat taken aback or disappointed. For me, when I met Gordie, he was bigger and better than I thought.

"When I had an opportunity to be around his record and break his record, I found it really fascinating to be around him, ask him questions and talk about stories."

As Gretzky has said, the "right" people were on the ice when the opportunity came to make scoring history in the Vancouver game. Luc Robitaille and Jari Kurri, his long-time linemate in Edmonton and L.A., were on the move, Robitaille taking the puck across the Vancouver blue line. He dropped it to Gretzky, who went cross ice to Marty McSorley, who was part of the Gretzky trade to L.A. When McSorley returned it through the slot, Gretzky had Canucks' goalie Kirk McLean down and out.

The L.A. Forum went wild and the game stopped for another ceremony. Gretzky had passed Howe's goal mark in his 15th NHL season, while Howe had taken 26 seasons to accumulate his 801. Gretzky was not done of course, playing until 1999 and completing his career with 894 goals.

That record should stand for a while, but then a lot of people thought the same about Howe's record.

12

BOBBY ORR'S GREATEST SEASON

The 1969–70 NHL season ended perfectly, with Bobby Orr flying through the air like Superman after he scored the Stanley Cup–winning goal.

Orr had soared through an incredible, superheroic campaign of 90 regular-season and playoff games, and what a way to finish it off.

"Bobby Orr, behind the net to Sanderson," renowned broadcaster Dan Kelly hollered over the airwaves. "To Orr. Bobby Orr . . . scores and the Boston Bruins have won the Stanley Cup."

A millisecond after Orr deposited his championship winner behind St. Louis Blues goalie Glenn Hall, defence-man Noel Picard tripped No. 4, sending him airborne. Photographer Ray Lussier of the Boston *Record-American* captured the remarkable image, producing one of the most striking photos in hockey history.

The Bruins had swept St. Louis for their first Stanley Cup championship since 1941.

"There was a lot of chatter that we hadn't won in 29 years back then," then Bruins coach Harry Sinden said. "There obviously were only six teams, and chances were you should have won more often.

"But the Montreal Canadiens and Toronto Maple Leafs had a real advantage because all the top players were in their backyard. The Detroit Red Wings also were pretty good because they were so close to Canada."

Sinden had a point. Between 1940 and 1969, the Bruins, Chicago Blackhawks, and New York Rangers won only one title apiece. Montreal (12), Toronto (10), and Detroit (5) combined to win the other 27 times.

"Thank God Toronto screwed up and a guy like Orr slipped through to us," Sinden chuckled.

In his first three seasons, Orr had already established himself as the game's best defenceman. He followed up his Calder Trophy in 1966–67 with back-to-back Norris Trophies.

Who won the Norris in Orr's rookie season? That would be Harry Howell of the New York Rangers. But with 13 goals and 41 points in 61 games, Orr outscored and outpointed his Rangers counterpart, who racked up 12 goals and 40 points in 70 games.

Not only did Howell win the Norris Trophy that season, but he and Pierre Pilote of Chicago were named the first-team all-star defencemen, while Orr and Tim Horton of the Toronto Maple Leafs settled for second-team honours.

In 1968–69, Orr set a record for points by a defenceman, with 64. That season ended in a defeat by the Montreal Canadiens in the semifinals, and a 21-year-old Orr had the Stanley Cup on his mind as he arrived at camp for his fourth

Bobby Orr flies through the air, after scoring the Stanley Cup-winning
goal against the St. Louis Blues and being tripped by defenceman
Noel Picard. (Le Studio du Hockey/Hockey Hall of Fame)

NHL season. During that extraordinary year, he would almost double his point total, scoring 33 goals and 87 assists for 120 points, in the process becoming the first defenceman to win the scoring title. No blueliner had ever finished better than sixth in the race for the Art Ross Trophy.

In the Bruins' home opener against the Rangers on October 12, Orr checked in with assists on goals by Fred Stanfield and John McKenzie, the latter being the game winner in a 2–1 victory. His first goal of the season came in the Bruins' fourth game, the finale of a back-to-back set with the Pittsburgh Penguins. The Bruins were 3–0–1 after four games and Orr already had seven points.

Embarking on a five-game road trip, the Bruins ran their unbeaten streak to 6–0–1 before losing in Toronto and Montreal. Although the Canadiens had their way with Boston, winning by a 9–2 margin on November 1, Orr still managed to register an assist. The next night, as Boston hosted the Maple Leafs, Orr had three assists in the 4–4 draw.

By mid-November, Orr already had 4 goals and 29 points in 16 games. The din picked up around the league about what he was doing. He took chances offensively, but skated so well that he always had enough time and space to get back defensively.

Orr's most productive outing came on December 20, when he assisted on five goals in a 6–4 win against Pittsburgh. In the Bruins' 40th game of the year, a 6–3 win at home against the Los Angeles Kings on January 15, his 51st helper set a record for assists by a defenceman.

Three nights later, Orr surpassed his own record for total points by a defenceman, recording his 65th point in a 6–3 win against Montreal at Boston Garden. A month later, he broke his record for goals by a defenceman, scoring number 22 in game 56, a 5–5 tie in Los Angeles. Yet another milestone was reached in a 5–5 draw against the Red Wings at home. Orr scored twice and assisted on two other goals to become the first defenceman to reach 100 points in a season. The date

was March 15, it was the Bruins' 67th game, and they still had nine more to play.

Over the final weekend of the regular season, Orr registered three assists in two games against the last-place Maple Leafs to push his Hart Trophy–calibre totals to 33 goals and 87 assists.

He also had 125 penalty minutes, notable because, among the NHL's top 12 scorers, only two others—McKenzie and Rangers left wing Dave Balon—topped the 100-penalty-minute mark.

Bobby Orr, the first player to win the Art Ross, Norris, Hart, and Conn Smythe Trophies in the same season. (Lewis Portnoy/Hockey Hall of Fame)

The Bruins finished with a record of 40–17–9, good for 99 points, but were denied first place in the East Division. The Chicago Blackhawks had also amassed 99 points, but with five more wins than their New England rivals. It didn't matter. After the New York Rangers won Games 3 and 4 of their quarter-final series against Boston, the Bruins reeled off 10 consecutive wins to eliminate New York, defeat Chicago in the semis, and sweep the Blues in the final.

Orr was the easy choice for the Conn Smythe Trophy as the playoff MVP. All he did was score nine times and register 20 points in 14 games. Bobby Orr thus became the first player to win the Art Ross, Norris, Hart, and Conn Smythe Trophies in the same season.

"He was fantastic when he came into the league," Sinden said. "It was hard to imagine he could get any better. It was hard to believe he could improve on his first three seasons.

"That [1969–70] was the season he established himself as the best player ever and I doubt there will ever be a player like him again."

Two months after winning the Stanley Cup, Bobby Orr (left) and fellow Bruin Ed Johnston ride in a celebratory parade on July 4, 1970 in Orr's hometown of Parry Sound, Ontario. (Le Studio du Hockey/Hockey Hall of Fame)

13

THE ACE BAILEY BENEFIT GAME

Over the years, the NHL's annual All-Star game has essentially been a celebration of the sport. A chance to take a break in the middle of a long season to showcase hockey's greatest players.

But in the beginning, in many ways, it was a celebration of life.

In particular, one player's life.

It all started during a game on December 12, 1933, when the Toronto Maple Leafs were in Boston to play the Bruins. Games between those two teams frequently turned rough.

In the second period, Leafs defenceman Red Horner hit legendary Bruins defenceman Eddie Shore with a solid hip check that left Shore sore and mad.

Seeking revenge, as the play moved back up the ice Shore charged into Leafs forward Irvine "Ace" Bailey from behind. Bailey was launched into the air and landed on the ice on the right side of his forehead. Bailey was unconscious, his body convulsing, his life in very real danger.

Horner was quoted years later as saying, "I thought to myself, 'That's the end of Ace.'"

With Bailey in convulsions, Horner—who was pretty mean himself—decked Shore with a punch that laid him out.

Bailey eventually regained consciousness after the game, but soon afterward he passed out again.

Doctors determined his skull had been fractured and he had suffered a cerebral hemorrhage. He was rushed to hospital and underwent two operations to relieve the pressure on the brain, but his condition was worse than the doctors had feared and a priest was called to administer last rites.

Incredibly, Bailey started slowly to improve, and a few days later he came out of his coma.

Bailey did indeed survive, and by early January he was well enough to meet with the media. Midway through the month, he left the hospital.

Bailey would shrug the hit off as almost being accidental and forgave Shore. He had little recollection of what had happened.

"I didn't see Eddie and Eddie didn't see me and we crashed. That's all," Bailey was quoted as saying.

Both Bailey and the Leafs were left with staggering hospital bills, and Bailey was left without future income, his hockey career over.

While the Bruins turned over $6,741 in gate receipts from a December game to help offset the costs, the NHL came up with the idea of playing an exhibition match between the Maple Leafs and a group of All-Stars to benefit Bailey. The big question, of course, was whether Shore, one of the best players in the league, would be named to the All-Star team, and if so, how he would be received by Leafs fans.

Well, Shore was named and in fact was in the starting lineup, wearing a leather helmet.

The game was played on February 14, 1934 in a packed Maple Leaf Gardens. Toronto, wearing sweaters with the word *ACE* and a small Leaf crest, won, 7–3. Almost $21,000 was raised for Bailey.

But most significant about the night was what transpired just prior to the game. During the opening ceremonies, each player was introduced by Foster Hewitt, and then skated to greet Bailey. When Shore's name was called, the Gardens turned eerily quiet. But Bailey shook Shore's hand and the crowd erupted in applause.

The Leafs retired Bailey's No. 6, that night, making it the first number to be retired in league history, although in the 1960s Bailey asked winger Ron Ellis to wear his number, which he did from 1968 until 1981.

As for Shore, after he felled Bailey he was himself knocked out by the punch from Horner. He hit his head on the ice and required stitches to close the gash. Police investigated the Shore–Bailey incident, but no charges were laid and Shore was ultimately suspended for 16 games.

There were several more All-Star benefit games after that one, and beginning with the 1947–48 season the NHL staged All-Star games on an annual basis, albeit in many different formats.

The NHL All-Stars and the Toronto Maple Leafs before the Ace Bailey benefit game on February 14, 1934 at Maple Leaf Gardens in Toronto, where the Maple Leafs beat the All-Stars, 7–3. (Hockey Hall of Fame)

14

THE DONATION OF THE HART TROPHY

Next to the Stanley Cup, the most important and prestigious trophy to win in the National Hockey League is arguably the Hart Memorial Trophy, awarded annually "to the player adjudged to be the most valuable to his team" during the regular season. Voting for the award is conducted by members of the Professional Hockey Writers Association prior to the playoffs.

The original Hart Trophy was donated to the NHL in 1923 by Dr. David A. Hart, father of former coach and general manager of the Montreal Canadiens Cecil Hart. When Dr. Hart's trophy was retired to the Hockey Hall of Fame, the NHL replaced it with the Hart Memorial Trophy, first presented in 1960.

Cecil Hart was a descendant of Aaron Hart, a founder of Montreal and Canada's Jewish community in the 1760s. He coached the Canadiens from 1926–27 to 1931–32, winning the Stanley Cup in 1930 and 1931. He was fired in 1931 after a dispute with Canadiens owner Leo Dandurand. After the team was sold, new owner Ernest Savard rehired Hart in 1936 as coach and general manager. According to the Canadiens' historical website, a condition of Hart's rehiring was that the Habs reacquire the legendary, though aging, Howie Morenz from the New York Rangers.

Joe Thornton is the only winner to have played with two teams in the same season he won the Hart.

Morenz did return to Montreal, but tragically he suffered a severe broken leg in a game against Chicago and died due to complications caused by blood clots on March 8, 1937.

That season, Hart still managed to guide the Canadiens to a first-place finish in the Canadian Division, but they were eliminated in the semifinals by the Detroit Red Wings.

Hart resigned as coach and GM during the 1938–39 season, turning control over to Jules Dugal. He had accrued a regular-season coaching record with the Canadiens of 196–125–73, with 16 additional playoff wins.

Cecil Hart died after a lengthy illness in July 1940.

The first winner of the Hart Trophy, in the 1923–24 season, was Frank Nighbor of the Ottawa Senators. It was last awarded to Detroit superstar Gordie Howe, in 1960. The first winner of the Hart Memorial Trophy was Montreal star Bernie Geoffrion, in 1960–61.

Wayne Gretzky has won the Hart more times than any other player: nine. Eight of those wins came in consecutive seasons, from 1980 to 1987, as an Edmonton Oiler, and the ninth was as a Los Angeles King in 1989. Howe won it six times. Gretzky and Mark Messier (Edmonton and New York

Rangers) are the only players to have won the Hart Memorial Trophy with more than one team, and Joe Thornton is the only winner to have played with two teams in the same season he won the Hart.

Eddie Shore won the trophy four times, one more than Bobby Orr, while the Buffalo Sabres' Dominik Hasek is the only goaltender to win it twice.

Most winners of the Hart were later inducted into the Hockey Hall of Fame, but not all of them, making the award the definitive statement of any player's rise to the pinnacle of the sport, no matter how long or short his stay.

Gordie Howe, NHL president Clarence Campbell, and Detroit Red Wings owner Bruce Norris in a pre-game presentation of the Hart Memorial Trophy, which Howe won for the 1962–63 season, as well as the Art Ross Trophy. (James McCarthy/Hockey Hall of Fame)

15

THE CREATION OF THE "ORIGINAL SIX"

World War II had a profound effect on the NHL. When the global conflict broke out before the start of the 1939–40 season, a seven-team league populated almost exclusively by Canadian-born players quickly showed its true colours. Military personnel were given ticket discounts, and pre-game ceremonies in Toronto and Montreal reflected the patriotism sweeping the country. Maple Leafs owner Conn Smythe, a hero in the first world war, applied to have his officer's commission reinstated and began forming an artillery battalion picked from the ranks of local sportsmen and his Maple Leaf Gardens employees.

But as able-bodied players began signing up for training in various services over the next couple of years, the toll on Montreal, Toronto, Boston, Detroit, Chicago, and the New York Rangers and Americans began to show. In the case of the Cup champion Bruins, a whole No. 1 forward line left the team. Milt Schmidt, Woody Dumart, and Bobby Bauer enlisted in the Royal Canadian Air Force soon after the attack on Pearl Harbor drew America into the fight.

Rosters became younger in a hurry. Bep Guidolin was called up by the Bruins as a 16-year-old, making him the youngest NHLer ever, while Eric Prentice, Ted "Teeder" Kennedy, and Ross Johnstone became the youngest to suit up for the Leafs, all 17. But the loss of so many stars was hurting hockey, especially in American markets.

While the Canadian and U.S. governments had decided not to ask the NHL to cancel play, as the games were judged a morale booster, it became harder for fans to make it to and from the rinks, because of wartime restrictions and blackouts. Train travel was also cut back to save energy for the war effort, resulting in the end of NHL regular-season overtime.

Many of those factors caused big headaches for the New York Americans. Sharing Madison Square Garden with the Rangers, their record was a league-worst 8–29–11 in 1940–41. Already in debt, the team had to sell its remaining stars for badly needed cash.

Manager Red Dutton tried to revive fortunes by rebranding the club as the Brooklyn Americans, hoping to lure in that borough's large population and take advantage of the thousands of wartime workers at the Brooklyn Navy Yard. But a plan to build a rink in the borough failed, and the team folded in the summer of '42.

> Canadian and U.S. governments had decided not to ask the NHL to cancel play, as the games were judged a morale booster.

Milt Schmidt shoots on Canadiens goaltender Claude Bourque in the final game of the regular season on March 17, 1940 at the Boston Garden. The Bruins beat the Canadiens 7–2. (Le Studio du Hockey/Hockey Hall of Fame)

Red Wings forward Norm Ullman battles for possession of the puck from Blackhawks centre Bill Hay. (Le Studio du Hockey/Hockey Hall of Fame)

A streamlined six-team league, with a schedule lengthened to 50 games, was created, and a golden era for the sport was ushered in. This period also saw the passing of NHL president Frank Calder, who had been at the league's helm since its inception in 1917. His replacement was the well-respected Dutton, though he only held the post for three years.

Former referee Clarence Campbell, who had been a Canadian lieutenant-colonel in Europe, then began a term as president that would see the "Original Six," all of which are still playing, through until expansion in 1966–67. Though outnumbered, the two Canadian teams would win 19 Cups between 1943 and 1967; meanwhile Detroit would earn five and Chicago one.

The New York Rangers faced off against the Toronto Maple Leafs at Madison Square Garden on December 29, 1940. The home team claimed a 3-2 victory. (Le Studio du Hockey/Hockey Hall of Fame)

THE RUSSIAN FIVE

The winged wheel of the Detroit Red Wings was rolling in the right direction in the early to mid-1990s. Captain Steve Yzerman had been surrounded with young stars like Sergei Fedorov through the draft, and key players like goaltender Mike Vernon, a Stanley Cup champion with Calgary in 1989, via trades.

But despite winning the Presidents' Trophy in the spring of 1995, the Red Wings hit a pothole in their quest to end a four-decade Stanley Cup drought. The New Jersey Devils swept them in the championship series. There was more work to be done.

A few months later, on October 24, 1995, Detroit management made a bold move that was more significant than the bare facts suggested. They traded sniper Ray Sheppard, who had scored 152 goals in 274 games for Detroit, to the San Jose Sharks in exchange for Igor Larionov.

Larionov was six weeks shy of his 35th birthday, but he provided Red Wings head coach Scotty Bowman with an opportunity to give his team a unique look, courtesy of a unit called the Russian Five.

Three nights after acquiring Larionov, Bowman employed a five-man unit composed of only Russians. Larionov played between Fedorov and left wing Vyacheslav Kozlov, with Vladimir Konstantinov and Viacheslav Fetisov on defence.

Kozlov and Larionov scored goals in the 3–0 win on the road against the Calgary Flames in Larionov's debut with the Red Wings.

Bowman didn't use his Russian Five all the time. He mixed up his lines to keep the opposition off balance. But when the Red Wings won the Stanley Cup against the Philadelphia Flyers in 1997, the combination of Larionov, Fedorov, Kozlov, Konstantinov, and Fetisov played a vital role.

"We didn't want to use them together every shift," Bowman said. "Sometimes we waited until the second or third period, sometimes we waited to use them at important times in games, like overtime. Sometimes we didn't use them at all together in games because we didn't want to give our opponents an opportunity to figure them out."

Bowman had watched too many Soviet teams arrive in North America and dominate with five-man units playing a skillful puck-possession game.

"In the system they were brought up in, they didn't believe in shooting the puck often," Bowman said. "They would rather move it around until one of them was freed up."

It was evident from that first outing that all five were comfortable with being thrown together from time to time. After all, with the exception of Kozlov, all had played together for CSKA Moscow in the late 1980s. Larionov and

Fetisov were part of a Soviet powerhouse that won Olympic gold in 1984 and 1988, World Championships in 1982, 1983, 1986, and 1987, and the Canada Cup in 1981. The team's dominant Green Unit consisted of Larionov between Vladimir Krutov and Sergei Makarov up front, with Fetisov and Alexei Kasatonov on the blue line.

Detroit's Russian Five gave the Flyers fits in the 1997 Stanley Cup final sweep. Philadelphia defenceman Paul Coffey, a future Hall of Famer, remarked that facing the Russian Five and its focus on puck control was like facing "five Gretzkys on the ice at one time."

Meanwhile, winning an NHL championship was one accomplishment each member of the Russian Five had been missing.

"I feel better right now than I have after winning any world championship or Olympics," Konstantinov said after the Red Wings' first Stanley Cup championship in 42 years. "I can't even explain what this means to me. It's better than anything I have ever done in hockey."

Unfortunately, the time together for the Russian Five

The Russian Five: Viacheslav Fetisov, Sergei Fedorov, Vladimir Konstantinov, Vyacheslav Kozlov, and Igor Larionov. (B. Bennett/Contributor/Getty Images)

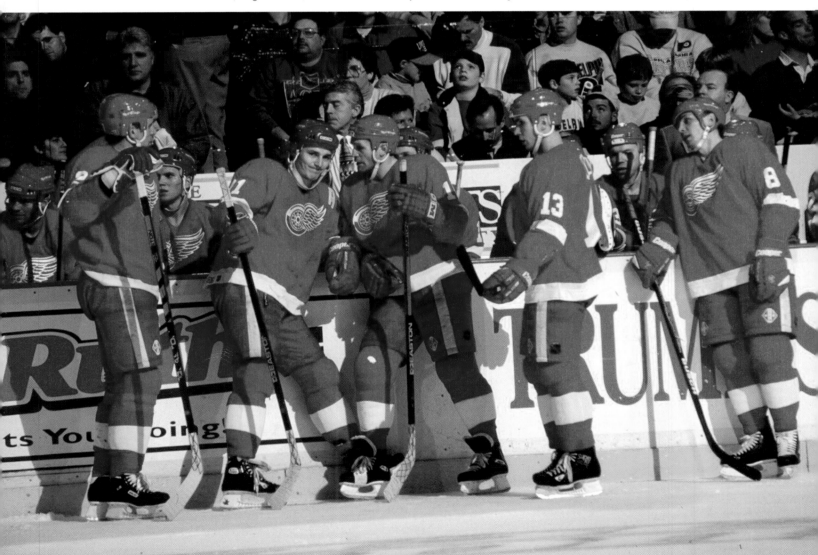

was cut short. After a team party and golf outing in suburban Detroit six days after the Stanley Cup final series ended, Konstantinov, Fetisov, and masseur Sergei Mnatsakonov were hurt when a limousine carrying the three crashed into a tree.

While Fetisov recovered from a bruised lung in time to play one final season with the 1997–98 Red Wings, Konstantinov and Mnatsakonov suffered severe head injuries. At 30, Konstantinov's career was over.

The Red Wings never could replace Konstantinov, a Norris Trophy nominee in his final season. But they did acquire Dmitri Mironov at the 1998 trade deadline to give the team a Russian Five II.

Detroit went on to successfully defend its Stanley Cup title in a sweep of the Washington Capitals that spring. Joining the Red Wings for their on-ice celebration in Washington was Konstantinov, in a wheelchair, clad in a Detroit sweater and baseball cap and wearing an ear-to-ear smile.

"I was very, very happy and excited to see his smile," Fedorov said after the game. "It was very inspirational to see him in the building."

Vladimir Konstantinov holds the Stanley Cup surrounded by former teammates Viacheslav Fetisov, Vyacheslav Kozlov, Igor Larionov, and Steve Yzerman after a car accident ended his career. (Dave Sandford/Hockey Hall of Fame)

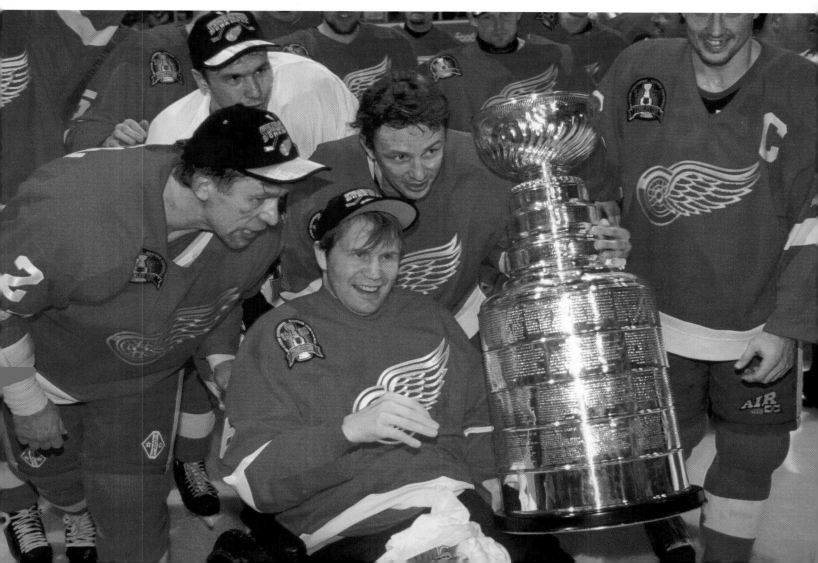

Henri Richard with Coach Hector "Toe" Blake during the 1955–56 season, Richard's rookie campaign. (Le Studio du Hockey/Hockey Hall of Fame)

HENRI RICHARD WINS 11 CUPS

Henri Richard did not follow his famous brother Maurice to the NHL until 13 years after the Rocket started his career, but his timing was perfect.

He debuted in 1955, the same season the Montreal Canadiens began a record run of five consecutive Stanley Cups. That put the "Pocket Rocket" on his way to a record 11 Stanley Cup wins by a player—the last of them in 1973, when he was 37 years old.

Fellow Hall of Famer Ray Bourque was closing in on age 41 when he finally won his first Cup in 2001, and he needed a change of teams to do it. Richard came into a dynasty and missed the playoffs just once in his magnificent career.

Henri always insisted he felt no pressure playing alongside his big brother (the Rocket was three inches taller and 10 pounds heavier), from his first appearance alongside him at the Habs' training camp in 1955. Many thought team management was simply being kind to Maurice by inviting his younger sibling, who was 19 and still had another year of junior eligibility.

But having put up 109 points in 54 games with the Montreal Junior Canadiens in 1953–54, Henri seemed ready for bigger things. His speed and hockey acumen impressed the veteran Habs (they grew frustrated trying to get the puck off him in workouts), earning him a job in 1955–56 at centre and the immediate approval of fans.

Henri's rookie classmates included defenceman Jean-Guy Talbot and winger Claude Provost, both of whom would also enjoy a long run of success through the 1950s and '60s.

Henri was a first-team all-star by 1958, one of two years in which he led the NHL in assists, and soon showed a knack for scoring in the spring. In an era when teams only played two rounds to win the Cup, Richard had at least two points in each of his 18 trips to the postseason.

The 1959–60 Habs, considered the best team of the five that won consecutive Cups, benefited from nine playoff assists by Richard in their eight-game sweep of Chicago and Toronto. The 4–0 Cup-clinching victory in Game 4 against the Leafs also saw Henri score the goal on which Maurice collected his 126th and last NHL playoff point.

While the Rocket would later lament that he quit the game too early at 38, the 24-year-old Henri was in his prime.

Though Chicago and Toronto successfully prevented Montreal from capturing a title over the next four years, the mid-1960s brought the arrival of Sam Pollock as GM and a renewed focus on winning the Cup. Young Yvan Cournoyer and tough Ted Harris joined incumbent stars Richard, Jean Beliveau, and an important acquisition, Dick Duff.

Henri Richard in game action against the Toronto Maple Leafs. (Frank Prazak/Hockey Hall of Fame)

Montreal was sipping from the Cup again in 1965 and repeated in '66, courtesy of a somewhat controversial overtime Cup winner by Richard in Game 6 against Detroit. After he was tripped up on a rush by Gary Bergman, Richard and the Wings defenceman both crashed into Detroit goalie Roger Crozier. The puck crossed the line propelled by Richard's elbow. At coach Toe Blake's urging, the Canadiens swarmed over the boards to celebrate before the Wings could protest.

Two years later, the league's expansion era opened with Montreal easily handling the West Division champion St. Louis Blues in back-to-back finals. Meanwhile, Blake gave way to Claude Ruel as coach, but Richard did not adapt well to the coach who followed Ruel about a third of the way into 1970–71: Maritimer Al MacNeil.

Though Montreal was back in 40-win territory after missing the playoffs the year before, things did not go smoothly for them in the 1971 final against the Blackhawks. The Habs fell behind, three games to two, and faced defeat at home. MacNeil's search for scoring prompted a series of line changes that left Richard out in the cold.

The Canadiens got out of town that night with a 4–3 win, but that was only half the story as Montreal reporters clustered around Richard after the game. He denounced MacNeil as the worst coach he'd ever played for and accused him of favouring English-speaking players.

Richard might as well have plopped MacNeil on top of a stack of dynamite and lit the fuse. Montreal won Game 7 on the road, with Richard scoring twice, and while MacNeil hoped to take language studies in the summer to improve relations with his players and the press, he was reassigned to the farm team in Halifax. Scotty Bowman came aboard to set the stage for Richard's last Cup.

Richard inherited the captaincy from the retiring Beliveau, which allowed him to share another unique honour with his brother as they became the first brothers to wear the *C* for the same team. Two years later, Montreal was back in the final against the Hawks. As the Canadiens took a 3–2 series lead into Chicago Stadium, Richard was poised to pass both Beliveau and Red Kelly by playing in his 165th playoff game.

The Canadiens won the high-scoring series, Richard managed 10 points in 17 games, and he was first in line to receive the Stanley Cup—in his case, for an incredible 11th time. Only Bill Russell of the Boston Celtics had won as many pro titles. When a contented Richard retired a couple of years later to run his own tavern, there were simply not enough fingers on which to put his championship rings.

Henri Richard, post-retirement, poses in his old Canadiens uniform with the Stanley Cup. (Le Studio du Hockey/Hockey Hall of Fame)

18

THE FIRST GOALIE GLOVE

Before there could be a glove save, there had to be a goalie glove.

Credit Emile Francis, the future NHL coach and executive, with devising and popularizing a mitt that goalies could use to snatch bullet-like shots out of the air. Francis fashioned it from the glove he used as a baseball shortstop around his hometown of North Battleford, Saskatchewan.

After Francis's father died when he was eight years old, an uncle who played senior men's hockey brought the boy to see a few of his games. The uncle was a defenceman, but Francis could not take his eyes off the goaltender. Though Francis had considered playing centre, once he realized that playing goal meant 60 minutes on the ice with no time watching from the bench, he settled on his favourite position. He showed such fine catching ability and quick reflexes playing junior that a sportswriter nicknamed him "The Cat."

Property of the Chicago Blackhawks, Francis made his way through the minors using a Rawlings first baseman's glove, a model made for George McQuinn of the New York Yankees. Francis asked his trainer to have a shoemaker sew a protective cuff around it, making it bigger and more effective than the trappers used by goalies at the time, which

Francis made his way through the minors using a Rawlings first baseman's glove.

were five-fingered and poorly webbed.

After Francis joined the Hawks in 1946–47, the unusual glove was the first thing Detroit coach Jack Adams noticed about the new kid across the ice. In the pre-game warm-up, Adams called over referee King Clancy and demanded that Francis take off the glove, which the goalie refused to do, as he had no spare.

Rather than cancel the game, Clancy let Francis play with the mitt, and when both men were in Montreal a day later, they sought out league president Clarence Campbell for a ruling. Intrigued by Francis's ingenuity, Campbell let The Cat keep his glove, and soon every goalie in the league was pestering sporting goods manufacturers to replicate the new catcher.

A couple of years later, Murray Dowey, goalie for the RCAF Flyers at the 1948 Winter Olympics, wore a similar glove at St. Moritz, and Swiss fans flocked to the arena just to watch him catch pucks in practice.

Francis continued to popularize the glove until his NHL career ended with the New York Rangers in 1951–52. He spent another decade in the minors.

While goalies took his innovation to enormous proportions as decades went on, adding oversized cuffs and extra webbing, there was eventually a league crackdown on equipment that brought the gloves down to accepted dimensions.

But in a 2016 interview, Francis joked that goalies' catchers still looked like "a bushel basket" compared to his first attempt more than half a century ago.

Emile "The Cat" Francis, who fashioned the first goalie glove, with the Chicago trainer Ed Froelich helping him suit up. (Imperial Oil–Turofsky/ Hockey Hall of Fame)

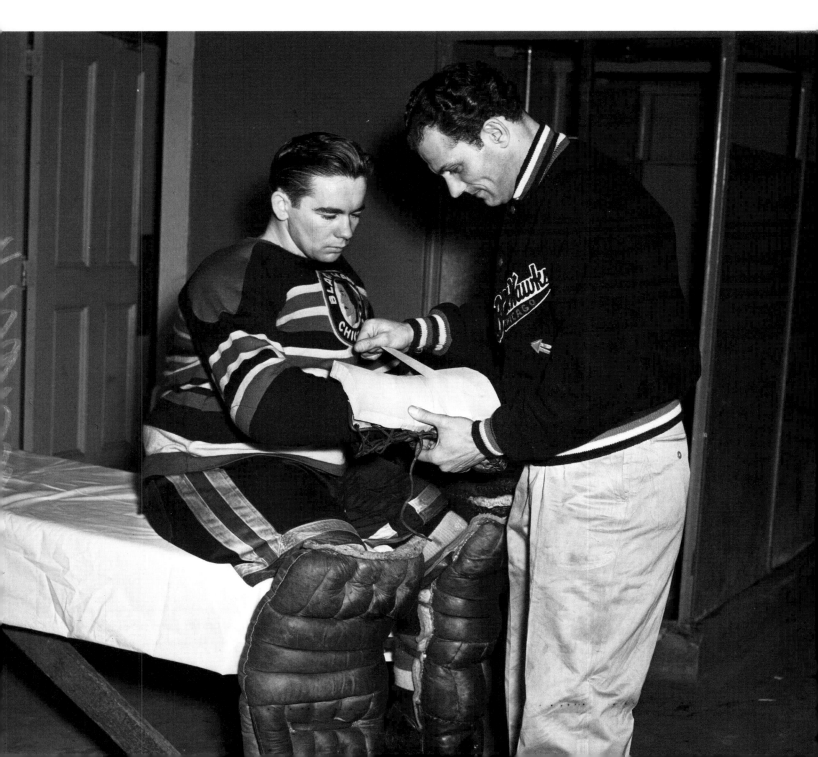

The first player selected in the NHL's amateur draft, Garry Monahan was taken by the Montreal Canadiens and played 748 NHL games for several teams, including the Toronto Maple Leafs. (Lewis Portnoy/Hockey Hall of Fame)

19

THE AMATEUR DRAFT BEGINS

The original NHL Amateur Draft in 1963 was such an unspectacular event that Garry Monahan, the player chosen first overall by the Montreal Canadiens, did not even know it had taken place.

The NHL had decided to introduce an amateur draft because league president Clarence Campbell wanted to do away with the sponsorship of junior clubs by NHL teams. Many believed the practice gave Toronto and Montreal an unfair head start in signing young talent, and it was eventually terminated in 1968.

"I was 16, and I don't remember any talk of any draft," Monahan told the *Montreal Gazette*. "When they phoned me and said they had drafted me, I didn't know what they were talking about. It had to be explained to me."

When the phone rang in the Monahan home in the Toronto suburb of Scarborough that day, Canadiens general manager Sam Pollock was on the other end.

"What did I know?" said Monahan, then a centre with the St. Michael's College School Buzzers in Toronto. "I didn't know anything. I didn't know there was a draft. Certainly, my parents and my older brother didn't know. The phone rang after the fact, and I don't even remember if it was the next day

or the next week. We were all sort of flabbergasted.

"My recollection is that my dad then told Sammy, 'You mean Pat, Garry's [18-year-old] brother?' Pat was the better player."

Prior to the 1963 draft, teams signed players to A, B, or C forms and placed the young talents with junior teams. An A form committed a player to a tryout; a B form gave the team an option to sign the player at a later date; and a C form—the most common—gave the team the right to sign the player to a pro contract at age 18.

For example, even though Bobby Orr was only 15 years old at the time of the 1963 NHL Amateur Draft, he was not available to be selected because the Boston Bruins had already signed him to a C form and he had already completed his first season with the Oshawa Generals.

Campbell wanted to get rid of the sponsorship system so that every team had an equal opportunity to land the best junior-age players.

After three days of NHL meetings, the draft took place on June 5, 1963, at the Queen Elizabeth Hotel in Montreal. The only people present were representatives of the league and of the six teams. It consisted of four rounds, and teams

Only five of the 21 selections went on to play in the NHL.

selected from a pool of players scheduled to celebrate their 17th birthdays between August 1, 1963, and July 31, 1964, and who were not already on a team's sponsorship list.

The first draft order was Montreal, Detroit, Boston, New York, Chicago, and Toronto. (Based on their last-place finish in 1962–63, the Bruins were awarded their choice of pick, but saved their chance to select higher for another, more talent-rich year.) The following year, the teams would rotate so that Detroit got the first pick, with Montreal choosing sixth.

In total, 21 players were chosen. The Red Wings decided not to draft in the third and fourth rounds, while the Blackhawks opted out of the fourth round. Only five of the 21 selections went on to play in the NHL: Monahan, Pete Mahovlich (Detroit, second overall), Walt McKechnie (Toronto, sixth), Jim McKenny (Toronto, 17th), and Gerry Meehan (Toronto, 21st). But those five averaged 772 regular-season games in the NHL, with McKechnie leading the way at 955.

Mahovlich was the most accomplished, with four Stanley Cup wins with the Canadiens. He was also a member of the successful Canadian teams in the 1972 Summit Series and 1976 Canada Cup.

The draft only warranted four paragraphs' coverage in the *Montreal Star*, primarily because of a blockbuster trade between the Canadiens and Rangers that sent seven-time Vezina Trophy winner Jacques Plante and forwards Donnie Marshall and Phil Goyette to the Rangers in exchange for goalie Gump Worsley and forwards Dave Balon, Len Ronson, and Leon Rochefort.

Monahan played 748 games with Montreal, Detroit, Los Angeles, Toronto, and Vancouver. Breaking into the Canadiens roster out of junior would have been a tough task, because Montreal had plenty of depth down the middle with Jean Beliveau, Henri Richard, Ralph Backstrom, and Jacques Lemaire. Monahan played only 14 games with Montreal in his first two seasons as a pro, but practised with the Canadiens as they won Stanley Cups in 1967–68 and 1968–69.

In his NHL debut, against the Bruins on October 21, 1967, he warmed the bench for two and a half periods before Canadiens coach Toe Blake sent him out for his first shift. Monahan was hit in the face with the puck as the result of a return pass from a teammate.

"It hit me flat, on the cheekbone near the bridge of my nose, and cut me in three different places," he said. "Down I went. I remember dropping my gloves. There was [defenceman] J.C. Tremblay, and I recall grabbing at my sweater as I sunk to my knees, out cold.

"They dragged me off after a shift of about 10 seconds. That was it."

In a strange twist, Monahan was traded to Detroit, along with Doug Piper, for his former St. Mike's teammate Mahovlich and Bart Crashley—exactly six years and a day after the Canadiens drafted Monahan.

"Sammy finally realized his mistake," Monahan said, jokingly. "So he traded me for Peter."

20

BILL BARILKO'S CUP-WINNING GOAL

t has inspired countless television features, at least one book, an iconic song, and even talk of a movie.

The tale of Bill Barilko and his 1951 Stanley Cup–winning overtime goal just never gets old, particularly in Toronto, where his No. 5 banner hangs from the Air Canada Centre rafters.

One of the many Leaf greats to come from mining country in Northern Ontario, the Timmins-born Barilko first sought his hockey fortune in the minors. In the mid-1940s, fate first took him and his brother Alex to California, where the game was catching on and the ruggedly handsome Bill became a fan favourite with the Hollywood Wolves.

Recommended to the Leafs when injuries struck their defence in 1946–47, "Bashing Bill" was called up and became an integral part of a Toronto team on the cusp of winning four championships in the next five years. In the spring of '51, in a series against Montreal in which the first four games all went to overtime, Barilko's big moment arrived on the evening of April 21.

After a late goal by the Leafs' Tod Sloan made Game 5 2–2 and forced extra time yet again, Barilko joined the rush, a habit that manager Conn Smythe disliked so much he'd threatened to fine any rearguard who did it. Barilko back-handed the Cup winner past Gerry McNeil of the Canadiens

at 2:53. Maple Leaf Gardens erupted and Barilko was a national hero, at least in English Canada.

But as the Tragically Hip would sing decades later, it was the last goal he ever scored. A few months later, the small plane that he and a friend took on a fishing trip in bush country failed to return. One of the biggest air searches of its kind followed, without success.

Barilko's family held out hope as long as possible, his mother seeking help from a tea leaf reader and refusing to give up, because "Bill will be famous again someday."

Theories were put forward that the 24-year-old Barilko had been secretly mining gold or was on some covert Cold War mission for the Canadian government. But his equipment remained untouched in its stall as the Leafs began training camp.

In June 1962, a few months after the Leafs had won the Cup for the first time in 11 years, the plane's wreckage and the two bodies were discovered by chance in thick muskeg. The public quickly made a connection between the end of the Cup drought and Barilko's discovery, a fascination that continues to this day.

In 2015, the Hockey Hall Of Fame learned it might not have the puck with which Barilko scored his legendary goal after all. The legitimacy of the disc long thought to be the one he shot, reportedly given to a young fan at rinkside by referee Bill Chadwick, was challenged by the Donohue family of Hamilton, Ontario.

Only a teenager at the time of the Leafs' Cup win, the late Harry Donohue had always maintained he'd walked onto the ice to retrieve the puck after asking permission from his father and an usher. A rare photo surfaced showing an unidentified young man walking toward the Montreal net while the Leafs celebrated, the puck still in the net. The orange crest on the Donohue puck matches the style used that season, but the Donohues kept it on their mantel and told very few people of its existence until Harry's passing.

The moment when Bill Barilko scored his famous, Cup-winning overtime goal in Game 5 of the Stanley Cup Final on April 21, 1951. (Imperial Oil–Turofsky/Hockey Hall of Fame)

Bill Barilko rides triumphantly on the shoulders of his teammates after winning the Stanley Cup. Four months later he died in a plane crash. (Imperial Oil–Turofsky/Hockey Hall of Fame)

21

TED LINDSAY HOISTS THE CUP

Ted Lindsay enjoyed a memorable final few weeks to the 1949–50 season.

In his sixth NHL year, Terrible Ted claimed his only Art Ross Trophy, with 23 goals and 78 points in 69 regular-season games. He also celebrated his first of four Stanley Cups with the Detroit Red Wings.

But that spring, Lindsay also began a wonderful tradition for the team that wins the Stanley Cup.

After Pete Babando scored in double overtime to give the Red Wings a victory in the seventh game against the New York Rangers at the Detroit Olympia, the Cup was put on a table for its usual subdued on-ice presentation, this season to Red Wings general manager Jack Adams.

This time, however, after the formalities had finished, Lindsay skated over and snatched the Cup off its pedestal, hoisted it over his head, and took the prized trophy for a victory lap.

To explain what he was thinking that evening, Lindsay stated he had simply wanted to take the celebration to the fans. It was, after all, Detroit's first championship since 1943.

"I never thought I was starting a tradition," Lindsay said. "I wanted to recognize who paid my salary. It was the fans in the seats.

"After they presented the Cup to Jack Adams, they put

it on a table with a tablecloth. I saw it sitting there and I went over and picked it up and took it over to the boards. Adams probably thought, 'What's that idiot going to do with that Cup?' He didn't know if I was going to throw it or whatever.

"I took it over and had it so people could see the names on the Cup. I went around the ice. I didn't think I was starting a tradition. I was just taking care of the people that paid my salary."

The following season, the NHL changed its ways. When the Toronto Maple Leafs defeated the Montreal Canadiens in five games, the Cup was presented to the captain, Ted Kennedy.

"He raised it and went around with it, and they said Ted Lindsay started that tradition. I'm honoured to have my name with it," Lindsay said.

The late 1940s and early 1950s were good times for Lindsay and the Red Wings. They finished first overall in the regular season seven times in a row from 1948–49 to 1954–55, won four Stanley Cups, and advanced to five Stanley Cup finals.

A big part of Detroit's success was the famed Production Line, with Lindsay on the left side, Sid Abel in the middle, and Gordie Howe on right wing.

"People always come up to me and ask what it was like

to play with Gordie Howe," said Lindsay, who had two seasons under his belt before Howe was a rookie in 1946–47. "I tell them, 'You should ask him what it was like to play with me. I was here first.'

"I truly believe Gordie was the best player of all time. He really grew as a player in his first few years with us."

The five-foot-eight, 160-pound Lindsay was no slouch himself. He was a nine-time NHL all-star who played a combined 1,201 games (1,068 regular-season games and 133 in the playoffs) and was inducted into the Hockey Hall of Fame in 1966.

The Red Wings won the Stanley Cup in 1951–52, when Abel was still the team captain. Then Abel retired and Lindsay captained the club when the Red Wings won back-to-back championships in 1953–54 and 1954–55.

The Red Wings didn't win another Stanley Cup until 1996–97. When they had their banner-raising ceremony at the home opener the following season at Joe Louis Arena, there were Lindsay and Howe, handing the Stanley Cup to Detroit captain Steve Yzerman to begin the pre-game festivities.

By then, the tradition Lindsay began more than four decades earlier had taken on a new twist. When the Edmonton Oilers won their third of five titles, in 1986–87, captain Wayne Gretzky took the Stanley Cup from NHL president John Ziegler and then handed it to Oilers defenceman Steve Smith.

It had been a long, difficult year for Smith. Thirteen months earlier, in Game 7 of the Smythe Division final against Calgary, the rookie defenceman had tried to make a pass from the side of the Edmonton goal, through the middle to his partner. The puck caromed off the leg of Oilers goalie Grant Fuhr and into the net, clinching the series for the Flames. The six-foot-four Smith was brought to tears. He was inconsolable.

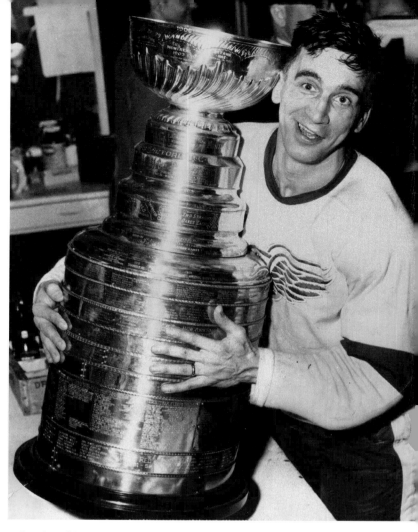

Ted Lindsay of the Detroit Red Wings embraces the Stanley Cup.
(Le Studio du Hockey/Hockey Hall of Fame)

Gretzky's gesture the following spring might have started a trend.

"I just gave it to the biggest guy in the crowd, and that was Steve," the humble Gretzky said at the time, with a sly smile.

In all likelihood it was the first time a captain receiving the Cup already had in mind the next teammate who'd get it. Many more premeditated hand-offs would follow. For his part, Gretzky claims it was only because by 1987 the presentation of the Cup had become so much of a presentation that he even had time to think about who would get it next.

Rene Lecavalier calls a game for French-language television broadcast *La soirée du hockey*. (Hockey Hall of Fame)

22

THE FIRST TV BROADCASTS

n Canada's Sports Hall of Fame, tucked between CFL star Pep Leadlay and skier Kerrin Lee-Gartner, is Rene Lecavalier.

He never scored a goal, stopped a shot, or coached a game, yet hockey fans, especially those in Quebec, considered him to be as famous as any of the Montreal Canadiens—and perhaps even the team itself.

When the Habs won their first of six Stanley Cups during the 1950s, Lecavalier was there—or at least his voice on the TV set was there—for thousands of Quebecers, and throughout their years of success in the '60s and '70s as well.

Lecavalier was the first person to call a televised hockey game in Canada, which he did for the Canadian Broadcasting Corporation's French-language outlet on October 11, 1952. While the CBC had conducted its initial experiments with closed-circuit hockey telecasts from Maple Leaf Gardens in Toronto earlier that year, the Montreal affiliate was able to iron out the bugs faster and get on the air.

So with Gordie Howe and the Red Wings at the Forum, it was "lights, camera, action," only a short while after TV had established itself as a popular medium in the vast nation.

Amazingly, the debut of *La soirée du hockey* did not mark the first time hockey had been beamed into living rooms. The British had tried it for a couple of periods in 1938 from a rink in London. An experimental station in New York City showed a Rangers–Canadiens game in 1940 to a test audience of 300 fans, a prelude to the Rangers' home games being seen locally on a regular basis beginning in 1946. And Hollywood was quick to get in on the act after the war, with KTLA in Los Angeles finding an audience for Pacific Coast Hockey League games.

Around 1949, the NHL began to seriously consider the idea of televised games. The old guard, such as league president Clarence Campbell, feared televised games might have a negative impact on attendance, just as TV had cut into box-office receipts at movie theatres. Why not join games in progress, then, so rinks would still sell out to the diehard fans who wouldn't want to miss half the game?

The CBC also fretted about hockey interfering with its regular broadcast lineup.

For all this handwringing, if a network was going to showcase the national pastime, it needed to deliver the highest quality product. In the producer's chair in Montreal, and very much aware of the need to impress television audiences with the best possible substitute for the real thing, was Gerald Renaud. Just 24, he was well versed in the game as sports editor of the French-language Ottawa paper *Le Droit* and host of a radio show on CKCH, across the river in Hull.

A relative in the broadcast business had suggested that Renaud apply for the new hockey position, and the young producer brought plenty of creative enthusiasm to the job.

Hardly anyone had televised hockey before him, so Renaud followed his instincts as to what viewers would like to see: the whole ice, a medium shot, and a close-up. He had three cameras positioned around centre ice to deliver the various angles.

With Rocket Richard, Bernie Geoffrion, Doug Harvey, Butch Bouchard, Elmer Lach, and Jacques Plante providing the content, Renaud wished to convey the speed and grace of the Habs, bringing them right into living rooms across the province and in Atlantic Canada, even if the TV sets of the day had only tiny black-and-white screens.

Behind the microphone was Lecavalier, a former war correspondent in the North African theatre and a cultural affairs radio host. He didn't just do "*lance et compte*" (he shoots, he scores!) but put his journalism background to work creating a narrative that enhanced each game and made the stars of *Les Glorieux* shine even brighter.

Sportswriter Frank Orr noted that Lecavalier was the first to dispense with the English hockey phrases that French broadcasters mangled when trying to force into their own language. He adopted his own calls that sounded much smoother to the French-Canadian ear ("puck" became "*rondelle*," for example). Several linguistic experts credited Lecavalier with helping his audience with their vocabulary, thus helping preserve the language in Canada. Lecavalier retired in 1985 and passed away in 1999.

Referees called six penalties in the goalless first period between the Canadiens and Wings in that first game, while Lach, with an assist from Richard, opened the scoring at the 4:39 mark of the second. Alex Delvecchio tied the score before the game was joined in progress by the television broadcast.

The stage was set for Montreal's Billy Reay to make history. The future coach of the Toronto Maple Leafs and Chicago Blackhawks scored the first goal to be televised in Canada: a power-play marker scored with Red Wings defenceman Marcel Pronovost in the penalty box.

Three weeks later in Toronto, television history was made again, in English.

Rene Lecavalier with Bernie Geoffrion, Maurice Richard and their wives. (Studio Alain Brouillard/Hockey Hall of Fame)

HOCKEY NIGHT IN CANADA IS BORN

Unlike the popular radio transmissions of Toronto Maple Leaf games, for which broadcaster Foster Hewitt's gondola was constructed at a specific height to suit his preferred line of sight, televised Toronto hockey experienced a difficult beginning.

The fledgling television branch of the CBC, which was about to launch its first two stations, in Toronto and Montreal, experimented with broadcasts of junior hockey during the 1952 Memorial Cup final at Maple Leaf Gardens. Foster Hewitt called a 10-2 win by Guelph over Regina to a small group of technicians at CBC headquarters via closed circuit.

While Leafs owner Conn Smythe understood the power of radio, when he saw the closed-circuit game he thought it was awful and that Toronto fans would never accept it.

He also fretted that televised hockey might affect attendance at the sold-out arena, and he certainly didn't want the bulky cameras blocking the view of paying customers.

Some accounts suggest that Smythe believed televised games might help to grow the game down the road, but when the CBC first began to broadcast games from the Gardens, it waited until 9:30 p.m.—an hour after the opening faceoff—to go on the air.

Producer George Retzlaff, who was a technical director from Winnipeg, was charged with the task of getting the

Gardens and the Leafs ready for the new medium. He listened patiently as Smythe urged him to restrict camera positions to the gondola high above the ice, or have one at each end that would trade angles, but likely disorient viewers.

Knowing he was soon to be televised, Hewitt had reason to be nervous, too. Some critics believed he overdramatized parts of his radio commentary, and they wondered how he would fare when a visual record held him to a higher standard. But Hewitt vowed to keep his keen play-by-play observations the same for television as they had been on radio.

Three weeks after the first nationally televised game in league history originated from the Forum in Montreal, Retzlaff and his three-camera team in Toronto were ready to make history of their own. The date was November 1, 1952. At 9:30 p.m., a 0–0 game between the Boston Bruins and Toronto Maple Leafs—playing their sixth home game of the season—was joined in progress in the second period. *Hockey Night in Canada* was on the air, witnessed by a Canadian public that had begun purchasing TV sets by the thousands. Imperial Oil was the sponsor, as it had been on radio.

The first thing viewers saw was the end of a Leaf goal celebration. According to a report in the *Globe and Mail*, the coverage began roughly 10 seconds after centre Bobby Hassard, from Lloydminster, Saskatchewan, had beaten Bruins goalie

"Sugar" Jim Henry. Teammate Max Bentley's goal eight minutes later was seen in its entirety—the first of thousands to follow—as Toronto won, 3–2.

The truncated broadcast that night evolved into a ratings machine, drawing huge audiences for Leaf games in the Toronto market and throughout English Canada. TV ad money flowed in, and the Gardens, which housed a tiny studio, became a magical Saturday-night kingdom.

According to reports, Imperial Oil paid only $100 per televised game that first season; within a few years, the sponsor renewed those rights for $150,000 in a three-year deal.

Hockey became the unifying force of a diverse country, as families and friends gathered in front of the TV set at home, the local pub, the legion hall, or wherever the game was shown.

Legendary broadcaster Foster Hewitt calls a game from his famous gondola in an early edition of *Hockey Night in Canada*. (Doug Griffin/Contributor/ Getty Images)

The legendary Stan Mikita was one of the first NHLers to use a curved blade on his stick. (Le Studio du Hockey/Hockey Hall of Fame)

THE BASICS: STICKS AND SKATES

No statistic can tell you how many shoes were ruined by early hockey players. "Blades" were literally just that—crude steel runners clamped onto street shoes, then removed for the long, wet walk home in sodden socks.

At the birth of the NHL, hockey sticks were reasonably referred to as "lumber" because the primitive piece of equipment was thick, heavy and constructed with a single piece of wood, its blade wide and flat, its shaft as flexible as a length of steel pipe.

Hockey skates and sticks are among the few items of equipment that have been with the NHL since the league's birth in 1917. Other equipment has been introduced over the decades to improve the safety of the players and the quality of the game itself. But the skates and stick, with the puck and the goal net, have been with the NHL forever.

Skates today will never be confused with the animal bones that people in modern-day Finland fashioned to help them hunt some 5,000 years ago. Centuries later, the Dutch fashioned their own crude skates for quick transit along their network of canals. Workbench science modified the design to eventually include a steel blade mounted on a block of wood that skaters strapped to their shoes.

When blacksmiths in Nova Scotia weren't shoeing horses in the late 1800s, they were advancing the skate by more finely honing the steel blade for the pond-skaters who were participating in the fledgling, rules-free game of hockey.

By the early 1900s, the blade had become more robust, crewed and later riveted onto a soft leather boot that afforded little protection from other blades and the slashing sticks that could easily slice through them.

But the leather skate and carbon-steel blade provided the template for decades of hockey. While safety caps on the heels of blades would be added and newer, lighter materials would be used, the basic design remained unchanged through the NHL's Original Six era, from the early 1940s into deep in the 1960s.

For a time, hard-molded plastic boots found a following among NHL players. These featured plastic brackets holding a thin blade to reduce weight. No longer were skates manufactured on a blacksmith's bench, but in laboratories with the aid of computers.

Today's NHL skate is feather-light and virtually bulletproof, a quantum leap even from what was worn a couple of decades ago. The lightest model, which can withstand the slash of another player's skate or a 100 mph slap shot, might weigh just a pound and a half.

Just as light, and every bit as much a marvel of science, is today's stick.

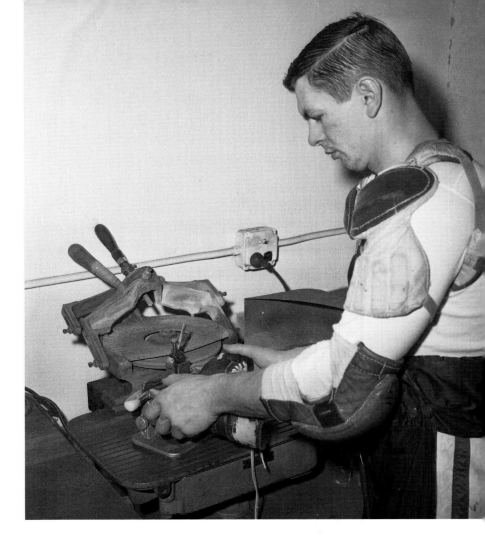

Mikita sharpens his own skates. (Le Studio du Hockey/ Hockey Hall of Fame)

The earliest players used what almost amounted to tree branches. The Mi'kmaq First Nations people of Canada's maritime provinces and Quebec's Gaspé Peninsula made an art of carving sticks from the hornbeam tree, the blade turned up to appear like a modern field-hockey stick.

Birch, ash and elm would become the woods of choice into the turn of the 20th century. In time, the two-piece stick appeared; its revolutionary design saw the blade inserted and glued into the shaft.

By the 1930s into the 1940s the two-piece stick had become the NHL skater's model of choice, the fat blade and thick, solid shaft making it practically a sledgehammer. But it was durable, indeed almost indestructible, something that pleased more than one cost-conscious team owner.

Chicago Blackhawks forward Stan Mikita broke a stick during a 1960s practice and accidentally discovered the curved blade, to the horror of goaltenders. Shots coming off the self-bent banana blades of Mikita, teammate Bobby Hull and others instantly became unpredictable unguided missiles.

Scientists worked with new materials. The lightweight aluminum shaft cut by half the weight in a player's hands. Aluminum sticks were used by players in the late 1980s, but when superstar Wayne Gretzky signed a deal with Easton in the early 1990s to use and endorse an aluminum stick, the wood stick at last became a relic.

Today's multiproperty composite sticks weigh next to nothing and have tremendous flex to whip the puck. They are a dream for players, though their fragility and cost (high-end models can retail for upwards of $300) compare poorly to the heavy lumber of days gone by and would have been a budget nightmare for team owners of yesteryear.

25

PULLING THE GOALIE

Newspaper accounts of the day didn't explain the motivation behind the move, except to call it an "amazing manoeuvre."

Imagine if it had actually worked!

The amazing manoeuvre occurred in a semifinal playoff game on March 26, 1931, at Boston Garden. With 40 seconds remaining in the second game of the best-of-five series, and the Montreal Canadiens leading 1–0, Bruins coach and general manager Art Ross removed goaltender Tiny Thompson, replacing him with a sixth skater (all six were forwards).

It is widely believed to be the first time a coach pulled a goaltender for an extra attacker, and it has been reported that the player who came off the bench was Red Beattie.

The Bruins didn't score, but the innovation was soon emulated by other coaches.

Although it was long believed that the first empty-net goal wasn't scored until the early 1940s, it actually took less than a year from that first try, and once again it involved the Bruins, Ross, and Thompson.

On January 12, 1932, at Boston Garden, the Rangers and Bruins were tied 3–3 in overtime. Back then, teams played a full 10-minute overtime period, not sudden death.

"At the end of the day, you're trying to find a way to win," said Keenan. "You're doing everything possible and not giving up."

According to wire service reports, it was Rangers forward Cecil Dillon who settled the outcome and scored the empty-net goal.

"Cecil Dillon, speedy Ranger spare, was the deciding factor in forcing the Bruins to bow," read the Associated Press story. "He broke a 3–3 tie early in the overtime by caging a pass from Frank Boucher and during the final minute after Manager Art Ross pulled out Goaler Tiny Thompson to put six forwards in action. Cecil hooked the rubber near his goal, beat every Bruin down the ice and drove home the final score without opposition."

Though the win was notable because it featured the first empty-net goal, that wasn't indicated in the game story. Of more significance at the time, it seemed, was that the Rangers' victory was their first in three seasons in Boston, breaking a "Garden jinx." The game was also the Bruins' fifth straight "extra-session clash."

One of the craziest instances of pulling the goalie involved the Canadiens and the Chicago Blackhawks in the final game of the 1969–70 season. That afternoon, the Rangers had easily beaten Detroit, 9–5, to pull even with fourth-place

Boston Bruins goalie Cecil "Tiny" Thompson was pulled from the net for an extra skater, allowing the NHL's first empty-net goal. (Le Studio du Hockey/Hockey Hall of Fame)

Montreal in the East Division standings. (Too easily, said the Habs. The Red Wings had clinched a playoff berth the night before and effectively had nothing to play for against New York.) To ensure a spot in the postseason, the Habs needed only to win or tie—or, if they should lose, to score at least five goals. That's because both teams had 38 wins, so the tie would be broken based on total goals scored.

With about 10 minutes remaining in the third period, the Blackhawks scored a couple of goals to take a 5–2 lead. Montreal coach Claude Ruel then pulled goalie Rogatien Vachon for a sixth attacker—keeping him out of the net unless there was a faceoff in the Habs' zone or after Chicago scored—in an attempt to produce the three goals. Instead, Chicago went on to score five more goals and win the game, 10–2. The Canadiens, winners of the two previous Stanley Cup championships, missed the playoffs for the first time since 1947–48.

For many years, coaches would wait until the final minute or so in the third period to pull their goalie. But over the years, that strategy became a lot bolder. Today, it's typical to see a team pull the goalie with several minutes remaining, depending on the score and circumstance.

"I remember a game, we were playing in Toronto, and Pat Quinn is yelling from the Leafs bench that we had too many men on the ice," said Mike Keenan, who coached several NHL teams between 1984 and 2009. "It was the second period, we were down a couple, so I pulled the goalie. I thought we might surprise them and we did. A lot of times, depending on the score and the time in the game, if we had a five-on-three power play I would go with six [skaters].

While the intent of pulling the goalie is to add a sixth skater and improve the probability of scoring the goal or goals needed to tie or win a game, the strategy doesn't always work.

"At the end of the day, you're trying to find a way to win. You're doing everything possible and not giving up."

And as the game evolved and the puckhandling skills of goaltenders improved, an empty net brought with it an additional risk factor.

A total of 14 goalies have been credited with scoring a goal in the NHL, although seven of them did so by being the last player to touch the puck before the opposing team inadvertently scored into its own net. But the other seven goals were the result of the goalie taking aim and hitting the empty net.

The first to do it was Ron Hextall of the Philadelphia Flyers, who was so gifted at handling the puck that it was often said he was like having a third defenceman on the ice. In his second NHL season, Hextall scored on December 8, 1987. He duplicated the feat the following season, in a playoff game on April 11, 1989, against the Washington Capitals. The Flyers were leading by a couple of goals and the Capitals, on a power play, pulled their goalie in an attempt to reduce the deficit. Instead, Hextall scored a shorthanded goal.

"The team was really pumped to try and get him that first goal," recalled Keenan, who was then coaching the Flyers. "We were always giving him the puck. We were probably risking icing, but it was a big thrill for the whole team. He could really shoot the puck well, probably better than some of our defencemen.

"We encouraged him during play to use his puck-handling skills to head-man the puck, or help us clear the zone. I remember [Mark] Howe once said to me that Hexy would add 20 years to his career because he would never have to skate back to retrieve pucks."

The all-time leader in goals by a goaltender is New Jersey Devils star Martin Brodeur, who scored three in his career, although two of them were own goals by the opposition. The one on which he shot the puck came against his hometown team, the Montreal Canadiens, in a playoff game on April 17, 1997.

THE NEW YORK ISLANDERS' DYNASTY

The ultra-competitive winger, the forward who pushed the New York Islanders into contention and on their way to four Stanley Cup victories in a row, could most often be found near the bottom of team scoring. That player was one Robert Thore Nystrom. Without him, and teammates like him, the star-studded Islanders might not have become the dynasty they were.

Born in Stockholm, Sweden, Nystrom and his family moved to Canada when he was four, and as a teenager he exhibited enough talent and determination in his two seasons of junior hockey with the Calgary Centennials to be selected by the Islanders in the third round (33rd overall) of the 1972 NHL draft.

On May 24, 1980, Nystrom squared his debt to the Islanders for their faith, redirecting a pass from John Tonelli seven minutes and 11 seconds into overtime. The Islanders had defeated the Philadelphia Flyers in six games to win the coveted Stanley Cup.

Nystrom had a flair for the dramatic. He scored 39 times in 157 career playoff games, and four of those goals were in overtime, including his Stanley Cup–clinching goal.

"I'll never forget what it meant to me," Nystrom told

> "I was a journeyman. I was by no means a star. That goal will stay with me forever."

Newsday. "I was a journeyman. I was by no means a star. That goal will stay with me forever."

The goal was a relief to the Islanders. They had entered the NHL as an expansion team in 1972 and swiftly developed into a contender. In their third season, they began a run of three straight trips to the semifinals, losing each time to the eventual Stanley Cup champion. Then there was a painful quarter-final exit in a seven-game loss to the Toronto Maple Leafs in 1978, and—the most devastating of all—a six-game loss to the hated rival New York Rangers in the semifinals in 1979.

The critics wondered whether this talented team, with Bryan Trottier, Mike Bossy, Denis Potvin, and Billy Smith in the lineup, could win a title.

"We were known as chokers," Lorne Henning said. "We were all starting to feel the heat. The sense of it was we had to win [in 1980] because it might be our last chance."

Funny how things work out. After a run of four consecutive years in which they topped 100 points, the Islanders finished the 1979–80 regular season with a middling record of 39–28–19 for 91 points.

General manager Bill Torrey, however, had made some tweaks to his roster that would pay handsome dividends in the

New York Islanders coach Al Arbour watches keenly from behind the bench. (Graphic Artists Hockey Hall of Fame)

playoffs. Rookie forwards Duane Sutter and Anders Kallur, as well as defenceman Ken Morrow—who joined the club after helping the United States to its Miracle on Ice gold medal win at the 1980 Lake Placid Olympics—became key performers.

Torrey also went after Maple Leafs forward Darryl Sittler, but the asking price of Clark Gillies was too high. The Islanders instead landed second-line centre Butch Goring in a trade with the Los Angeles Kings that sent the first-ever Islander, popular forward Billy Harris, and defenceman Dave Lewis to Hollywood.

The roster adjustments were enough to alter the Islanders' own springtime script.

In 1980, they knocked off the Kings, 3–1, in the preliminary round; the Boston Bruins, 4–1, in the quarter-finals; and the Buffalo Sabres in six games in the semis. In the final, the Islanders built up a 3–1 series lead before the Flyers forced a sixth game, in which Nystrom scored his championship winner.

Nystrom knows that, even though he provided the heroics that evening at Nassau Coliseum on Long Island, the Islanders received contributions from everyone on the roster, as well as head coach Al Arbour and the team's architect, Torrey.

"The team always came first," Arbour once told the *New York Post*. "We won the Cups not because of Mike Bossy, Bryan Trottier, and Denis Potvin, but also because of people like Bobby Nystrom, Garry Howatt, and John Tonelli."

To play out their string of four Stanley Cups, the Islanders beat the Minnesota North Stars, 4 games to 1, in 1981, and then swept the Vancouver Canucks and Edmonton Oilers in the 1982 and 1983 finals, respectively.

Opposite: Surrounded by jubilant teammates and photographers, Denis Potvin of the New York Islanders hoists the Stanley Cup on May 24, 1980 at the Nassau Veterans Memorial Coliseum in Uniondale, New York. (Peter S. Mecca/Hockey Hall of Fame)

Left: Hall of Famer Bryan Trottier was a key member of the Islanders dynasty between 1980 and 1983. (Lewis Portnoy/Hockey Hall of Fame)

In total, the Islanders won 60 of 78 postseason games in their four-year Stanley Cup run, went an incredible 12–1 in overtime outings, and faced the brink of elimination only once in a series.

That close call came in the best-of-five preliminary round against the Pittsburgh Penguins in 1982. In Game 5, the Penguins held a 3–1 lead with less than five and a half minutes remaining in the third period.

Islanders defenceman Mike McEwen scored at the 13:33 mark and Tonelli tied the game with 2:21 left in regulation time. Tonelli scored again in overtime to send his teammates into the next round.

"The Penguins scared us half to death," Tonelli said. "Down two goals with five-and-a-half minutes left is not the best spot to be in.

"But we've experienced such situations, though all we could do was keep saying, 'Keep it going! C'mon, all the way!' And things like that. You do this to overcome your true feelings of hopelessness, though we never gave up."

Seven members of the never-give-up gang were inducted into the Hockey Hall of Fame: Arbour, Bossy, Gillies, Potvin, Smith, Torrey, and Trottier.

Sixteen Islanders played on all of the four Stanley Cup–winning teams: Bossy, Bob Bourne, Gillies, Goring, Kallur, Gord Lane, Dave Langevin, Wayne Merrick, Morrow, Nystrom, Stefan Persson, Potvin, Smith, Sutter, Tonelli, and Trottier.

"We went through so much together," Potvin told *Newsday*. "It became important not to let the guy next to you down. Friendships evolved. We cared about each other. We'd developed a kinship."

"We were well balanced," Bossy added. "Everyone had an important role. To me, we were the epitome of a team."

27

THE RICHARD RIOT

Sixty years ago, the NHL grounded the Rocket, but ignited the riot that came to symbolize the passion and adoration Quebec had for its greatest hockey player.

While the Montreal Forum is gone, old-timers can still point to the stores and buildings along Rue Ste. Catherine that were damaged during a tense 24 hours in 1955, starting when the Habs' St. Patrick's Day game against visiting Detroit was forfeited.

The Richard Riot stemmed from NHL president Clarence Campbell's controversial call to suspend Maurice Richard for the balance of the 1954–55 season after an incident in Boston four days earlier.

As fine a scorer as Richard was—his 50 goals in 50 games had secured his legend a decade earlier—he had a very short fuse. And that fuse was lit after he was high-sticked and badly cut by the Bruins' Hal Laycoe.

Never mind that Laycoe was an ex-Canadien and a former roommate and tennis partner of Richard's; the Rocket chased him down and clubbed him twice with his stick. During the ensuing fight, linesman Cliff Thompson tried to intervene and was punched by Richard.

With Richard already on the league's watch list for

More than $500,000 worth of damage was done as windows were broken and shops were looted.

an incident with an official earlier in the season, Campbell threw the book at him. The ban put Richard out of the race for what would have been his only Art Ross Trophy, and all but prevented Montreal from stopping Gordie Howe and the Red Wings from winning another Stanley Cup.

For fans in the province of Quebec, Campbell had just defied a god—a native Montrealer and source of immense pride.

"[Richard] gave us all hope," said author Roch Carrier, who wrote *The Hockey Sweater*. "French Canadians are no longer to be condemned to be hewers of wood and drawers of water, to be servants, employees. We, too, are champions of the world."

Richard immediately regretted hitting Thompson, but felt the official was in over his head trying to handle the Laycoe incident. Indeed, Thompson never worked another league game.

But Richard also felt railroaded at the hearing by Laycoe and referee Frank Udvari, both of whom didn't say "the right things" in his opinion. With no video in those days, Richard and Montreal coach Dick Irvin lost their case.

When news of the suspension broke, phones at Campbell's Montreal office began ringing off the hook with threats of

NHL president Clarence Campbell is confronted in his seat between periods at the Montreal Forum on March 17, 1955, the night of the infamous Richard Riot.(Le Studio du Hockey/ Hockey Hall of Fame)

bodily harm. Montreal newspapers blasted the decision and created an ugly backdrop for the Wings' visit on March 17.

Campbell was urged by police not to attend the sold-out match, as about 10,000 protesters gathered outside the Forum carrying signs and effigies of him. But the former army officer, who had been part of the Allied prosecution team at the Nuremberg war trials, was not intimidated as he took a seat in the stands amid loud booing.

The perfect storm ensued as the Wings rolled to a 4–1 lead and the crowd turned its fury on the president. A ripe tomato splattered Campbell and a female friend. One man reached out as if to shake hands, only to throw a punch at the NHL president.

After a tear gas bomb was set off, forcing the evacuation of the building, a shaken Campbell awarded the game to Detroit. That's when the real carnage began outside.

"The people were going crazy," Habs forward Dickie Moore recalled. "You never knew what they'd do next, maybe blow the place up."

More than $500,000 worth of damage was done as windows were broken and shops were looted. If the rioters didn't have hard projectiles to throw, they used their rain galoshes. The Habs and Wings were kept in their dressing rooms as the riot raged. About 70 people were arrested.

"That was a disgraceful exhibition to a [sport] that fellows like myself have worked 38 years to build," Wings manager Jack Adams told CFPL television in London, Ontario, the next day as the Wings changed trains en route home.

"I blame the papers for building [the crowd's anger] up. They're partly to blame for making a hero out of Richard. When one man thinks he's bigger than the game, it's pretty near time to do something."

It took another full day for the anger to subside in the streets, helped by a public radio address by Richard on March 19, pleading for calm.

Montreal made the Cup final, where they lost to Detroit. Richard never forgot either the lost chance at winning a scoring derby or what would have been the first of a record six consecutive Cups for the Canadiens (they would win the next five).

"Rocket never spoke about those things, but I know it hurt him," Moore said. "But the person who probably was affected by the Riot after him was Boom Boom Geoffrion. He won the scoring title that should've been Rocket's, and he was booed in Montreal for a long time after."

28

THE CUP COMES TO CALIFORNIA

The Anaheim Ducks were in the midst of celebrating their 2007 Stanley Cup victory when a congratulatory message was read aloud: "[Your] perseverance and determination in defeating the Ottawa Senators is a testament to the greatness of California's world-class sports teams."

It was signed, "Governor Arnold Schwarzenegger."

Well, the Ducks weren't likely thinking of impressing the Terminator in their bid for a title, but the hockey world certainly took notice of the only Stanley Cup to be awarded in the Golden State since the Los Angeles Kings first brought NHL hockey to California back in 1967.

And within 20 years of Wayne Gretzky arriving on the West Coast to touch off a new wave of interest in the game, the expansion Ducks, San Jose Sharks, and a flood of minor-pro and grassroots hockey had followed. Now the venerable Cup had crossed the continent for a victory party.

"Canada loves their hockey, and from what I heard out there, we have quite a few fans who love their hockey out here, too," said captain and Conn Smythe Trophy winner Scott Niedermayer amid the confetti and fireworks at the Honda Center.

Gretzky and the Kings had come close, winning Game 1 of the 1993 final against the Montreal Canadiens before the roof fell in. But Montreal would remain the last Canadian team to win the Cup for over two decades, as the balance of power shifted south of the border, to New York, Detroit, New Jersey, Dallas, Colorado, Tampa Bay, Carolina—into the Sunbelt, but not yet as far west as California.

That changed after the cancelled 2004–05 season. Anaheim had made the final in 2003, losing to New Jersey, but then missed the playoffs altogether in 2004. After the lockout, new general manager Brian Burke and his new coach, Randy Carlyle, guided the Ducks to a club record 98-point run and a trip to the Western Conference final, where they lost to Edmonton. The following year, they were favoured by many to go all the way.

With good reason. The Ducks had Jean-Sebastien Giguere and Ilya Bryzgalov in goal, while strong role players Chris Kunitz, Sammy Pahlsson, Rob Niedermayer, and Andy McDonald were willing and able. The scoring punch came from a couple of kids who'd leapt out of junior in western Canada and the Ontario Hockey League: Ryan Getzlaf and Corey Perry.

Burke sought to add to the arsenal. Scott Niedermayer, signed as a free agent from the New Jersey Devils, took less money and brought his three Cup rings to Anaheim. His dream was to win a Cup with his brother, and the Ducks named him captain immediately. Burke also brought back unrestricted free agent Teemu Selanne, despite him posting some rather ordinary numbers since leaving the Ducks in 2001.

These were exactly the kind of players Carlyle wanted on his team to get it through the treacherous waters of the Western Conference. But the biggest and best acquisition was yet to come: giant defenceman Chris Pronger, acquired via trade from Edmonton. Once April 2007 arrived, and with it a second chance to reach the final, the Ducks were looking and sounding like winners. They had already dropped the adjective *Mighty* from their nickname and changed their logo and colours.

As spring loomed, seven Western Conference teams had 100 or more points: in order, Detroit, Nashville, Anaheim, San Jose, Dallas, Vancouver, and Minnesota. Five of those teams had allowed fewer goals than the Ducks. But Anaheim defeated Minnesota, Vancouver, and Detroit—never needing more than six games—to arrive in the final against a Canadian team, the Senators.

Ottawa had joined the NHL just ahead of Ducks in 1992 and enjoyed plenty of support across the Great White North. But the Ducks played a traditional, muscular brand of hockey, bolstered by their offensive prowess, that many purists enjoyed. The Ducks were the playoffs' most penalized team, but had been able to kill most of them off. They also

Teemu Selanne celebrates in the dressing room after the Anaheim Ducks win the 2007 Stanley Cup. (Craig Campbell/Hockey Hall of Fame)

had five more Canadian-born players than the Euro-rich Sens—who were coached, coincidentally, by Anaheim's former GM, Bryan Murray.

Schwarzenegger dropped the puck for Game 1. Enjoying home-ice advantage and some of the Hollywood vibe, Anaheim took both ends of the California portion of the series, 3–2 and 1–0, the latter on a late Pahlsson goal.

Ottawa got into the win column back home, a Game 3 victory that was marred by a Pronger hit on Dean McAmmond that saw the big defender get suspended. Game 4 had its rough moments as well, but two Andy McDonald goals and another late strike by Dustin Penner put Anaheim in position to win at home.

McDonald and Rob Niedermayer scored early in Game 5, with Travis Moen, Francois Beauchemin, and Corey Perry stretching the lead to a decisive 6–2. For Scott Niedermayer, receiving the Cup from commissioner Gary Bettman was a familiar ritual, but for every other Duck in that game, more than 17,000 fans in the arena, and the 36 million living in the state at the time, June 6, 2007, was the first contact with Stanley.

As the story goes, Schwarzenegger phoned Canadian prime minister Stephen Harper in Ottawa to tease him about the win with a twist on his signature line, telling the PM, "We'll be back." But while Anaheim has yet to repeat as Cup champs, they at least made history in SoCal.

Brothers Rob and Scott Niedermeyer follow their Cup-carrying teammate Chris Pronger through a crowd of celebrating Ducks fans. (Jeff Gross/Staff/ Getty Images Sport)

29

KING CLANCY PLAYS ALL
SIX POSITIONS IN ONE GAME

Before Bert Campaneris of the Kansas City A's played every position in a baseball game in 1965, hockey gave the world King Clancy.

It was in a Stanley Cup final game between his Ottawa Senators and the Edmonton Eskimos, played on March 31, 1923, that accomplished young defenceman Francis Michael "King" Clancy made his NHL debut in every other position on the ice. Clancy played both points on the blue line and rotated through left, right, and centre up front. Then, in the third period, goaltender Clint Benedict was called for a minor penalty, in the days when goalies had to serve their two minutes.

Clancy, one of only 10 men on the team in the era of minimal rosters, dropped back to guard the net.

Among the Edmonton snipers was 24-goal scorer Duke Keats, but the Senators survived the penalty, winning 1–0 to clinch the Cup in the two-game series. Edmonton, representing the Western Canada Hockey League, was credited with 68 shots on goal in the game.

It took the NHL a long time to adjust the rule that governed substitutions when goalies were assessed penalties. A teammate was eventually allowed to take the netminder's stick, blocker, and glove (but not his pads), and stand in the crease.

On March 15, 1932, in Boston, Clancy was once more in net, this time for the Maple Leafs, after Lorne Chabot was penalized. Rotating with teammates Red Horner and Alex Levinsky, each gave up a goal in a 6–2 loss.

Later, the league decreed that a penalty shot would be called in lieu of sending the goalie to the box. Finally, in 1949–50, the current rule was adopted, calling for a team to send off a forward or defenceman who is on the ice at the time the penalty is called.

The Ottawa-born Clancy wouldn't only cover all positions on the ice. After retiring as a player (and referee), he served the Toronto Maple Leafs as coach, assistant coach, and assistant general manager, blazing a trail followed by many great players in the future who found second careers behind the benches and in the executive suites of the teams for which they had once been stars.

Opposite: A portrait of Francis Michael "King" Clancy, as a member of the Ottawa Senators. Clancy was the first person to play all six positions during one game.(Le Studio du Hockey/Hockey Hall of Fame)

MONTREAL WINS FIVE CUPS IN A ROW

I n today's NHL, the "Stanley Cup window" opens and closes quickly. Teams build for a one-year title shot and need many factors to go right during that nine-month period.

Before the Pittsburgh Penguins's victories in 2016 and 2017, the Detroit Red Wings were the last to win back-to-back Cups, nearly 20 years before. In the salary cap era, a repeat of the Edmonton and New York Islander runs in the 1980s, or of Montreal in the late 1970s, is unlikely, let alone a collection to rival the mighty five-time-champion Montreal Canadiens of 1955–60.

The year 1955 was an eventful one for the Canadiens and the entire city of Montreal. In March, Rocket Richard was suspended for the balance of the season and the playoffs for hitting an official, not only triggering a public riot, but weakening the Habs lineup considerably in what became a seven-game loss to Detroit in the Stanley Cup final.

General manager Frank Selke had patiently put the elements of a winner together, drawing on his famed farm system to build a strong lineup that complemented Richard and young Jean Beliveau. But after the loss to Detroit, Selke came to the conclusion that coach Dick Irvin was no longer the right man to get the team—which had only one title to its name in the previous decade—back on top.

Believing Irvin had become too belligerent, he looked for a more easy-going replacement. An obvious choice was Toe Blake—a Montreal star in the 1930s and '40s, but in 1955 a man at loggerheads with Selke. A few years earlier, a dispute between the two men had prompted Blake to quit his job as coach of a Habs minor-league affiliate. Richard, however, lobbied for his old teammate, and Selke relented.

Blake knew how to handle players and tactics, and with all the talent Selke had assembled, the Canadiens became unstoppable. In 1955–56, four Montreal players were first-team all-stars: goalie Jacques Plante, defenceman Doug Harvey, Beliveau at centre, and Richard at right wing. The Canadiens lost only two playoff games, besting Detroit in the final.

Richard became captain the next year, upon Butch Bouchard's retirement, and had his last truly memorable regular season, registering 62 points, and his last all-star nod: right wing on the second team. Bernie Geoffrion dominated playoff scoring, with 18 points in 10 games, as the Habs beat the Rangers in the semifinals and Boston in the final, again losing just two games in the process.

Concurrent with Montreal's run of riches was Harvey's string of Norris Trophy wins. In 1957–58 he was designated the league's top defenceman for the fourth time in the five-year history of that relatively new award. This season, the Bruins had Montreal knotted at two games apiece in the

(left to right) Goal-scoring Montreal Canadiens Alain Brian "Ab" McDonald,
Ralph Backstrom, and Bernie Geoffrion celebrate after beating the Toronto
Maple Leafs, 3–2, in the Stanley Cup Final on April 16, 1959.
(Imperial Oil–Turofsky/Hockey Hall of Fame)

final, but Richard, who had recovered from a severe cut to a leg tendon at midseason, scored an overtime winner in Game 5, part of his 11-goal postseason burst.

Punch Imlach's upstart Maple Leafs provided the opposition in the 1959 title round, but Montreal had now added the Pocket Rocket, Henri Richard, and accounted for half the positions on the two all-star teams: the latest Norris winner, Tom Johnson, plus Harvey, the younger Richard, Beliveau, left winger Dickie Moore, and Plante. The Leafs managed one win in the series.

Selke would call the last of the five Cup entries the best of all. Despite another push from the Leafs and the arrival of high-scoring winger Bobby Hull in Chicago, the Habs rolled through eight playoff games without a loss. Though Richard played little that spring and scored only once in the playoffs, he didn't retire until the following September,

a decision reluctantly made at training camp.

As broadcaster Dick Irvin Jr. pointed out, the Canadiens were also darn impressive in the regular season throughout those five fantastic campaigns. Four times they finished in first place, by margins of 24, 19, 18, and 13 points. The only team to come in ahead of them in the six-team league were the '56–57 Wings, who were six points up but lost to Boston in the opening round.

All good things must come to an end. Though Montreal again took top spot in the 1960–61 season, it finally met its match in the opening round. In a bitterly contested series, the hungry Blackhawks used muscle more than finesse to beat the Canadiens in six games. Chicago coach Rudy Pilous was magnanimous in victory.

"We simply cannot believe it. We have beaten a famous team, the champions."

(left to right) Montreal Canadiens Jacques Plante and Maurice Richard pose with the Stanley Cup on April 14, 1960 at Maple Leaf Gardens, after beating Toronto four games straight. (Imperial Oil–Turofsky/Hockey Hall of Fame)

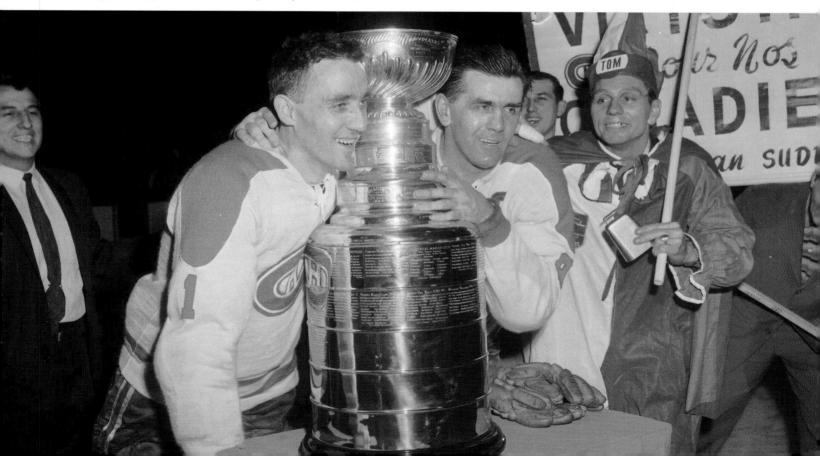

31

TRADING FRANK MAHOVLICH

Huge multiplayer trades often signify a shakeup or even the rebirth of a franchise. But for the Toronto Maple Leafs and their fans, a seven-player deal in March 1968 would come to be associated with the end of a golden era.

Frank Mahovlich was coming off a Calder Trophy–winning season in 1957–58 when Punch Imlach joined the Leafs, first as assistant GM and later as general manager/coach. The relationship between player and executive in the early years was wonderful, as the Leafs took three straight Stanley Cups between 1962 and 1964. But then it changed.

Mahovlich went from the high of a 48-goal 1960–61 season to a stay in hospital during the '64–65 season for what the team claimed was exhaustion, but what Mahovlich later revealed was depression brought on in large part by the coach's haranguing.

"The first four years were great, the last four weren't so great," Mahovlich said. "He just wasn't the guy I once knew."

Imlach, who seemed to delight in prodding all his players with a dictatorial delivery, always thought he could get more out of Mahovlich. The latter believed he was better off letting his talent do the talking and sticking to scoring.

"Mahovlich and [baseball's] Joe DiMaggio . . . those guys are just so fluid and graceful that it looks like they're not giving you everything," opined coach and broadcaster Harry Neale. He compared the disparagement of the Big M to the criticisms captain Mats Sundin would face in Toronto the 1990s and 2000s.

To be fair to Imlach, Toronto's media and fans also had high expectations of the superstar winger, who was infamously offered to the Blackhawks in 1962 for a then-unheard-of sum of $1 million before saner heads prevailed. Leaf teammates said Mahovlich took any derogatory comments to heart instead of letting them slide, which meant that when Toronto fans occasionally booed him, he could go into a personal funk.

The Leafs' Cup streak ended when they failed to reach even the final in 1965 or 1966. The Imlach–Mahovlich cold war worsened. The two men would go weeks or months without speaking, and then the silence might be broken only by Imlach belittling the Big M. The coach also seemed to delight in deliberately mispronouncing Mahovlich's surname.

The Leafs' last title, in 1967, was something of an upset. Though Mahovlich registered 10 points in the playoffs,

"The first four years were great, the last four weren't so great," Mahovlich said. "He just wasn't the guy I once knew."

his 46 in the regular season was a seven-year low. The next season saw the Leafs begin to slide, in part because the club sold off farm teams and Imlach was ill prepared for the expansion draft, which robbed the Leafs of depth.

Mahovlich was having a better year personally, but that also enhanced his trade value. On March 3, 1968, Imlach stunned the hockey world. Mahovlich, Peter Stemkowski, Garry Unger, and the rights to defenceman Carl Brewer—another Imlach target—were sent to the Detroit Red Wings for forwards Norm Ullman, Paul Henderson, and Floyd Smith.

Neither team would go far in the playoffs despite the deal, though Ullman would lead the Leafs in scoring three times and end up in the Hall of Fame. Ullman's greatest contribution on a larger scale lay in making effective scorers out of wingers Henderson and Ron Ellis, bringing them to the attention of the organizers of Team Canada '72. Smith would end his career in Buffalo, but returned to the Leaf fold as a respected amateur scout before being pressed briefly into service as coach in 1979 and general manager in the late 1980s.

Detroit made the playoffs once in the years immediately following the deal. Stemkowski's biggest seasons would be as a New York Ranger, while Unger embarked on a record-setting streak of consecutive games that would continue through his years with St. Louis and Atlanta.

For Mahovlich, the deal was liberating. He scored 49 goals in his first full season on a line with Gordie Howe and Alex Delvecchio, and registered 196 points in 198 games with Detroit.

Involved in a second major trade, midway through the 1970–71 season Mahovlich found himself en route to the

Despite their acrimonious relationship, Frank Mahovlich is all smiles with coach Punch Imlach after Mahovlich scored two goals and had one assist on January 6, 1960, at Maple Leaf Gardens, where the Leafs beat the Detroit Red Wings, 3-1. (Imperial Oil–Turofsky/Hockey Hall of Fame)

Montreal Canadiens. This deal brought Mickey Redmond and Guy Charron to Motown. Mahovlich's tenure in Montreal would be a happy time for the winger. He played with brother Peter on a team that would win the Cup in his first season and again in 1973, giving him six in all.

In the spring of 1974, at age 38, he ended his last NHL season with a flourish, totalling 80 points, and then went "home" to Toronto to play for the Toros of the World Hockey Association.

As for Imlach, the Leafs' losing ways cost him his job in 1969. He came back to the NHL via the Buffalo Sabres, and a decade later was restored as GM in Toronto under the unstable ownership of Harold Ballard. That, too, led to a major falling-out with another team legend, captain Darryl Sittler.

Frank Mahovlich playing for the Montreal Canadiens at the Forum in Montreal after the relationship with Imlach deteriorated past saving. (Frank Prazak/Hockey Hall of Fame)

GORDIE HOWE'S RETURN TO THE NHL

Watching the great Gordie Howe, with his all-around game and toughness, was an exciting experience.

The NHL got a powerful reminder of this fact when Mr. Hockey made a triumphant return to the league for one final season, eight years after he retired for the first time.

Howe had played his final game for the Detroit Red Wings on April 4, 1971, after enduring a painful season in which he'd missed 15 games with sore ribs, a broken nose, and a stubborn wrist problem. He also disliked the Red Wings' rookie coach, Ned Harkness.

So after four Stanley Cup championships, six Hart Trophies, and six Art Ross Trophies in 25 seasons with Detroit, Howe stepped away from the game at the age of 43 before training camp commenced in the fall.

The gentleman from Floral, Saskatchewan, took a job in the team's front office. The Red Wings retired his No. 9, and he was inducted into the Hockey Hall of Fame.

But after two years on the sidelines, Howe unretired to realize a dream of playing with sons Mark and Marty with the Houston Aeros of the World Hockey Association. After two Avco Cup titles and a whole lot of memories playing alongside his boys—in four seasons with the Aeros and two

"I said if Gordie didn't play, I wouldn't coach," Bowman told the Detroit Free Press.

more with the New England Whalers—Howe found himself back in the NHL.

The WHA had folded, but the NHL elected to absorb Howe and the Whalers, Wayne Gretzky and the Edmonton Oilers, the Quebec Nordiques, and the Winnipeg Jets for the 1979–80 season.

Howe was back in the NHL at 51.

But one final lap around the league as a member of the Hartford Whalers—as they were called in the NHL—almost didn't happen for Howe. He suffered from dizzy spells in training camp, but the mysterious condition disappeared in time for the Whalers' season opener, a 4–1 loss in Minnesota to the North Stars.

Howe began the season also dealing with the disappointment that his son Marty had not made the team out of training camp and was starting the season in the AHL with the Springfield Indians. Then Marty broke his arm, delaying a possible return to the Whalers.

The older Howe managed to score the first goal of his NHL return during the Whalers' second game, a 3–3 draw on the road against the Pittsburgh Penguins.

On Halloween, Howe and his Hartford teammate Dave Keon, then 39, made a memorable return to Maple Leaf

Left: Gordie Howe (centre) with his sons Mark and Marty as members of the World Hockey Association's Houston Aeros during the 1973-74 season. (O - Pee-Chee/Hockey Hall of Fame)

Opposite: Gordie Howe playing for the Hartford Whalers at the Checkerdome in St. Louis, three months before he retired at age 52. (Steven Goldstein/Hockey Hall of Fame)

Gardens, where Keon had starred for 15 seasons. Each scored in the Whalers' 4–2 win over the Toronto Maple Leafs.

But the highlight was Gordie Howe's return to Detroit for the NHL's All-Star game on February 5, 1980, at Joe Louis Arena. The Whalers had already visited Detroit, beating the Red Wings, 6–4, on January 12. But the all-star game was a much bigger affair. It included a smidgen of controversy when Scotty Bowman, then with the Buffalo Sabres and also the coach of the Prince of Wales Conference all-star team, decided to include Howe on his side.

"I said if Gordie didn't play, I wouldn't coach," Bowman told the *Detroit Free Press.* "It was natural for him to play that game in Detroit. I didn't care what anybody thought. I knew he could still play, and it turned out perfect."

The Red Wings faithful appreciated Bowman's resolve. After public address announcer John Bell introduced Detroit defenceman Reed Larson, it was Howe's turn.

"And from the Hartford Whalers, representing all of hockey with great distinction for five decades, number nine," Bell announced.

The then NHL-record crowd of 21,002 rose to its feet and gave No. 9 a standing ovation that lasted more than four minutes, chanting, "Gordie, Gordie, Gordie." The crowd only halted its applause when Bell began to introduce anthem singers Roger Doucet and Roger Whittaker.

Howe was clearly uncomfortable with the rousing reception and at one point confered with his friend Red Wings trainer Lefty Wilson.

"I had the same feelings for the fans as they had toward me," Howe said. "I was very emotional and the fans were getting to me, so I skated over to Lefty Wilson on the bench and asked for help so I would be normal again.

"Lefty was bilingual. He spoke English and profanity. He said something to me I can't repeat, and it worked."

It was Howe's 23rd all-star game—an NHL record—and a young Wayne Gretzky's first. The Great One was held off the scoresheet that day, while Howe provided a perfect ending. He assisted on Real Cloutier's late goal to give the Wales team a 6–3 win.

"When Scotty picked me to play, he really stuck his nose out because I later learned there was opposition to me playing," Howe said. "I have so much respect for that man."

Mr. Hockey had 11 goals at the all-star break. He scored his 800th career NHL goal on February 29, early in the third period against St. Louis Blues goalie Mike Liut in a 3–0 win for Hartford. Two new teammates joined him to finish the season: Bobby Hull, traded to the Whalers by the Winnipeg Jets, and son Marty, who was finally promoted with six games left in the season.

Howe returned to Joe Louis Arena for one final game on March 12. He delighted the home crowd with an assist on Keon's opening goal midway through the first period of a 4–4 tie.

The Red Wings visited Hartford for the regular-season finale. Howe scored his 801st and final regular-season goal in the second period of a 5–3 win. In total, Howe played in all 80 of the Whalers games, scoring 15 times and finishing with 41 points.

It was on to the playoffs for a first-round date with the Montreal Canadiens, who were coming off four Stanley Cup wins in a row and exhibited their postseason prowess with a three-game sweep of Hartford.

Howe, however, made sure he gave hockey fans one final thrill with a backhand goal that beat Montreal goalie Denis Herron in the third period of Game 2, his final outing at the Montreal Forum.

It was Howe's first Stanley Cup playoff goal in a decade, and the Canadiens supporters stood and gave him one last hurrah.

After his 26th NHL season concluded and he had played into his fifth decade, Howe retired for good on June 4, 1980, at age 52.

"It's not an easy task to retire," he said at his farewell press conference. "No one teaches you how. I found that out when I tried it the first time. I'm not a quitter. But I will now quit the game of hockey."

33

MOSIENKO'S FASTEST THREE GOALS

Any list of Chicago scoring records brings to the fore such revered names as brothers Max and Doug Bentley, 50-goal man Bobby Hull, and 2016 Art Ross Trophy winner Patrick Kane.

But another, perhaps lesser-known name will always be in the conversation. Because for all the high-scoring dazzle of his peers on that list, Bill Mosienko's scoring record—still intact 65 years later and counting—may never be broken.

Mosienko needed just 21 seconds to score three times. Only Jean Beliveau has come close, and it took him more than twice as long—44 seconds—to complete a hat trick.

The son of a Ukranian-born Canadian Pacific Railway worker in Winnipeg's North End, Mosienko grew up one of 14 children. Only five foot eight, the right winger was nonetheless a well-known player on the local Monarchs in the late 1930s.

Winnipeg-born Blackhawk Joe Cooper spotted Mosienko during a trip home, and Bill was soon under contract. Unable at first to cross into the U.S. due to the outbreak of World War II, Mosienko didn't join the Hawks until February 1942. When he finally made his debut, he scored two goals—coincidentally, 21 seconds apart—against the Rangers. With so many NHL players on military duty, his status was enhanced.

Becoming a full-time NHLer in 1943–44, Mosienko compiled 60 goals over the next two seasons. He was twice a second-team all-star behind Rocket Richard. That Mosienko scored at least 15 goals in almost every season he played was also remarkable because the Hawks of the '40s and '50s were among the weakest of the Original Six. But they did have the Bentley brothers at the time, and Mosienko joined them for a while to form the Pony Line.

In the spring of 1952, Mosienko was just shy of 30 years of age as his team arrived in New York for its last game of the season. It had already been an interesting year, one that began with a special exhibition game played before the visiting Princess Elizabeth when Chicago faced Toronto at Maple Leaf Gardens.

In New York, he had dinner with an old friend who happened to own a collection of books about hockey. As he perused a list of scoring feats, Mosienko remarked that he'd like to see his name among them some day.

The stage was not exactly set for hockey history when game time rolled around. Both the Hawks and Rangers were playoff orphans, and New York management didn't even sell tickets for the upper reaches of MSG, limiting the crowd to about 7,000. New York gave the start to minor leaguer Lorne Anderson and jumped out to a 6–2 lead.

Bill Mosienko proudly holds his hat-trick pucks after scoring three goals in just 21 seconds. (Le Studio du Hockey/Hockey Hall of Fame)

Mosienko was out with centre Gus Bodnar when the latter set him up for a low wrist shot that hit its mark at 6:09. Bodnar controlled the next faceoff and quickly found Mosienko coming down the wing for another quality shot, making it 2–0 at 6:20. The next goal took even less time. On a similar play, Bodnar this time got the puck to left winger George Gee, who relayed it to Mosienko for a third goal, exploiting a weakness on that side of the ice due to an apparent injury to Rangers defenceman Hy Buller.

Mosienko had just broken a 14-year-old record held by Detroit's Carl Liscombe, who'd needed a minute and 52 seconds to score his three.

"It was all a surprise it happened," Bodnar said. "The way he was lining up, all I had to do was get him the puck."

Blackhawks coach Ebbie Goodfellow tried to get the

Bill Mosienko's scoring record—still intact 65 years later and counting—may never be broken.

trio off the ice after the third goal, but they insisted they weren't the least bit tired. Mosienko in particular wanted to stay. A try for a fourth consecutive goal on a similar set-up hit the post, or else it would have been four goals in 28 seconds.

Mosienko described the feeling back on the Chicago bench after his third goal as "like being on Cloud Nine."

Anderson had been playing with the New York Rovers of the Eastern League, and like Dave Reece, the Boston goalie who never played another NHL minute after Darryl Sittler's 10-point game in 1976, he was done in the NHL after this match. He played only two more games as a pro, in that year's Eastern League playoffs.

Mosienko was modest about his fame. When his career ended in 1955, he went back to Winnipeg to run a bowling alley. He passed away in 1994.

Bill Mosienko carves up the ice for an action shot. (Imperial Oil–Turofsky/Hockey Hall of Fame)

34

HOCKEY GETS A SECOND REFEREE

After reaching a high-water mark of better than eight goals a game in 1981–82, NHL scoring began to drop off. By 1990–91, teams were scoring an average of just under seven goals a game, and in the lockout season of 1994–95, it dropped below six for the first time in a quarter century.

This lack of offence gave rise to the idea that the game needed an extra set of eyes on the ice to help catch all the obstruction and other fouls that players were committing to deter scoring chances.

A two-referee system had long been debated but never implemented. One reason it didn't gain traction for the longest while was the belief that players were getting bigger, while rinks weren't getting any larger—still the same 200-by-85-foot measurements used since the 19th century—so there simply wasn't room on the ice for another official.

However, starting with the 1998–99 season, each team would play 20 games under the two-ref system. The league didn't really have to change a lot of policy or deal with logistics to bring in extra zebras, because playoff games at that point had a second referee standing by, usually watching the game on TV in a separate room to provide backup when plays needed to be reviewed.

What the league had to do was create a set of guidelines for the positioning of the second official—which territory he would cover as play moved up ice—as well as who would make penalty calls and how any differences in interpretation of the rules would be handled.

The test run was a hit: penalties were reduced, while shots on net and scoring came back to a degree. Games also took less time to play as opponents spent less time hacking and whacking behind the play.

There was also a drop in major fouls, an indication that players, knowing there was more chance of getting caught, were changing their habits.

As for the question of whether the ice would get congested, one referee was now able to get so far in front of the play, while the other remained well behind, that more room actually opened up.

The 1998–99 season was the first in a three-year span in which the NHL would add four new teams, in Atlanta, Columbus, Minnesota, and Nashville. At first, there were questions as to whether the league might have to import a few referees from Europe to cover the extra games, but younger officials were recruited from the AHL and other minor leagues, while former players were encouraged to try officiating as a new line of work.

In 1999–2000, clubs played 50 of their 82 regular-season games with two referees, and finally, in 2000–01, all games were played under the four-official system (two refs and two linesmen).

"All the things we were worried about—too many penalties, games being too long—never came to pass," Bryan Lewis, the former director of officiating said.

With penalties down, games were ending an average of seven minutes earlier. As the game became faster with the removal of the red line and the crackdown on obstruction, two referees made it easier to officiate the game.

Of course, having two referees also allowed for one official to take over if the other was hurt, or give the linesmen a hand if one of them had an issue.

But after nearly 20 years, it's hard to think of NHL games without double vision.

Opposite: The NHL first tried using two referees during the 1998-99 season. By 2000-01 all 82 games were played with four on-ice officials. (Rusty Barton/ Hockey Hall of Fame)

35

BELIVEAU WINS THE CONN SMYTHE TROPHY

I n the spring of 1964, as the Toronto Maple Leafs were closing in on their third straight Stanley Cup, NHL president Clarence Campbell had an idea.

Hockey offered no reward to the best performer over the two playoff rounds needed to win a championship. Often, the league's MVP—the winner of the Hart Trophy—did not survive a single playoff round. Campbell looked around at other sports and noted that baseball had a World Series MVP award, and the stars of the NFL and CFL championship games were also recognized. Why not an award for the league's best performer in the postseason?

The notion came at a time when Leaf patriarch Conn Smythe had begun to step back from a front-line role with the team. Smythe had organized the purchase of the club in 1927 to keep it from leaving Toronto. Under his leadership, the Leafs had won 10 Cups and operated what most considered to be a model franchise out of historic Maple Leaf Gardens, which he built during the Great Depression.

Smythe was immediately put forward as the namesake

> Many found it amusing—ironic, even—that the first recipient of the Conn Smythe Trophy played for the team the Leafs boss probably detested most: the Montreal Canadiens.

of the new award by his son Stafford and others. With no objections, a trophy depicting a model of the Gardens set against a giant maple leaf was approved in time for the 1965 playoffs.

Many found it amusing—ironic, even—that the first recipient of the Conn Smythe Trophy played for the team the Leafs boss probably detested most: the Montreal Canadiens. Just the same, respect was universal for the first winner of the trophy, classy Canadiens centre Jean Beliveau.

In the 1965 semifinal between the Leafs and Habs, Beliveau scored the game-winning goal in Game 2 at the Forum, one of three goals and three assists he would produce as his solid Montreal squad won the series in five games and broke Toronto's hold on the Cup.

But Beliveau saved his best for the Cup final against Bobby Hull, Stan Mikita, and the Chicago Blackhawks.

That series went the distance, but Beliveau seemed to be there every time his team needed a big goal, including the first strike in Game 7 as Montreal clinched the Cup with a 4–0 victory.

The date was May 1—the latest a Cup Final game had yet been played—when the shining new trophy made its debut at the Forum. After Beliveau was named winner by a vote of writers covering the final—he'd scored 16 points in 13 playoff games—the ever-polite "Gros Bill" carefully placed it back on the table with the Stanley Cup.

Another year would pass before a Leaf—the only one to date—would win the Conn Smythe Trophy. Crafty centre Dave Keon received it after a classic double upset of Chicago and Montreal in 1967. He only had eight points that April and May, but the writers were quick to point to the contribution his speed, penalty-killing prowess, and great two-way play made to Toronto's championship.

A series of firsts quickly became associated with the trophy. In 1966, Detroit goaltender Roger Crozier won it despite the Red Wings losing to the Habs in the final. Glenn Hall repeated the feat in 1968, after playing three rounds with the expansion St. Louis Blues, who also lost in the final.

A defenceman won for the first time in 1969: Serge Savard of the Canadiens. The first double winner was Bobby Orr, in 1970 and '72. Orr's feat was sandwiched around rookie goalie Ken Dryden's exploits in 1971—Dryden won it with just a few regular-season games under his belt, a full year before he earned the Calder Trophy as rookie of the year.

To date, nine Montreal players have won the Conn Smythe, including Bob Gainey in 1979, the only left winger in the group.

The trophy was mostly won by a member of the Cup–winning team in the '70s and '80s—usually Montreal, Philadelphia, the New York Islanders, and Edmonton—though it should be noted that Reggie Leach's 19 playoff goals for the Flyers in 1976 made him an easy choice despite his club's loss to Montreal in the final, during which he scored four times.

Goalie Ron Hextall was recognized for almost winning the Flyers a Cup in 1987 against the Oilers, and in the last instance

Montreal's Jean Beliveau, captain of the 1965 Cup-winning Canadiens, is congratulated by Chicago's Bobby Hull. (Studio Alain Brouillard/ Hockey Hall of Fame)

of a non-winner getting the nod, goalie Jean-Sebastien Giguere of the Anaheim Ducks had his name etched on the Smythe Trophy in 2003 despite his team's loss to the New Jersey Devils.

Patrick Roy won the Conn Smythe Trophy three times, after backstopping two different teams, Montreal and Colorado, to Cup championships in three different decades—in 1986 and 1993 with the Canadiens, and 2001 with the Avalanche.

Beginning in the late 1980s, teams had to win four full best-of-seven rounds to win a Cup. The NHL's footprint also continued to expand, and as it did so, the names on the Smythe Trophy began to reflect that fact: American defenceman Brian Leetch won it with the Rangers in 1994, as did U.S.–born goalies Tim Thomas (with Boston in 2011) and Jonathan Quick (Los Angeles in 2012). Nicklas Lidstrom of the Red Wings had 16 points in 23 games to become the first European-born-and-trained winner, shooting down the myth that those from the other side of the pond had no stomach for two months of hard-driving playoffs.

Bob Baun, who played two games for the
Toronto Maple Leafs on a broken leg.
(Imperial Oil–Turofsky/Hockey Hall of Fame)

BOB BAUN BREAKS A LEG

n the spring of 1964, Toronto Maple Leaf Bobby Baun earned his place in hockey lore.

That April, Baun and the Leafs were playing the Detroit Red Wings in the Stanley Cup final. Heading into Game 6, the Red Wings were leading the series, three games to two, and the score was tied, 3–3, midway through the third period.

Toronto was killing a penalty when a faceoff was called in the Leafs zone. Off the draw, Baun blocked a Gordie Howe shot that struck the side of his right leg, near the ankle, and the defenceman eventually collapsed to the ice. He managed to play on for a while, but later claimed that a puck battle with Howe put additional strain on the leg, which gave out and forced him to the ice again.

He was unable to put any weight on the injured leg and was taken off on a stretcher.

The full extent of the injury was not immediately determined, but Baun had a pretty good idea of what was wrong. The doctors assured him he would not do any more damage to the leg if he returned to play. The question was how much pain he could endure.

Baun had the ankle wrapped and frozen and he returned

to the Leafs bench for overtime. With the freezing, he was able to stand on the leg again without severe pain.

It was then that he called off defenceman Larry Hillman and went out on the ice with his partner, Carl Brewer.

Baun was known more for his bruising style of play than his offensive abilities. He never possessed a great shot and he scored very few goals. He had just 37 in 964 regular-season games over a 17-year career, and just 3 in 96 playoff games. But one of those playoff goals would never be forgotten.

In the second minute of overtime, the Wings tried to clear the puck out of their zone, but Baun managed to stop it at the blue line. He then launched a rolling puck that hit the stick of Wings defenceman Bill Gadsby and deflected up and over goaltender Terry Sawchuk to give the Leafs the win and force Game 7 back at Maple Leaf Gardens.

Baun described the shot as being "a triple flutter blast, with a follow-up blooper."

Whatever it was, it sent the Leafs home looking to win a third consecutive Stanley Cup, while the Red Wings were still a victory away from winning their first Cup since 1955.

Despite the pain, and despite knowing deep down what

> Baun described the shot as being "a triple flutter blast, with a follow-up blooper."

was likely wrong with his leg, Baun avoided the doctors between games and kept his foot in a pail of ice. He once again had the leg taped and frozen so that he could somehow play Game 7.

The Leafs wound up winning, 4–0, to capture the Cup. Baun was named one of the game's three stars.

Baun wasn't the only injured Leaf playing in that series. Red Kelly, a former Wing, was playing on a damaged knee that required special treatment to allow him to play. Kelly scored in that seventh game, after which he passed out from the pain. Andy Bathgate also played with pulled stomach muscles.

It was only after the Cup win that Baun finally went for X-rays, which confirmed he had a hairline fracture of the right fibula. So Baun had scored the overtime goal in Game 6 and played the seventh game on a broken leg.

Years later, he would joke, "It was the best break I ever had."

A few days after the Cup win, Toronto held a parade to celebrate the victory. While climbing into one of the convertible cars, Baun slipped and re-injured his broken right leg.

Toronto's Bob Baun mixes it up with Terry Harper of the Montreal Canadiens. (Frank Prazak/Hockey Hall of Fame)

37

WAYNE GRETZKY'S GREAT GOODBYE

The headline writers called it "The Great Goodbye."

It was the final NHL game the remarkable Wayne Gretzky, arguably the greatest player ever, would play.

The date was April 18, and fittingly enough the year was 1999. A Sunday afternoon at Madison Square Garden in New York. Gretzky and the Rangers versus the Pittsburgh Penguins.

The ending was somewhat disappointing, or unspectacular, in that Gretzky, playing his 1,487th regular-season game, finished with an assist on the Rangers' only goal, scored by Brian Leetch, in a 2–1 overtime loss.

And No. 99 was sitting on the bench when Jaromir Jagr scored to give the Penguins the victory. Afterward, Jagr asked Gretzky for his stick.

His final game in Canada had been played a few days earlier, on April 15, a 2–2 tie in Ottawa, and the fans begged him to stay for one more season.

Once the game in New York was over and his career was in the books—mostly the record books—the fans rose to give the Great One a standing ovation. He did a lap around the ice with his teammates, then another on his own, giving the fans and his family and friends a grand wave before leaving the ice for the final time.

Gretzky finished his illustrious career at the age of 38, owning almost every offensive record in the game. He won the Stanley Cup four times, the Art Ross Trophy as the league's leading scorer 10 times, and the Hart Trophy as the league's most valuable player nine times.

The list goes on . . .

At one point he owned or shared 61 NHL scoring records. Gretzky set a regular-season record with 215 points in 1985–86. He scored 50 goals in an amazing 39 games in 1981–82. He had a 51-game point streak in 1983–84.

And, like only the great ones can, he changed the game. Gretzky often worked magic from behind the opposing goal, either darting around to score himself, or setting up teammates. It was a piece of ice that became known as his "office."

Gretzky made his NHL debut at the age of 18 on October 10, 1979, at the old Chicago Stadium. In this, their first NHL game, the Oilers lost the game, but Gretzky earned the first of his 2,857 career points, assisting on a Kevin Lowe goal at 9:49 of the first period.

He scored his first goal four nights later, in his third game, beating Vancouver Canucks goaltender Glen Hanlon on the power play at 18:51 of the third period. He went on to accumulate 137 points, including 51 goals, in his rookie season, winning the first of eight straight Hart Trophies.

But of all the magical moments in his 21-year pro career, "I would say my last game in New York was my greatest day in hockey," he said a few years ago. "Everything you enjoy about the sport of hockey as a kid, driving to practice with Mom [Phyllis] and Dad [Walter], driving to the game with Mom and Dad, looking in the stands and seeing your mom and dad and your friends, that all came together in that last game in New York.

"My dad and I hadn't driven to a rink in years and years, but we drove to the rink together that morning. It was sort of the same conversation on the way to that game as it was when I was eight years old. 'Make sure you work hard, make sure you backcheck.' I'm sitting there going, 'Wow.'

"It was an emotional day for me, to be able to look up into the stands and see my mom and dad, my family and friends. It just brought back sort of all the memories I had as a kid playing hockey and that's why—listen, nothing compares to winning—but as an emotional day, that was the greatest day of my life. It put the ribbon on my career, pulled it all together.

Wayne Gretzky skates through centre ice at New York's Madison Square Garden during his final NHL game, April 18, 1999. (Dave Sandford/Hockey Hall of Fame)

The Great One hangs up his skates.
(Dave Sandford/Hockey Hall of Fame)

"I knew then there was no difference between playing as an eight-year-old and going to a game and being a professional hockey player at 38 and playing your last game. The feeling was still the same, the excitement was still the same, the relationship with your family the same, the game itself was the same, the only thing difference is I wasn't quite as good as I used to be. That's what I remember most.

"I had no second thoughts that day about retiring. I wasn't scared of retiring from the game of hockey and the practices and everything that goes with hockey. What I knew was that I was completely done with preparing for a season, three or four hours a day of getting ready to be physically ready to go in September. I knew I wasn't mentally ready to do that anymore and that's why I never had any second thoughts."

Gretzky had contemplated retiring several years earlier, while he was playing with the Los Angeles Kings after they were defeated by Montreal Canadiens in the 1993 Stanley Cup final. At the time, he said: "I don't want to be remembered as a has-been. I want to go out playing as well as any player in the game, if not better."

After the disappointment of that loss had passed, Gretzky decided to continue playing, eventually moving on to St. Louis and finally the Rangers.

"The last thing my dad said to me when we got to the rink—I think his exact words were, 'You know, I'd really like to watch you play one more year.' And I was, 'Whoa,' that was the most pressure I felt. You know, because he was a fan like everyone else and he was a big fan of mine. He didn't want me to retire, and I think it hurt him more than anyone else. But I was ready. I got nine goals that year. That was it, nine goals.

"On the drive home, my dad was pretty down about it, so he didn't press it again. But I knew it was time and, like I said, I had no regrets. I remember sitting on the bench with 30 seconds left in regulation and [coach] John Muckler

called a time out. I'm thinking, 'I've got 30 seconds to go' . . . But that day just brought it full circle for me."

Gretzky finished his career with 894 goals and 1,963 regular-season assists. He had more assists than the No. 2 all-time scorer, Gordie Howe, had total points (1,850).

And he had a profound influence on the game, both of how it was played and by putting hockey on the map in the United States, helping to grow its popularity, after he was traded to L.A.

During a ceremony prior to that final game, NHL commissioner Gary Bettman announced that the number 99 had been retired leaguewide, the first time a player had been honoured that way.

"When you take off that sweater, your jersey, after today's game, you will be the last player in the NHL to ever wear 99," said Bettman. "You have always been and always will be the Great One, and there will never be another."

The Hockey Hall of Fame also announced it was waiving the three-year waiting period for induction and that Gretzky would be the last to receive that exemption.

Asked to name the greatest performance of his career, Gretzky once said it was the second game of the 1987 Canada Cup final against the Soviet Union, a 6–5 overtime win for Canada.

"I didn't score a goal that night [he had five assists], but it was the best game I ever played," he said.

Back in 1979, when Gretzky was with Edmonton in the World Hockey Association, Oilers owner Peter Pocklington marked Gretzky's 18th birthday by throwing a pre-game party on the ice at Northlands Coliseum. He presented the young player with a 21-year personal services contract reportedly worth $5 million.

"It looks like I'm here for life," Gretzky said that night. "I'm locked up until 1999."

The Great One eventually moved on from Edmonton, of course, but he was locked up as an NHL player until 1999.

38

THE ISLANDERS'
19 CONSECUTIVE SERIES WINS

The New York Islanders were a beaten but extremely proud bunch as they returned to their dressing room in the bowels of Northlands Coliseum in the spring of 1984.

The Edmonton Oilers had defeated the Islanders in five games in the Stanley Cup final to end a remarkable run for Bryan Trottier, Mike Bossy, Denis Potvin, and company. The Islanders had won an NHL-record 19 consecutive playoff series, resulting in four Stanley Cup championships in a row.

After a convincing 6–1 victory in Game 2 at home to draw even in the 1984 final, the Islanders had renewed hope that there might be a fifth consecutive title. But the Oilers proved they were up to the task in Edmonton, winning three straight and outscoring the defending champions from Long Island, 19–6.

So as the clock ticked down on the end of the Islanders dynasty, they had plenty of time to reflect on their fabulous four championships and their drive for five.

"I felt no shame turning the Cup over to them," said Islanders captain Potvin after the series finale. "I'm damn proud. Several [Oilers] talked about idolizing us as we shook hands. One great team turned the Cup over to a team that was great all year. They deserved it."

The Islanders' streak began in April 1980. General

manager Bill Torrey had put together a talented group, but they were coming off two early-round playoff exits, and doubt had crept in as to whether they had the nerve to succeed in the pressure-packed playoffs.

In 1977–78, the Islanders had finished third overall in the regular season with 111 points, behind the Montreal Canadiens (129) and Boston Bruins (113). But the Habs and Bruins continued their winning ways in the playoffs to advance to the final. The Islanders blew a 2–0 series lead in the quarter-finals against Toronto, and lost in Game 7 when Lanny McDonald scored in overtime to give the Maple Leafs a surprise appearance in the semifinals.

The following year, the Islanders won the Presidents' Trophy with 116 points, one better than the Canadiens. But Montreal went on to win its fourth consecutive Stanley Cup, while the Islanders were again surprised, this time in a six-game semifinal loss to the New York Rangers, a team that had finished a whopping 25 points behind the Islanders in the regular season.

The heat was on coach Al Arbour and his players in the spring of 1980. The Islanders entered the postseason as the fifth seed and went up against the 12th-seed Los Angeles Kings.

The teams split the first two games on Long Island, and the Kings held a 3–1 lead after two periods in Game 3 in Los

Mike Bossy celebrates his overtime goal in Game 1 of the 1982 Stanley Cup Final against the Vancouver Canucks. (Paul Bereswill/Hockey Hall of Fame)

Angeles. However, Clark Gillies and Butch Goring tied the game in the third period, and defenceman Ken Morrow won it in overtime. The Islanders clinched the series the next evening with a stress-free 6–0 win, and the victory put them on cruise control for the next four—and almost five—years.

During their remarkable run of 19 consecutive playoff series wins, the Islanders played an exhausting 99 games, going 72–27. They swept five series and enjoyed an incredible 13–1 record in overtime games. Goaltender Billy Smith registered five shutouts, and the team arrived at the rink facing elimination only three times, including Game 5 of their championship series against the Oilers in 1984.

In 1982, the Pittsburgh Penguins had the Islanders down 3–1 in the best-of-five opening-round series. But another great escape occurred when defenceman Mike McEwen and forward John Tonelli scored in the final 5:27 of regulation time, and Tonelli scored 6:19 into overtime for the series win.

In 1984, the Islanders almost fell victim to the Rangers

once again. In the final game of the opening round, Don Maloney scored with 39 seconds remaining in the third period to force overtime. But Morrow delivered the decisive blow once again with a sudden-death winner 8:56 into the extra period.

The 1984 final was a rematch of the previous championship series, in which the Islanders had had little difficulty sweeping the young and talented Oilers.

In later years, Wayne Gretzky would often tell the story of how he and Kevin Lowe walked past the Islanders dressing room after the last game of the 1983 final, noting that there was not much celebrating going on; the veteran Islanders were nursing bumps and bruises sustained after four gruelling rounds.

"The players themselves were so exhausted, so tired, and had so many ice packs, we could really see the price they paid," Gretzky recalled. "Guys like Denis Potvin, I could see, were really beat up.

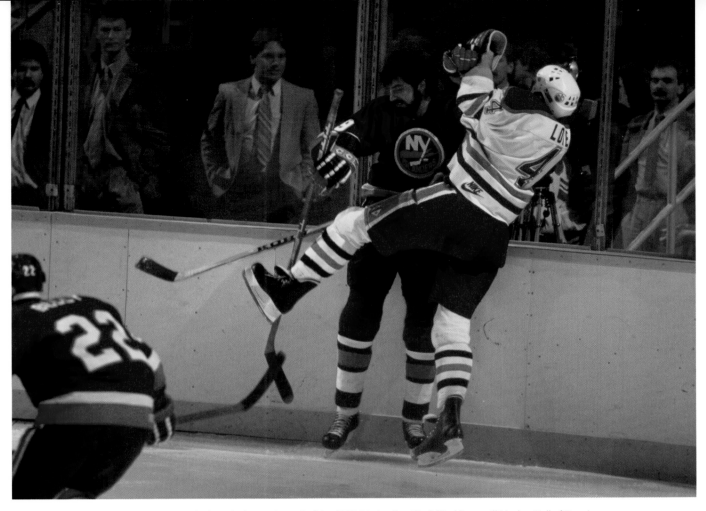

Clark Gillies and Kevin Lowe crash against the boards during Game 4 of the 1984 Stanley Cup Final. (Paul Bereswill/Hockey Hall of Fame)

"And we were fine. No problems at all. We got on the bus and Kevin said, 'That's the difference.' They were wounded. We lost and we were fine."

But the Oilers were also better prepared the second time. They added an unemployed Roger Neilson to break down film for the team in the playoffs. Neilson had steered the Vancouver Canucks to the 1982 final against the Islanders.

The Islanders had been effective in standing up the Oilers at the blue line in 1983, forcing Edmonton to play a dump-and-chase game. Billy Smith only allowed six goals in the sweep.

But in 1984, the Oilers' skill and speed were on full display. When Kevin McClelland scored the game's lone goal in the series opener, the Oilers seemed to gain confidence against Smith, and despite a loss in Game 2, they finished off the final with dominant wins of 7–2, 7–2, and 5–2.

"I just thought we would never see the day that we had to shake hands and say congratulations," Bob Nystrom said in his postgame remarks. "That was a very difficult thing to do."

The Islanders were simply worn out from a terrific five-year run.

"We had so much adversity, injuries, and other things," Arbour noted. "I had to play a lot of guys far too much in other series. It eventually took a toll and we had nothing else to give."

39

THE TORONTO MAPLE LEAFS COME BACK FROM THREE GAMES DOWN

One of the marvels of the Stanley Cup tournament is that the improbable occasionally happens. Like when a team appears to be down and out, yet somehow musters enough momentum to storm from behind to take a best-of-seven series after losing the first three games.

It has happened only four times in NHL history. The Toronto Maple Leafs were the first to do it, in 1942 against the Detroit Red Wings.

The NHL waited another 33 years until the New York Islanders turned the trick against the Pittsburgh Penguins, and it was another 35 years before the Philadelphia Flyers pulled off the unbelievable against the Boston Bruins.

The fourth team was the Los Angeles Kings, against the San Jose Sharks in 2014.

The Maple Leafs were not only the first to pull off the miracle comeback, but Syl Apps, Turk Broda, and their teammates remain the only club to accomplish the feat in the Stanley Cup final.

"We won it the hard way," said Toronto head coach Hap Day, who had captained the Maple Leafs to their most recent Stanley Cup win a decade earlier. "I had my doubts right up until that final bell rang."

After losing the first three games by scores of 3–2 and 4–2 in Toronto and 5–2 in Detroit, Day made two lineup changes for Game 4, subbing in Don Metz and Hank Goldup for Gordie Drillon and Bucko McDonald. Still, the Maple Leafs were on the verge of being swept when they fell behind, 2–0, in the second period.

However, Toronto managed to draw even before the end of the second period on goals by Bob Davidson and Lorne Carr. Detroit's Carl Liscombe and Toronto's Apps traded goals in the third period before Nick Metz, Don's older brother, scored the eventual game winner for the Maple Leafs with seven minutes remaining.

There were all kinds of shenanigans in the final minute. Referee Mel Harwood gave Red Wings right wing Eddie Wares a misconduct, but Wares refused to leave the ice. Detroit coach Jack Adams verbally lashed out at Harwood and then punched the official in the face. NHL president Frank Calder handed out multiple fines and suspended Adams indefinitely. Ebbie Goodfellow coached Detroit for the rest of the series.

The Maple Leafs returned home to hammer the Red Wings, 9–3, and Don Metz led the way with three goals and two assists. He also scored the first goal in Game 6, in Detroit, which Toronto won, 3–0, to set up the seventh and deciding game.

A then-record crowd of 16,218 fans packed Maple Leaf

Syl Apps of the Toronto Maple Leafs with the Stanley Cup after Toronto made history on April 18, 1942, by beating Detroit, 3–1, to win the series. (Imperial Oil–Turofsky/Hockey Hall of Fame)

Gardens to witness history in Game 7. After a goalless opening 20 minutes, Detroit's Syd Howe scored the lone goal of the second period. But it wasn't long before Toronto's Sweeney Schriner sandwiched two goals in the third period around Pete Langelle's series clincher, scored in the midst of a goalmouth scramble.

The Maple Leafs not only made history with the comeback, but rookie Gaye Stewart became the youngest-ever Stanley Cup winner at the age of 18 years, nine months. John McCreedy added the prized NHL championship to his 1936–37 Memorial Cup win with the Winnipeg Monarchs and the 1939–40 Allan Cup title he had won with the Kirkland Lake Blue Devils. Toronto's escape from nearly certain defeat proved the improbable was indeed possible, an accomplishment that would be cited in many dressing room speeches but rarely equalled.

In the spring of 1975, the expansion Islanders were in their third year of existence and had made the playoffs for the first time. After getting by the rival New York Rangers in the best-of-three preliminary round, the Islanders lost three close games to open their quarter-final series with the Pittsburgh Penguins, by scores of 5–4, 3–1, and 6–4.

The Islanders credited coach Al Arbour for the turnaround. He decided to bench goaltender Billy Smith in favour of Glenn "Chico" Resch and brought the players together for an inspirational on-ice speech during practice before Game 4.

"Al had us all in the corner of the rink and he said, 'If anybody on this team doesn't think we can beat Pittsburgh, they'd just as soon go in, take off their equipment, and leave,'" recalled Islanders rookie John Tonelli. "Obviously, there was not a mass exodus. We laughed about it. We said, 'He's serious.'"

The Islanders won the next three games by scores of 3–1, 4–2, and 4–1 to set up the dramatic series finale in Pittsburgh's Civic Arena.

In Game 7, captain Ed Westfall scored with 5:18

Leafs goalie Turk Broda with the Vezina Trophy for fewest goals against in 1942, after narrowly beating Frank Brimsek and Johnny Mowers for the award. (Imperial Oil–Turofsky/Hockey Hall of Fame)

remaining in the third period and Resch earned the shutout in the 1–0 win.

The Islanders almost duplicated the accomplishment in the next round, but lost in Game 7 to the eventual Stanley Cup champion Philadelphia Flyers.

In the spring of 2010, the Flyers not only found themselves down 3–0 in their second-round series with the Boston Bruins only to battle back to force a seventh game, but they fell behind 3–0 in the first period of the deciding game.

James van Riemsdyk, Scott Hartnell, and Danny Briere scored to pull Philadelphia even, setting the stage for Simon Gagne to register the series-deciding goal with 7:08 left in regulation time.

"All the adversity we had fought through, being down, 3–0 in the series, 3–0 in the game, to come back and win, it's absolutely incredible," said Hartnell, whose Flyers eventually lost in six games to the Chicago Blackhawks in the Stanley Cup final.

Jeff Carter and Mike Richards were part of that Flyers team, though Carter did not play against the Bruins in 2010 because of an injury. Nevertheless, he and Richards were both there four years later with the Kings, when Los Angeles managed to rebound after falling behind, 3–0, in the first round against San Jose. Anze Kopitar snapped a 1–1 tie late in the second period of Game 7 and in the third period the Kings cruised to a 5–1 win.

"That's when I feel our team played its best: when we have something to lose," Kings forward Justin Williams said. "We didn't want to go home. We didn't want an early summer. We enjoyed playing when the weather starts to get really hot."

The Kings went on to win the Stanley Cup in 2014, two years after they won their first NHL championship.

Frustration boils over in Boston as Milan Lucic (right) engages in a scrum with Simon Gagne of the Philadelphia Flyers. (Brian Babineau/Contributor/Getty Images)

40

BOSTON GETS ITS GARDEN

t was one of the most famous arenas in the history of the National Hockey League, known affectionately to locals simply as "The Gah-den." But it will come as a surprise to many that the building was originally conceived as "Boston Madison Square Garden."

When a new arena, the third iteration of Madison Square Garden, opened in New York in 1925, the builders' grandiose plan was to construct six more Madison Square Gardens across the United States. Ultimately, only the one in Boston was built, and the name was shortened to Boston Garden.

The 1920s were halcyon days for the burgeoning National Hockey League. Small, cozy rinks were replaced with "exposition buildings," as they were called. These were large, multipurpose structures designed to accommodate sporting events, car shows, conventions, and boxing matches. Combined with the expansion to 10 teams, this trend meant the NHL could boast grand, iconic arenas that produced greater revenues and often housed more people than the towns where the players were born.

Such lavish venues weren't cheap. In a 1929 letter to Stanford Zucker, a prospective owner from Cleveland, NHL president Frank Calder detailed that the Montreal Forum had cost $1.5 million to build, while construction expenditures for Madison Square Garden hovered around $6 million, including the downtown real estate on which it sat.

In April 1924, to spur his bid for an expansion team in the Massachusetts capital, Boston businessman Charles Francis Adams notified Calder of a group's intent to build a 15,000-seat arena in his city. Granted a franchise, which made the existing Boston Arena its temporary home, Adams received financing from Madison Square Garden Corporation and construction of the new rink began in December 1927. Built at a then record price of $10 million, Boston Garden opened with a prizefight on November 17, 1928.

> Built at a then record price of $10 million, Boston Garden opened with a prizefight on November 17, 1928.

The Garden hosted its first NHL game on November 20, a 1–0 Boston loss to the Montreal Canadiens. The Bruins' first season in their new digs ended in celebration four months later, as they defeated the New York Rangers, 2–1, on March 29, 1929, to sweep the two-game series and win their first Stanley Cup.

Former All-American college running back Huntington "Tack" Hardwick helped found Boston Garden and tried to convince Calder to add a second NHL tenant in 1929. Calder told Hardwick to work out an arrangement with Adams, but no deal was ever brokered. Hardwick eventually became a director of Boston Garden when a local consortium bought out Madison Square Garden's investment in 1934.

Like the four-leaf clover that represented the city with a rich Irish population base, Boston Garden was special, one-of-a-kind. It was perched above a train station in the north end of the city, and its rink was nine feet shorter than the other league surfaces. That distance was lost between the blue lines—players would carry the puck through the neutral zone at their peril.

The ice was also two feet narrower than other arenas. The result was a rink that seemingly had no corners. Boston offered visiting players nowhere to hide.

Also unique to the Garden was the overhanging balcony, where the famous "Gallery Gods" held court and were never shy about letting players know what they thought of their performances.

The great King Clancy, with Toronto in the 1930s, was the target of many barbs.

"Hey Clancy, we've got a town named after you: Marble-head!"

"Hey Clancy, there's a bus leaving in the morning. Be under it."

Boston Garden was also home to the Boston Celtics, one of the original franchises of the National Basketball Association. Even then, the arena had its own distinct flavour. Six years after the NBA formed in 1946, the Garden installed the original parquet floor from the Boston Arena, the Bruins' original home.

Just as the peculiarities of the ice surface gave the Bruins an advantage, so too did the parquet floor for the Celts. Familiarity may breed contempt, but it also brings knowledge. The home teams used the arena's quirks to their advantage and produced five Stanley Cup–winning teams and sixteen NBA champions, including a run by the Celtics of eight consecutive titles from 1959 through 1966.

The great moments live in history: Bobby Orr flying through the air to break the Bruins' 29-year Stanley Cup drought on May 10, 1970; Bob Cousy and John Havlicek leading the Celtics to 10 championships in 11 years in the 1950s and '60s; Larry Bird achieving a level of fame that transcended basketball in the 1980s.

There were also regrettable incidents along the way. A hit by Bruins star defenceman Eddie Shore on December 12, 1933, left Toronto's Ace Bailey with a fractured skull and in need of two brain operations. Shore was suspended for 16 games, at that time one-third of the 48-game regular-season schedule.

In the heat of battle during a game on March 13, 1955, Montreal's Rocket Richard punched a linesman in the face in an attempt to fight Boston's Hal Laycoe. That prompted NHL president Clarence Campbell to suspend the Canadiens superstar for the rest of the regular season and the entire play-offs. The suspension incited the wrath of Montreal fans and sparked the famous Richard Riot on St. Patrick's Day.

By the end of the Garden's glorious 67-year history, the antiquated building had run its course. It was the league's only building without air conditioning. Dressing rooms were small, plumbing was a major issue, and rats would unofficially boost the building's attendance. Electrical blackouts at critical times plagued the Garden in its later years—the Stanley Cup finals in 1988 and 1990, both against the Edmonton Oilers, suffered power-related interruptions.

The final game held at the venerable arena came on September 26, 1995, an exhibition between the Bruins and Montreal to bring the arena's existence full circle. Boston won 3–0. After the game, which was attended by many former Bruins, the banners were taken down and transported to their new home, a moment that closed out an era filled with too many great moments to count.

Boston Garden hosted hockey games from 1928 until 1995. (Le Studio du Hockey/Hockey Hall of Fame)

Marcel Dionne playing for the Los Angeles Kings. On April 10, 1982, he was determined his Kings wouldn't fall behind the Edmonton Oilers two games to one, despite the Oilers' 5-0 lead in Game 3 of the playoffs' opening round. (Paul Bereswill/Hockey Hall of Fame)

41

THE KINGS' MIRACLE ON MANCHESTER

Two thoughts were skating around Marcel Dionne's head as he and his Los Angeles Kings teammates stepped onto the ice for the third period of Game 3 of their first-round series against the Edmonton Oilers.

The Little Beaver, as Dionne was known during his Hall of Fame career, felt that even though the Kings were down 5–0, they had a faint chance to come back because the Oilers, known for their firewagon style of play, weren't airtight defensively.

Dionne also thought about how much he'd like to wipe the overconfident grin off the mug of Edmonton coach Glen Sather.

"They were pretty cocky," Dionne told the Madison Square Garden Network when the cable sports station revisited the April 10, 1982 playoff game that became known as the Miracle on Manchester.

"I remember looking over at Glen Sather and seeing him laughing. We weren't that bad. We may not have been great, but we had character players."

The Kings' character had been on full display in the opening two games of the best-of-five preliminary-round series in Edmonton. The heavily favoured Oilers had finished second overall in the regular season with 111 points, a whopping 48 points ahead of the 16th-place Kings. But Los Angeles

outscored the high-flying Oilers, 10–8, in the series opener, and briefly led Game 2 before losing, 3–2, in overtime.

The series shifted to the Forum, situated on Manchester Boulevard in the Los Angeles suburb of Inglewood, California. Wayne Gretzky, Mark Messier, Jari Kurri, Glenn Anderson, Paul Coffey, and Grant Fuhr put on a clinic in the opening 40 minutes.

Messier and Gretzky scored in the first period to build a 2–0 lead. Gretzky's third of five goals in the series was scored while teammate Dave Hunter was in the penalty box.

Hunter still had a seat in the penalty box when Edmonton defenceman Lee Fogolin made it 3–0 in the opening minute of the second period. Risto Siltanen and Gretzky had increased the Oilers' lead to 5–0 after the middle 20 minutes.

"If you would have asked me after the second period about our chances to come back, I would have said 'slim,'" Dionne said. "But we knew the Oilers had a tendency to play wide-open hockey. So our attitude, as we headed back to the ice, was 'We're not going to give up.'"

The Kings had some offensive firepower of their own, with the Triple Crown Line of Dionne, Dave Taylor, and Charlie Simmer, as well as Jim Fox, Bernie Nicholls, and defenceman Larry Murphy.

Messier once described the Kings' miraculous comeback

as a snowball rolling down a hill that the Oilers could not stop. It was defenceman Jay Wells who put the snowball in motion at 2:46 of the third period.

In 185 regular-season and playoff games with the Kings, Wells had only six goals to his credit. But his screened shot—Taylor was in front of Fuhr—gave his team a lift.

Nineteen-year-old rookie Doug Smith beat Oilers defenceman Kevin Lowe to a rebound at 5:58, but it wasn't until almost nine minutes later that Simmer scored off an Edmonton turnover to make it 5–3.

At the 15-minute mark, Oilers centre Garry Unger cut Los Angeles defender Dave Lewis in the face with a high stick. Unger was hit with a five-minute major, but Lewis retaliated and drew a roughing minor. With the teams playing four on four, Kings defenceman Mark Hardy surprised Fuhr off the rush, scoring the fourth Kings goal with 4:01 remaining in regulation time.

After Lewis's penalty had expired, Los Angeles had a full three minutes on the power play in which to tie the game. But the Kings struggled with the man advantage. Goalie Mario Lessard had to make a terrific stop on a shorthanded breakaway from Edmonton's Pat Hughes. And then L.A. coach Don Perry resorted to the old stalling tactic of changing goalkeepers. In went Doug Keans for Lessard with 1:37 left. Lessard went back in at the next whistle, and then was lifted for an extra attacker in the final minute.

On the dramatic game-tying goal, a deflected puck went to Gretzky along the side boards, but Fox was quick to get there and put enough pressure on No. 99 to steal the puck. He then fed a pass back to Hardy, whose shot from the high slot yielded a rebound to rookie Steve Bozek, who scored with five ticks left on the clock.

After a wild celebration, the game went to overtime. Messier missed an open net early in the extra period, and a few shifts later, Perry sent out his all-rookie line of Smith, Bozek, and Daryl Evans.

Smith faced Messier for a draw in the Oilers zone. The L.A. rookie barely won the faceoff, and as the puck slowly slid back behind Smith, Evans cruised in from the side boards and leaned into the game winner, 2:35 into overtime.

"There's no time to even think about the shot," Evans told the *Los Angeles Times*. "It was just close your eyes and hope it hits the net. It found a hole over Grant Fuhr's shoulder."

Evans remembered calling his parents in Toronto after the game. It was, of course, the wee hours of the morning back east, and they had gone to bed after two periods.

With all the emotion, the Kings could not have slept if they tried.

"It took me a long time to recuperate from that game," Dionne said. "I remember laughing and celebrating two hours after. The emotion that goes through you is incredible."

The Oilers tied the series with a 3–2 victory in Game 4, after which the two teams shared a flight back to Edmonton for the deciding game, to be played at Northlands Coliseum the following evening.

The Kings didn't reach their hotel in downtown Edmonton until 5 a.m. local time, but it was the Oilers who played as if they hadn't had a good night's sleep. They fell behind, 6–2, after two periods and were eliminated by a score of 7–4.

"I remember looking over at Glen Sather and seeing him laughing. We weren't that bad. We may not have been great, but we had character players."

42

PHIL ESPOSITO'S TRADE TO BOSTON

A sportswriter in Phil Esposito's hometown of Sault Ste. Marie, Ontario, described the young centre's 1967 trade from the Chicago Blackhawks to the Boston Bruins as "the biggest daylight holdup in the NHL trade market."

For decades afterward, the Blackhawks must have felt their hands were still in the air, though it had been with the best of intentions that they dealt away one of the NHL's top 10 scorers of all time.

Take yourself back to the end of the 1966–67 season, when Chicago finished in first place only to be upset that spring by the Toronto Maple Leafs, who went on to defeat Montreal for the Stanley Cup. In 1961 Chicago had won the only title not claimed by the two Canadian teams since 1955. Eager to get back on top, they went looking for much-needed help on defence.

They eyed Gilles Marotte of the Bruins, who was quickly gaining a reputation as a tough undersized blueliner. As the NHL's doormat at the time, Boston certainly valued Marotte, but also knew it had an even better defenceman about to burst through the NHL wall in Bobby Orr.

Chicago manager Tommy Ivan knew Marotte wouldn't come cheap, but thought he could kill two birds with one stone. Third-year centre Esposito had gone through the Leafs series without a single point. Though he'd spent some time centring Bobby Hull and had tied for seventh in NHL scoring that year with Phil Goyette of the Rangers, Esposito had struggled in the playoffs, leaving him with critics and doubters within the organization.

As the days ticked toward the NHL trade deadline in mid-May, teams were preparing for the June expansion draft, trying to get something now for players they might lose for nothing in the draft to the six new teams. Because of this, Ivan and his Boston counterpart, Milt Schmidt, began talking about the two principals and eventually added more names to the mix.

Schmidt would have been a winner in the deal just by getting Esposito, but Ivan surrendered two more forwards he thought he could live without: winger Ken Hodge and centre Fred Stanfield, who had been linemates on Chicago's sponsored junior team in St. Catharines.

Schmidt threw a centre, Pit Martin, into the deal so that Chicago could at least fill Esposito and Stanfield's position, and added minor-league goalie Jack Norris (the Hawks were about to lose Glenn Hall in the draft).

Shock gave way to anger when Esposito was told about the trade. The fact that the news was relayed by Hull instead of Ivan made him even angrier at Hawks management.

Phil Esposito of the Chicago Blackhawks shields the puck from Toronto Maple Leafs defenceman Allan Stanley. (Frank Prazak/Hockey Hall of Fame)

"Bobby had been in the office that day and he'd heard I was traded," Esposito recalled years later. "I kind of knew I was in trouble because I went into the office with an expense and Tommy didn't want to talk to me. Bobby called my mom, my mom called me, I called Bobby back.

"They didn't want me. That's not my fault that I was in the most one-sided trade in history. They were the stupid ones. They made the deal.

"Naturally, a guy is a bit shaken when something like this happens. It hurts a guy's pride."

Esposito arrived in Boston itching to prove himself. He proclaimed that the Bruins' eight-year playoff drought was

through and that a Stanley Cup would soon come their way.

Almost immediately, he, Hodge, and Wayne Cashman ushered in the era of the Big Bad Bruins, supplementing Orr's dazzling skills and rushes.

Esposito reached a career-high 35 goals in his first year in Boston and nearly beat Chicago's Stan Mikita for the league scoring title. In 1968–69, the Bruins and Esposito both hit 100 points, the latter winning the first of his five Art Ross Trophies, and Hodge had 90 points.

But the full impact of the trade hit Chicago in the spring of 1970. The Bruins swept them in the semifinals, with Orr and Esposito having claimed first and second place in the scoring race, and Stanfield having become a strong two-way centre. Boston brought the Cup to New England and would do so a second time in 1972. The Bruins wouldn't miss the playoffs again until 1997.

As for Marotte, he did bring a degree of toughness to the Chicago blue line, amassing more than 100 minutes in penalties in two seasons. But he did not alter the makeup of his team the same way Esposito, a dominant force in the Bruins dressing room, did his. The same year the Bruins won their first Cup, Chicago traded Marotte to Los Angeles. Martin stayed and became captain in the mid-1970s, but the Hawks gave way to the new order in the NHL after losing Cup finals to Montreal in '71 and '73.

"You always have second thoughts," Schmidt said years after the trade. "But this was one move I never regretted making. You only hope you're right and things work out the way you expected. I never expected this."

Esposito played his first season as a Boston Bruin in the 1967-68 season, and would be a force for the Bruins for years to come. (Frank Prazak/Hockey Hall of Fame)

43

GLENN HALL'S GOALTENDING STREAK

All Glenn Hall did was put together one incredible, unbeatable streak of consecutive complete games in goal.

All he did was play through illness, facial stitches, trips to the dentist, and slumps to give his team a chance to win, whether it was for the Detroit Red Wings, or later for the Chicago Blackhawks.

There had been great goalies before Hall and would be great goalies after him, but none of his fraternity completed 502 consecutive games—503 if you're counting consecutive starts. Not even close. Yet Hall likes to clown around when the subject of his superior streak comes up.

"You mean 552 games, don't you?" Hall once said with a chuckle, referring to the 49 straight Stanley Cup playoff games he suited up for during this run.

Hall added that if you included his minor-pro days with the Edmonton Flyers and Indianapolis Capitals, as well as his time in junior with the Windsor Spitfires, he performed in more than 1,000 games in a row.

Of course, this is stretching the truth, considering that his time in Edmonton in 1952–53 was interrupted by a brief

He was a 10-time all-star, won three Vezina Trophies, won the Calder Trophy, and was inducted into the Hockey Hall of Fame in 1975.

stint with the Red Wings to relieve an injured Terry Sawchuk.

Eventually, the Red Wings decided to trade Sawchuk to the Boston Bruins in June 1955, clearing the path for Hall to become the Wings' No. 1 netminder at age 24.

His streak began on October 6, 1955, with a 3–2 Red Wings loss to the team that he would eventually end his remarkable streak with, the Blackhawks.

After two full seasons playing in every game with Detroit, Hall was moved to the Blackhawks, along with Ted Lindsay, in a trade that sent Hank Bassen, Forbes Kennedy, Bill Preston, and Johnny Wilson to the Red Wings.

Hall played in every game of his first five seasons with Chicago, tying Georges Vezina's record of 328 consecutive regular-season appearances on January 24, 1960. But early in his sixth season, a back ailment ended Hall's streak.

On the day before the 13th game of the 1962–63 season, Hall was putting on his equipment prior to an afternoon practice. He bent down to fix a toe strap on his pad and felt a twinge in his lower back. He thought the adrenaline of practice would liberate him of the discomfort, but the pain did not subside.

The next evening at Chicago Stadium, his defence worked

Glenn Hall completed 502 consecutive games, the longest streak of any goaltender in NHL history. (Frank Prazak/Hockey Hall of Fame)

furiously to keep shots to a minimum. But Hall was in agony. During a stoppage in play 6:30 in, he skated over to the bench to advise Blackhawks coach Rudy Pilous that rookie backup goalie Denis DeJordy should get ready.

DeJordy had been summoned from the Blackhawks' AHL affiliate, the Buffalo Bisons, the night before. In those days, backup goalies sat in the stands in street clothes until they were needed. So DeJordy went to Chicago's dressing room to don his equipment.

After Bruins forward Murray Oliver scored at the 10:31 mark to tie the game at 1–1, Hall had had enough, even though that was the only recorded shot he faced that evening. He pulled himself and skated over to the bench. DeJordy, then 23, stepped in to make his NHL debut in a game that would finish in a 3–3 draw.

Hall's streak was over. It had lasted 30, 195 minutes and 43 seconds, including 65:12 of Stanley Cup postseason overtime play.

Now the question became: Could he ready himself to at least maintain his streak of consecutive games *played*? He had three days before a road match against the Montreal Canadiens to find out.

But, upon examination by team physician Dr. Myron Tremaine and trainer Nick Green, Hall discovered he had suffered a pinched nerve in his lower back. He needed recovery time. He did not accompany his teammates to Montreal.

He would, however, miss only four games that season.

"Unfortunately, it didn't get better like I thought it would because I didn't think it was that serious," he recalled. "Was I disappointed? Was I upset? I can't remember. It was

more than 50 years ago. I just remember I simply couldn't play because I was hurt. It's something you deal with and move on."

At the time, the NHL's iron-man streak belonged to one of the skaters Hall was traded for—Johnny Wilson—at 580 games.

Hall, known as Mr. Goalie, certainly enjoyed an eventful career. The 10-time all-star won three Vezina Trophies, the Calder Trophy in 1955–56, the Conn Smythe Trophy in 1967–68, and was inducted into the Hockey Hall of Fame in 1975.

His name was etched on the Stanley Cup three times. The first was as a call-up in the 1952 playoffs with Detroit, even though he never saw a moment of game time. Then, he played a central role with the upset-minded Blackhawks in 1961. Finally, in 1989, as Mike Vernon's goalie coach with the Calgary Flames.

In the Blackhawks' successful Stanley Cup run of 1961, he shut out the Canadiens in Games 5 and 6 to end Montreal's run of five straight titles, in a massive upset in the semifinal.

He finished his career playing with the expansion St. Louis Blues, and was in goal when Boston star Bobby Orr scored his famous overtime Cup-winning goal. He had previously surrendered the 500th career goal by Maurice "Rocket" Richard, on October 19, 1957.

In his hometown of Humboldt, Saskatchewan, there is a Glenn Hall Park on Glenn Hall Drive.

"I guess I have a lot to be proud of," Hall said. "The record is one of the accomplishments that I'm proud of."

43
100

Above: Glenn Hall played for the Detroit Red Wings and the Chicago Blackhawks during his remarkable streak, ultimately ending his career with the St. Louis Blues. (Imperial Oil–Turofsky/Hockey Hall of Fame)

Opposite: Hall plays the puck away from Toronto Maple Leafs forward Frank Mahovlich. (Frank Prazak/Hockey Hall of Fame)

Ray Bourque (left) and Colorado Avalanche captain Joe Sakic hoist the Cup during the celebration after Game 7 of the Stanley Cup Final on June 9, 2001. Colorado defeated the New Jersey Devils, 3-1. (Dave Sandford/Hockey Hall of Fame)

44

RAY BOURQUE WINS THE CUP

Denver Broncos quarterback John Elway never made a hand-off as quickly as Colorado Avalanche captain Joe Sakic did in 2001 with the Stanley Cup.

As NHL commissioner Gary Bettman and officials from the Hockey Hall of Fame brought the trophy to its centre-ice stage, cameras caught Sakic telling Ray Bourque to stand right beside him for the official presentation. Sakic briefly held the Cup, his second championship in 13 years, but quickly passed it to Bourque, the sentimental story of that playoff year.

In his 22-year career, the great defenceman had earned many honours in the game, save a big one: the coveted silver chalice. He broke into the NHL with the Boston Bruins in 1979, becoming their captain in 1988. Bourque loved Boston and the Bruins, and he repeatedly signed dollar figures that many considered to be less than the going rate because he believed they could win. He was a crucial part of the franchise's run of 29 consecutive playoff appearances—including trips to the final in 1988 and 1990—that ended with a failure to qualify in the spring of 1997.

Three years later, it seemed certain that the Bruins were trending in the wrong direction, and finally Bourque asked to be moved, preferably to an East Coast team. Instead, a match was found in the Rocky Mountains. Turned back in

the Western Conference final twice in the three years since they'd won their 1996 Cup, the Avs were looking for a workhorse on the blue line.

Bourque, a five-time Norris Trophy winner with his great skills and instincts still intact, was willing, and he became the principal in a five-player deal made just before the 2000 playoffs.

"In 20 and a half years in Boston, with all the troubles pro athletes have been in, Ray was never a problem," said Hall of Fame writer Kevin Paul Dupont of the *Boston Globe*. But Bourque, like local Red Sox legends Carl Yastrzemski and Ted Williams, had never won the big prize to cap his career.

Colorado still had the nucleus of its powerhouse: forwards Sakic and Peter Forsberg, and Patrick Roy in net. However, there was plenty of room for Bourque to give them one more weapon in the arsenal.

With 14 points in 14 regular-season games after the trade, Bourque was instantly a fan favourite. But a title that first year was not to be; the Avs lost with a heartbreaking clank of the puck off the post in a 3–2 loss to Dallas in Game 7 of the Western Conference final.

Bourque and the Avs were undaunted. The next autumn, baseball caps reading "Mission 16W" began to appear around Denver. The whole city was getting behind Bourque's quest to check off the 16 wins required to capture the Cup.

He played all but two games that season, earning 59 points, his best showing in years. Colorado had 118 points and won the Presidents' Trophy, finishing first overall.

But that was all a dress rehearsal for the spring. In the playoffs, the Avs swept Vancouver, survived a Game 7 scare against the Los Angeles Kings, and made it past St. Louis in five. That left them facing a showdown with the defending champion New Jersey Devils.

Bourque contributed an assist on the goal that won Game 3, but the Devils were able to take a 3–2 series lead. Roy shut them down in Game 6 to set the stage for a winner-take-all Game 7 at Denver's Pepsi Center. There was no way the Avs were passing up such a chance again, and they skated away with a 3–1 win and the Cup.

When it was over, when the Stanley Cup was on the ice, the crowd drowned out Bettman's congratulatory remarks as they chanted the 40-year-old Bourque's name. The roar in the rink increased as the defenceman, upon receiving the trophy, gave it a long-awaited kiss and did a little victory lap.

"What a feeling," he said later. "That's why we made the move. My family knew why I was making it, and now they're living the dream. Everyone I played with there has a little piece of this."

Louis Armstrong's "What a Wonderful World" played in the rink as Bourque waltzed around the ice with the coveted trophy. When he departed, with his mission finally accomplished, it was for the last time.

Ray Bourque played for the Boston Bruins from 1979 to 2000, winning the Norris Trophy five times. (Dave Sandford/Hockey Hall of Fame)

45

THE NHL ADOPTS VIDEO REVIEW

The world's fastest sport was in need of an assist—a little help from a second look.

As players were becoming faster by way of superior conditioning and skate technology, while using extra muscle and one-piece sticks to propel pucks harder, game officials were under pressure to keep up with the pace.

The increase from one referee to two (fully implemented in 2000–01) would help officials cover more ice, but even before that change, the league recognized that in hockey sometimes the naked eye—or even the stationary camera—can't tell the full story.

In the early 1990s, the NHL augmented the calls on the ice with video replay. At the time, the aim was to address two of the oldest bugaboos in the book: Did the puck cross the goal line? And if so, did it go in before time expired? From the old triumvirate of people—the referee, goal judge, and timekeeper—making those decisions, the process was now streamlined.

"When you can see a puck over the line with the clock superimposed [on the TV screen] with two-tenths of a second on it, there can be no arguments," said Bryan Lewis, in those days the league's director of officiating.

Each rink had to be equipped with overhead cameras, rigged at a slight angle to reveal just enough white space to show when a puck had completely crossed the red goal line and was a "good" goal. A booth in the press box was created where NHL supervisors could check the television feed.

Officials also monitored whether a puck had gone over the line prior to the net being dislodged, and whether it was directed into the net by a high stick, hand, or foot, or deflected in off an official.

One of the extensions of the video program was born out of a greater concern about protecting goalies from injuries via aggressive crease-crashers. For a while there was a zero-tolerance policy toward stepping even a foot in the blue paint unless the puck was there first.

"We want the players to think about that area as if it's a pit of alligators," said one league official.

But that policy came under scrutiny during the 1999 Stanley Cup final, when Brett Hull of the Dallas Stars clearly had a foot in the crease as he fired home the championship-winning goal against the Buffalo Sabres. The league, however, had made it clear to teams that players would be allowed to pursue a rebound into the paint.

With league expansion to 30 teams at the turn of the century, the review process was becoming unwieldy to operate, with so many incidents subject to different interpretations at each rink. In 2003, the league created a command centre, run out of its Toronto office, to monitor questionable goals and plays. Among the staff assigned every night to watch more than 10 games on some evenings were hockey operations executives such as Colin Campbell, Mike Murphy, and Kris King, each of whom had played in the league and could appreciate the nuances.

With a small number of trained personnel keeping an eye on games being played in the different time zones, the calls could be interpreted even more quickly and accurately, thus improving the flow of 1,230 regular-season games plus two months of playoffs.

In the massive "war room" is a 30-foot bank of high-definition TVs that can display various angles of a particular game. The array of TVs is dominated by a seven-by-four-foot main screen. Referees at arenas can be linked to the command centre via headset, allowing them to discuss any disputed goals and relay the verdict and reasoning to the teams.

The wide range of angles available, particularly when two networks are showing the same game, often allow the

Toronto office to make its ruling before the call comes in from the game officials.

Beginning with the 2015–16 season, coaches are allowed to challenge controversial goals if they believed the attacking team is offside, or guilty of goalie interference. A failed challenge results in the team giving up its time out, a restriction designed to keep coaches from abusing the system. On-ice officials are given mini iPads to help them work with the command centre to make their determination at the penalty bench.

The league retained the right to review any potentially troublesome play in the last minute of the third period or at any point during overtime of a regular-season or playoff game. But if an on-ice official makes a call, and the replay offers no irrefutable evidence of a misinterpreted ruling, the goal will stand.

"In the end, it's all about getting the calls correct," Murphy said. "That's what we want, that's what the officials want, that's what the teams want, and that's what the fans want."

Officials have had support on close calls from video replay since the early 1990s. (Ottawa Senators/Hockey Hall of Fame)

46

COACHING INNOVATIONS

n the late stages of a Boston Bruins–Montreal Maroons playoff game on March 26, 1931, fans in Boston Garden were aghast to see their team's net suddenly empty.

As time ticked down with Montreal clinging to a 1–0 lead, Boston coach Art Ross called goalie Tiny Thompson to the bench and put an extra attacker on the ice. The Bruins, perhaps unsure how to set up for the first-ever six-on-five, failed to score, while the Maroons were too discombobulated to hit the unattended cage.

Newspaper accounts of the game made references to Ross's "amazing manoeuver" to try and tie the game.

Within a year or two, the other seven teams in the NHL also tried pulling the goalie—just another example of how quickly a useful coaching innovation can catch on.

Such tweaks went back to the formation of the league in 1917. Goalies had already begun to figure out ways around the rule that forbid them from flopping to the ice—they faked injury or equipment problems. So, one of the first rule changes in the new league was to allow goalies to sprawl face-down to make a save.

The adoption of two blue lines changed skating patterns and the ways players passed the puck.

The Original Six years of the league added a variety of wrinkles. Teams experimented with using a forward on the point to increase the potency of the power play. In the Canadiens' dynasty years of the late 1950s, the other five teams gave up trying to defend against the Habs on a five-on-three; instead, they ganged up to force through a rule that, if a goal was scored with a team down two players, one of the minor penalties would end immediately.

Jacques Plante came out of his net to play pucks, which meant his team and the opposition had to adjust. In Toronto, Punch Imlach sometimes employed his biggest, strongest defencemen on draws, not to win the faceoff outright but to tie up the opposing centre.

Cerebral coaches such as Roger Neilson practically re-wrote the rule book. Coaching in junior, Neilson would pull his goalie but instruct him to leave his stick lying across the goal line before coming to the bench, as no regulation outlawed such a ploy. He was also the first coach to use video to review the game, employing high schoolers to set up cumbersome cameras in the seats.

In Philadelphia, Fred Shero hired Mike Nykoluk, the first full-time assistant coach. "The Fog" could also be found writing warning notes on the ceiling of the dressing room, because he knew bored players would inevitably look up there during team meetings.

Sometimes he'd deliberately diagram a drill that made

little or no sense, hoping a player would be alert enough to question him. Of course, his edict to "arrive first on the puck and in ill humour" also worked for a few years, before the Broad Street Bullies gave way to the Habs under Scotty Bowman, who made treating his players unpredictably a key tool for keeping the Canadiens sharp.

The arrival of Europeans and their big-ice mentality gradually seeped into North American strategy. A young Glen Sather took note of Bobby Hull, Anders Hedberg, and Ulf Nilsson with the Winnipeg Jets of the WHA, and the way they merged North American and European tactics, particularly on breakouts and transitions, rather than staying in their lanes. When Sather became coach of the Edmonton Oilers, he was blessed to work with a cast of free-wheeling youngsters. His team went after the puck deep in the opposition end and, in a few deft moves, would find themselves with a scoring chance.

It's a widely held belief among the coaching fraternity that coaching has always been copycat business. Teams will always try to mimic the strategies of the Stanley Cup champions.

Coaches are not the only ones breaking down a game, looking for new strategies. Two or three assistants are on the bench, entrusted with special teams or other departments, sometimes with an eye in the sky on game nights.

"The coaching today has just become so detailed that they don't leave any stone unturned," said analyst and former NHL defenceman Bob McGill. "If a player today says they were not prepared for the game, then it's on them, certainly not the coaching staff.

"They have assistants and video and they watch everything. You look at the tools they have right on the bench, iPads and tablets and TVs to see plays and check things. I just think the information they have today—and the information highway—is amazing. You can get an instant look at something to help a player if he makes a mistake.

"When I came in, there was no video, or maybe once in a while. Neilson started that, but when he left Toronto [in 1979], I don't recall going over any video for the longest time.

"Mike Keenan, for me, was the best practice coach ever. You look at Mike Babcock picking up on that in Toronto. You get on the ice, its go-go-go and you're done. You look up and realize they only practised 38 minutes, but no time was wasted.

"Keenan was that way: the first guy to make sure everyone had their own water bottles. So when it was time for a drink, it was like it was timed, too, and it was on to the next drill right away. He pushed us to be better every day and to expect more from yourself every day."

Then there is 21st-century analytics, perhaps the final frontier of innovation.

"Most coaches have always had an analytical mind," former Vancouver Canucks coach Willie Desjardins said. "When I was in Japan [coaching Tokyo Seibu], I had what I called 'success factors.' It was, 'If we do these things, we'll win.' And that was kind of an early sign of analytics, where you find something, and there's a correlation between that and your success. The key is what you measure, and then accurately measuring it."

Opposite: Fred Shero, coach of the Philadephia Flyers, 1971-78, was the first coach to hire an assistant coach full-time. (Frank Prazak/Hockey Hall of Fame)

Above: Mike Keenan was known around the league for his innovative practices. He coached the Philadelphia Flyers for four seasons, 1984-88. (Paul Bereswill/Hockey Hall of Fame)

47

HOCKEYTOWN AND JOE LOUIS ARENA

n the summer of 1982, Jim Devellano was standing in the middle of an empty Joe Louis Arena with a look of pain on his face.

"The Ilitch family had just purchased the team," the one-time general manager of the Detroit Red Wings recalled. "We'd just been to the box office and were horrified to find out on July 12 that we only had 2,100 season tickets [sold] for the coming season."

"The Joe" had opened in 1979—unfortunately, just as the franchise was struggling through the worst years of its post–Gordie Howe depression. Between 1971 and 1983, including the first four years after they left their old home at the Olympia, the Wings made the playoffs just once.

"I'm out at centre, with no ice in at that time of year, and look up at this 20,000-seat building and thought, 'My God, it's going to take a hell of a team to fill this place,'" continued Devellano. "I said to Marian Ilitch [wife of Red Wings owner Mike], 'I don't think we'll ever do it.' But sure enough, we were able to. Winning does that."

Detroit and its home arena were a very long way from being known as Hockeytown at that point, but fortunes began to turn almost immediately for the Ilitch family and Devellano during the 1983 draft. With the fourth pick, the Wings selected Steve Yzerman, and soon made him one of

the youngest captains in team history. Next, Detroit made moves to be battle-ready in the hard-nosed Norris Division, adding some muscle around Stevie Y.

"The first people who helped us get the really big crowds were Yzerman, Bob Probert, and Joe Kocur," Devellano said. "The team got a little bit better, we got feistier, and we eventually got the place full."

The Wings had almost moved to nearby Pontiac, Michigan, after their days at the downtown Olympia were through. Their home since 1927, the Olympia was antiquated and the neighbourhood had become economically depressed. But the city offered the Wings' owner at the time, Bruce Norris, a break on rent and parking if he would keep the team in town, playing at a site on the Detroit River waterfront that was ideal for a new arena.

The Wings played their final game at the Olympia, which had housed political conventions and even an Elvis concert, on December 15, 1979. It was a 4–4 tie with the Quebec Nordiques.

Joe Louis Arena, which cost $57 million (in U.S. funds) to erect, not only gave the team a more picturesque location by the water, but it was a quick trip for the many Wings fans across the river in Windsor, Ontario.

"Today, you'd say it looks like a really old-style building,"

Devallano said. "But it was [considered modern] when it opened, other than forgetting to put in a press box."

Indeed, press row—added at the last minute—represented one of the tightest squeezes in the league for members of the media, but in a way it was also a throwback to the Original Six era.

"Once the Ilitches took over the building, they took a lot of steps to make it a warmer place," Devellano added. "If you've ever walked the concourse there, you saw all the old pictures."

Wayne Gretzky, whose family were Wings fans, often had some of his best games there. The Joe was an all-round blue-collar environment, and he enjoyed the atmosphere.

"When I arrived, they had so few season tickets that the whole lower bowl was $12 a ticket," Devellano said. "We had to get fans in the seats and reinvent hockey. It wasn't

Hockeytown then, but we built it because of good players."

The Wings began making the playoffs regularly, and though there would be some postseason heartbreak along the way, they put together contending teams with a focus on the ultimate prize. Along the way, Joe Louis Arena was also the site of the 1980 all-star game (played before a then-record crowd of 21,002), the 1987 NHL draft (the first to be held in the U.S.), 50-goal and 100-point seasons for both Yzerman and Sergei Fedorov, as well as Nicklas Lidstrom's 1,000th point.

"I've spent 35 years there, and there would be no doubt in my mind what my favourite memory would be," Devellano said. "The first Stanley Cup. It came at home in 1997 against the Philadelphia Flyers. Darren McCarty scored to make it 2–1.

The Olympia was home to the Detroit Red Wings until their move to the Joe Louis Arena in 1979. (Hockey Hall of Fame)

"The other great memories were the retirement of Yzerman's jersey and the retirement of Lidstrom's jersey—simply because those two players made us the franchise we became."

The legendary Scotty Bowman would also hoist his last Cup as an NHL coach there in 2002, while Mike Babcock won his first six years later.

The arena also hosted college hockey, basketball, arena football, the Republican National Convention at which Ronald Reagan was nominated, and an Ontario Hockey League title for the Detroit Jr. Red Wings. Many legendary concerts were held there as well.

The Wings are moving to Little Caesar's Arena, built at a cost of more than $700 million, for the 2017–18 season.

With the Joe Louis Arena and the great Detroit teams that dominated the 1990s and 2000s, Detroit was aptly labelled as "Hockeytown." (Dave Sandford/Stringer/Getty Images Sport)

48

THE BRUINS END THEIR CUP DROUGHT

I f it's true that a team has to stomach—and learn from—a bitter defeat before it can figure out how to savour a victory, then the Boston Bruins rid themselves of a terrible aftertaste in the 2011 Stanley Cup playoffs.

The previous year had ended on a sour note for head coach Claude Julien's team. In the Eastern Conference semifinal against Philadelphia, Boston became just the third team in league history to squander a 3–0 lead in a playoff series.

The Bruins' 4–1 victory over the Flyers in Game 3 had given them a seemingly insurmountable series lead. But Flyers captain Mike Richards broke David Krejci's wrist with a devastating bodycheck in that game, knocking the gifted forward out of the 2010 playoffs. That proved to be the turning point in the series.

Philadelphia won the next four games, which included a 4–3 Game 7 victory in Boston, a game the Bruins had led, 3–0, during the first period.

And so the Bruins' Stanley Cup drought, dating back to 1972 and littered with crushing defeats, continued.

The memory of that collapse provided Boston with extra motivation over the summer of 2010. Then general manager Peter Chiarelli engineered a couple of key trades close to the

> The Bruins became the first team in NHL history to win three seven-game series en route to the Stanley Cup.

2010–11 trade deadline to help the Bruins win the Northeast Division. First, he acquired centre Chris Kelly from Ottawa on February 15, 2011. Three days later, he plucked forward Rich Peverley from Atlanta and defenceman Tomas Kaberle from Toronto. Kelly and Peverley substantially upgraded the third line and improved the Bruins' penalty killing, while Kaberle provided depth on the blue line.

As the opening round of the playoffs arrived, the Bruins were well prepared to face their longtime nemesis, the Montreal Canadiens. Or so they thought.

The Habs rolled into Boston and swept the first two games. The dazed Bruins recovered to take the next two in Montreal to even the series, and then took Game 5 at home, 2–1, only to see the Canadiens do the same two nights later in Montreal.

In a dramatic Game 7 in Boston, winger Nathan Horton beat Carey Price in overtime to advance the Bruins past their archrivals.

That set the stage for a rematch against Philadelphia, the team that had rallied from three games down to knock Boston out the previous spring. If revenge is a dish best served cold, the Bruins were more than happy to serve it on ice.

With Krejci healthy and on a march to the playoff scoring title, Boston swept the Flyers. Next up: the Tampa Bay Lightning in the Eastern Conference final.

Tampa was two periods away from a 2–0 series lead in Boston when Tyler Seguin provided the B's with a much-needed spark. The rookie's pair of goals spurred the Bruins to a 6–5 victory to even the series at a game apiece.

The series shifted back and forth until the seventh game in Boston. Horton's third-period goal was all goaltender Tim Thomas needed for a 1–0 victory that sent the Bruins to the Stanley Cup final against Vancouver.

Thomas was not your typical, cookie-cutter, butterfly netminder. Far from it. He was an unpredictable acrobat who defended his crease with the mentality of a linebacker. There was never a dull moment with the Flint, Michigan, native. There were rarely any goals against, either.

Thomas had survived a serpentine nine-year odyssey through Finland and Sweden, the International Hockey League, the East Coast Hockey League, and the American Hockey League to reach the NHL for good in 2005.

Six years later, the 2011 Stanley Cup final would tie a bow on one of the greatest years in league history: 35 regular-season wins with a goals-against average (GAA) of 2.00 and a .938 save percentage. Thomas upped the ante with a .940 save percentage and a GAA of 1.98 in the playoffs.

The Bruins goaltender was one of the few constants in

an extremely uneven and often bizarre series. After the first six games, the Canucks had three one-goal victories in Vancouver, while the Bruins had won their three home games by a combined 14 goals.

Thomas saved his best for last. The University of Vermont alum turned aside all 37 shots, as the Bruins won, 4–0. Patrice Bergeron and Brad Marchand had two goals each to lead Boston to its sixth Stanley Cup.

Thomas was awarded the Conn Smythe Trophy as the most valuable player in the playoffs and the Vezina Trophy as the league's best goaltender during the regular season. The Bruins became the first team in NHL history to win three seven-game series en route to the Stanley Cup.

And so the 39-year drought was over. After winning the Cup in 1972 in six games over the New York Rangers, the Bruins had been swept by the Canadiens in 1977 and lost to the Habs again a year later in six games. Then they ran into another dynasty, losing in four games to the Edmonton Oilers in 1988 and in five games to the Oilers two years later.

But after all those bitter lessons, in the summer of 2011 Boston was left with only the sweet taste of victory.

The Boston Bruins ended a 39-year Cup drought after beating the Vancouver Canucks in the 2011 Stanley Cup Final. (Dave Sandford/ Contributor/Getty Images)

49

THE FIRST SHOOTOUT

A tie was once considered a noble result in the NHL, but as coach Paul Maurice once observed, "At the end of the night, fans really want to see a winner and a loser."

So when the league took a year-long hiatus because of a labour disruption in 2004–05, it used the break to break the tie for good.

In the summer of 2005, the NHL adopted a rule that games not decided in regulation time or four-on-four overtime—which had itself become a bit stagnant, as almost 15 percent of games in 2003–04 had resulted in a tie—would be decided by a shootout.

The league borrowed the shootout idea from the International Ice Hockey Federation's penalty-shot tiebreaker, which the IIHF had in turn adapted in 1992 from European football. The NHL actually gave the shootout a trial run after the 2003 all-star game ended in a tie.

Two points in the NHL standings were still the prize when the shootout was approved, but the losing team would now get one.

All teams held shootouts during the 2005–06 preseason schedule to get used to the concept and streamline such protocols as player selection and cleaning of the ice. It didn't take long for the new format to face its first real test.

The Toronto Maple Leafs and Ottawa Senators ended the NHL season opener, played October 5 in Toronto, in a 2–2 draw, with nothing resolved in overtime. So coaches Pat Quinn and Bryan Murray went to their respective lists of shooters.

Ottawa's Daniel Alfredsson beat Ed Belfour on the very first attempt, while the Leafs had the misfortune to face the great goalie Dominik Hasek at the other end. One of the most unflappable goaltenders under shootout pressure, going back to the 1998 Nagano Olympics, "The Dominator" stopped a couple of new Leafs whom Quinn sent out, Jason Allison and Eric Lindros. Belfour blocked Martin Havlat, but Dany Heatley went five-hole and secured the win, leaving Jeff O'Neill stranded on deck for Toronto.

Coaches such as Quinn were skeptical of the shootout "gimmick." Two games later, the Leafs lost another shootout to the same team and would become one of the worst-performing clubs under the new format.

But teams with proven snipers had a ball. Anze Kopitar, Jonathan Toews, Pavel Datsyuk, and Patrick Kane each scored upward of 40 shootout goals during the ensuing years.

Unknowns such as Frans Nielsen, Jussi Jokinen, T.J. Oshie, Radim Vrbata, and Brad Boyes became clutch

Daniel Alfredsson of the Ottawa Senators scores against Ed Belfour of the Toronto Maple Leafs in the first-ever NHL shootout. (Dave Sandford/Getty Images)

players beyond 65 minutes. Vrbata took over the league lead in career shootout goals in the 2016–17 season, while Ilya Kovalchuk set a record with 11 in 2011–12, seven of which won games for his New Jersey Devils. The season before, Jarret Stoll of the Kings hit on nine of 10 attempts, a shooting percentage yet to be matched.

Two of the NHL's most dramatic outdoor games were decided in shootouts in snowy conditions, with Sidney Crosby of the Penguins and Toronto's Tyler Bozak delivering the winners. Crosby's came in the first Winter Classic, when he scored on Buffalo's Ryan Miller to give Pittsburgh a 2–1 win.

"The game on the line and to see this many people, I mean, it's mind-boggling," Crosby said. "The best way to describe it is the *Gladiator* movie."

Bozak's goal came before the largest crowd ever to watch a hockey game: 105,491 at the "Big House" at the University of Michigan. He keeps a framed photo of it in his off-season home in Denver.

"It's the coolest shot," Bozak said. "Me coming in on the shootout and all the fans in the background. Flurries are coming down too, so their goalie [the Red Wings'

Jimmy Howard] couldn't see the puck. Maybe I got lucky with that.

"It was an unforgettable experience, how it went for the team and me personally. Having the chance to win the game. The snow falling and all the fans . . . it was perfect."

Many goalies have also had their finest hour in shootouts. Vancouver's Ryan Miller took the NHL career lead in shootout saves into the 2016–17 season, with 55, two up on the New York Rangers' Henrik Lundqvist. Florida's Roberto Luongo, meanwhile, had faced almost 400 shootout attempts in his career.

There have been some creative moves to try and spice up the event. Shooters have come in both fast and slow, performed what look to be figure eights as they use up the lateral ice, or come in hard and braked before their release, hoping to cross up the goalie. Shooting from between the legs was also in vogue for a while.

Some old-schoolers may never appreciate the creativity of certain shooters. But even after the overtime format was changed to three on three, it was clear that the tiebreaker was here to stay. The excitement of the shootout is impossible to deny.

Aki Berg played parts of five seasons with the Los Angeles Kings before he was traded to the Toronto Maple Leafs, where he spent the rest of his NHL career.
(Dave Sandford/Hockey Hall of Fame)

THE DRAFT LOTTERY

Aki Berg will never be remembered as a premier NHL defenceman, and the late Lester M. Wintz will never be thought of as a major hockey executive. But they both have a place in league history.

The Finnish-born Berg was the first player chosen by a draft lottery winner: the Los Angeles Kings, in 1995. Wintz was a marketing executive with the Kings who happened to be in New York on a business trip on draft lottery day. With only a 4.2 percent chance of winning, the hockey department in L.A.—one of the 10 teams that qualified for the lottery by missing the playoffs—asked Wintz to make a perfunctory stop at the league office to represent the club.

He wound up getting a congratulatory handshake from commissioner Gary Bettman.

After the ping pong balls fell their way, the Kings took Berg third overall in 1995. Under the original lottery rules, a team couldn't move up more than four spots (or down more than one). Thus, only the five worst teams in the league had a shot at the top prize. Los Angeles had finished seventh from the bottom, and so moved up to third.

The idea behind the weighted draw was to prevent teams from deliberately finishing at the back of the pack to land the No. 1 pick, a concept the NBA had originated in 1985 to discourage "tanking." In 1992–93, the expansion Ottawa Senators narrowly finished last with a record of 10–70–4 and chose Alexandre Daigle. It didn't work so well for the Senators; Daigle ended up with just 172 points in 301 games before he was traded to Philadelphia.

In 1993–94 the Senators were a distant last, but the expansion Florida Panthers and Mighty Ducks of Anaheim got the first two picks, relegating Ottawa to No. 3 overall. They picked Czech centre Radek Bonk. A year later, the Senators landed in the basement yet again, and although the Kings won the first lottery, Ottawa held on to the first pick, which they used to select defenceman Bryan Berard. The 1995–96 season, the Senators' fourth in the league, resulted in another last-place finish, but this time they won the lottery and chose defenceman Chris Phillips.

In 2013 the league reconfigured the lottery to give all non-playoff teams—thanks to expansion to 30 teams, there were now 14 each season—a chance at the No. 1 pick. In each of the next three seasons, the cellar dwellers were nudged aside by teams with better records, most notably in 2015, when 28th-place Edmonton beat out Buffalo in the Connor McDavid sweepstakes. In 2016, two separate draws were added for the second and third picks. The 30th-place Toronto Maple Leafs proved luckiest, though, winning the lottery and the chance to choose Auston Matthews.

51

THE KITCHENER KIDS GO 1, 2, 3

When Milt Schmidt, Woody Dumart, and Bobby Bauer arrived at the Boston Bruins training camp for the 1939–40 NHL season, the Stanley Cup championship was still fresh in their memories. The Bruins had won their first title in a decade the previous spring.

The autumn of 1939 began the trio's second full season together in Boston. Growing up in the twin cities of Kitchener (Schmidt and Dumart) and Waterloo (Bauer) in southwestern Ontario, they had been teammates in junior with the Kitchener Greenshirts, and they began their professional careers together in 1936 with the Providence Reds of the International-American Hockey League.

Buoyed by their successful Stanley Cup run in the spring of 1939, Schmidt, Dumart, and Bauer embarked on a season to remember. They finished one, two, and three in scoring to spearhead the Bruins to a first-overall finish and a 31–12–5 record. Schmidt, a centre, won the league scoring race with 22 goals and 52 points in 48 games. Left wing Dumart (22 goals, 21 assists) and right wing Bauer (17 goals, 26 assists) tied with 43 points.

"We were so proud of that accomplishment," Schmidt recalled. "I'm often asked why we played so well together, and I believe it was because we were so close, good friends off the ice."

Schmidt, Dumart, and Bauer shared a one-room apartment in nearby Brookline, Massachusetts. It made for a cozy setting for the three to discuss their play, their opponents, and the game.

"We were hardworking guys, but we were just kids," Schmidt said. "We didn't go out much, so we would go back to our place and analyze our play and the games."

The three had always been linemates in junior with Kitchener or in Providence, but Bruins head coach and general manager Art Ross put them together for good in 1937.

"We clicked because we each contributed something different to make the whole line effective," Dumart said. "Milt was the guy with speed and Bobby had the finesse, the knack of going between the player and the boards. I was up and down my wing and I could really let that wrist shot go."

Unfortunately for the terrific trio, they were unable to carry their regular-season success into the playoffs and defend their championship. The New York Rangers, led by another Kitchener native, defenceman Ott Heller, shut down the Kids' line and defeated Boston in six games in the first round of the playoffs. Schmidt did not register a point in the six-game series, while Dumart and Bauer were limited to a goal apiece. New York shut out the Bruins three times in the first five games.

(left to right) The Boston Bruins' Bobby Bauer, Milt Schmidt, and Woody Dumart.
(Imperial Oil–Turofsky/Hockey Hall of Fame)

The line's one-two-three accomplishment in the 1939–40 scoring race was not matched until the Detroit Red Wings' Production Line of Ted Lindsay, Sid Abel, and Gordie Howe claimed the top three spots in 1949–50.

In 1940–41, only Bauer finished in the top 10 in league scoring, but all three performed better in the playoffs, with Schmidt leading the way with five goals and 11 points in 11 games. The Bruins defeated the Toronto Maple Leafs in seven games in the semifinals and swept the Red Wings in the final.

It would be the final NHL championship for the Kitchener Kids. In the midst of the 1941–42 season—and World War II—all three enlisted in the Royal Canadian Air Force.

"Bobby, Woody, and I had long talks with Art Ross," recalled Schmidt. "He had a son who was in the Royal Canadian Air Force, and we thought if it was good enough for Art Jr., then it was good enough for us."

Before reporting for duty, they played in Montreal against the Canadiens on February 11, 1942, and departed in style as they combined for 10 points in an 8–1 win. Players from both teams carried the three off the ice on their shoulders.

Schmidt, Dumart, and Bauer would win the Allan Cup with the RCAF Flyers a couple of months later as they trained in Ottawa, but they would not play in the NHL together again until the 1945–46 season.

"It sure was good to be back again," said Schmidt. "When we got home, there was nothing but ovations, which we appreciated."

They would only enjoy two more seasons as a line, because Bauer retired at the end of 1946–47 at the age of 32.

Schmidt went on to win the Hart Trophy in 1950–51, and the three were eventually reunited in the Hockey Hall of Fame, with Schmidt being inducted in 1961, followed by Dumart in 1992 and Bauer in 1996.

Bauer passed away in 1964 due to a heart attack. Schmidt and Dumart, however, were in Toronto with the Bauer family when the late Bruins forward was inducted.

"I had been hoping he'd get in for a long time," a 79-year-old Dumart said at the time. "Bobby really deserved it, and we're all thrilled. Even in his last year, he scored more than 30 goals."

"All I can say is that between Woody and myself, we are just elated that Bobby has been chosen to be inducted," Schmidt added. "It seems so many years ago now we were just three young guys. It was never in our thoughts to be at this stage.

"It's been like a dream come true, to have all three of us in the Hockey Hall of Fame. I know he's up there, looking down on all of us and enjoying it."

The line's one-two-three accomplishment in the 1939–40 scoring race was not matched until the Detroit Red Wings' Production Line of Ted Lindsay, Sid Abel, and Gordie Howe claimed the top three spots in 1949–50.

52

DOUG GILMOUR AND HOCKEY'S BIGGEST TRADE

Rick Wamsley was on an exercise bike on the morning of January 2, 1992, trying to sweat his way through a New Year's hangover.

After beating the Montreal Canadiens at home on New Year's Eve, the goalie's Calgary Flames had a few days off before facing the Edmonton Oilers, and it was supposed to be a quiet time. But teammate Doug Gilmour had bolted from the club the day before, headed home in a bitter pay dispute, and there was a feeling that something would give sooner rather than later.

It was then that Wamsley got a call from general manager Doug Risebrough, telling him he'd been traded. "Toronto," was all he was told, and one of the first people he rang up to find out more was Gilmour. He, too, had been called by Risebrough and told he'd been dealt to the Maple Leafs, but given no further details.

As the next hour unfolded, the two sudden ex-Flames gradually pieced together what would be the largest trade in NHL history: five for five—involving 10 players in all. Back in Toronto, as a Leaf official read all the names involved to the media, there was genuine shock at the seemingly endless list.

When fully put together, Gilmour, Wamsley, defencemen Jamie Macoun and Ric Nattress, and forward prospect Kent Manderville were ticketed for the Leafs in exchange for forward Gary Leeman, muscleman winger Craig Berube, defencemen Michel Petit and Alex Godynyuk, and goalie Jeff Reese.

"It was a unique situation and we were very fortunate it worked out," said Toronto general manager Cliff Fletcher, who had been the Flames' only GM from the franchise's creation in 1972 up to the previous year, when he took on the immense rebuilding challenge in T.O. "When you win just 10 of your first 40 games, you know you have holes to fill. I know these new guys well. I would never make a deal of this magnitude if I wasn't sure."

The big 10-player deal was announced on January 2, but it had actually been agreed to the day before. It couldn't be made official on New Year's Day because the NHL offices were closed.

Fletcher, who had guided Calgary to the Stanley Cup championship in 1989, had already made one significant deal with Edmonton that 1991–92 season to reshape his roster. Meanwhile, his Flames successor, Risebrough, was looking to make his own landmark deal. When he and Gilmour locked horns in salary arbitration, and the latter received what he thought was a substandard one-year award, it set the stage for the forward's exit. At a team function a couple of

days before the trade, Gilmour brought a video camera, knowing he was through in Cowtown.

The Flames and Leafs had kicked tires on various players in the summer, but after the seven-player deal with the Oilers that netted goalie Grant Fuhr and winger Glenn Anderson, talks cooled. The standoff between Gilmour and Risebrough rekindled interest, while Fletcher was humiliated by his team's 12–1 loss in Pittsburgh on December 26, which underlined the need for dramatic change.

Fletcher knew the Flames roster well, but Calgary had ex-Leaf GM Gerry McNamara on staff as a pro scout. As far as he had been told, the Hartford Whalers were the team the Flames were speaking to, in a deal that would bring forwards Pat Verbeek and Jim McKenzie for Gilmour alone. Then, out of the blue, McNamara got a call from the hockey office, asking his opinions on several Leafs such as Leeman and Reese, and he realized something bigger was afoot.

"My [philosophy] is to put yourself in the other GM's shoes," Fletcher said in reflecting on the deal. "Try and understand whether he thinks it's a good fit or not."

But from the moment the clubs signed off on the deal, observers were calling it a huge win for the Leafs. Though Gilmour's impact wouldn't be fully realized until the following season, when he, Macoun, and Manderville were part of a three-round playoff run, there was an immediate change in the temperature around Maple Leaf Gardens.

"Everyone knows we were floundering," said Toronto defenceman Dave Ellett on the 25th anniversary of the deal. "When they made that trade, Dougie came in, turned our team and the whole franchise around.

"I remember the first practice we had, and you could just feel the energy. Dougie made everyone else better— Wendel Clark and everyone who played with him. Suddenly, you had a guy who was feeding the puck at the right time.

"People talk about his stats, but he brought a lot more to the team than that. His leadership, playing in every situation, you can't put a value on that."

Gilmour and Fletcher quickly reached a new contract agreement, and the slick centre had two 100-point seasons as a Leaf and won the Selke Trophy in 1992–93. Under coach Pat Burns, Gilmour was the catalyst that put the Leafs within a win of their first Cup final appearance in almost 30 years. Toronto made it to the conference final the next season as well, with Gilmour becoming the franchise leader in playoff points and team captain before the magic began to fade in the mid-'90s.

Meanwhile Calgary soon found out that none of the pieces it had acquired fit its long-term plans. Leeman, who had scored 50 goals as a Leaf, hoped to be a difference maker with the Flames, but his goal of winning a Cup would be realized as a Montreal Canadien in 1993.

"The '80s were a difficult time [in Toronto]," Leeman told Sportsnet on the trade's 25th anniversary, "and [in] the early '90s they were starting to straighten things out a bit. Cliff asked me at the beginning of the [1991–92] season, he said, 'Do you wanna stay or go?'

"I asked to be traded, so I knew it was coming. Had I known the guys that were comin' this way, I might have wanted to stay."

In the changing NHL economic environment that followed, particularly once the salary-cap era began and no-trade clauses were invoked, Fletcher and his peers knew that the days of 10-player deals were likely past.

"There would have to be some strange circumstances," Fletcher said. "It's just the way the game is. With expansion, teams just don't have that kind of depth at every position. That deal was already considered unusual for its time, and teams don't trade as much these days."

Opposite: Doug Gilmour of the Toronto Maple Leafs prepares for a faceoff during the 1992-93 season. (Chris Relke/Hockey Hall of Fame)

53

SUTTERS VERSUS SUTTERS

The biggest day of the year in the Sutter household didn't come during the hockey season, but in early July, when the NHL schedule was announced. That's when Brian, Darryl, Duane, Brent, Rich, and Ron could see when they would cross paths in the coming season. And in July 1983, they learned that on October 30, Ron's Philadelphia Flyers were scheduled to meet Duane and Brent's New York Islanders.

Any time the Islanders and Flyers faced each other in the 1980s was a big deal. The Islanders had defeated Philadelphia in the 1979–80 final for their first of four consecutive Stanley Cups. But the clubs' considerable rivalry was about to intensify. A week before this particular game, the Flyers landed Rich Sutter in a trade, paving the way for a historic evening when four brothers would play in the same NHL game for the first time.

The Flyers already had Rich's twin brother, Ron, but the two had struggled early in their first full year in the NHL, playing separately after three successful seasons together in junior with the Lethbridge Broncos.

In their first season and a half in Lethbridge, one of the twins' teammates was older brother Brent. But Brent left the Broncos midway through the 1981–82 season to join his brother Duane with the New York Islanders. Brent and

Duane won a Stanley Cup that spring and celebrated another championship a year later.

The Islanders were five months removed from their fourth consecutive title, while the Flyers entered the evening on a six-game win streak. Even though the Philadelphia Eagles had hosted the Baltimore Colts across the parking lot at Veterans Stadium that afternoon, a capacity crowd of 17,191 spilled into the Spectrum to watch the Sutters go at it.

There wasn't much to celebrate for the home side, as Brent, Duane, and the Islanders had little difficulty that evening, departing with a 6–2 victory.

Brent scored twice and Duane collected a pair of assists as the Islanders jumped out to a 3–1 lead after the first period, and 4–2 after 40 minutes.

"After a shift, I would go back to the bench and think that it was just like playing hockey back home again," Ron recalled of that day. Although back home in the hayloft, their mother, Grace, would often snatch the tennis ball away from them if the games got too intense or chores on the family farm weren't done first.

Six out of seven sons of Grace and Louis Sutter played long and successful NHL careers. The oldest, Gary, was an outstanding player, too, but decided to stay home, go to school, and continue to work on the family ranch in Viking, Alberta.

"Gary would've been the best of all of us, and he's coached around home," Brent said. "But he wanted to finish his schooling, and he did . . . We're very proud of him."

Brian paved the way with the St. Louis Blues and was followed by Darryl, Duane, Brent, Ron, and Rich. They played in a combined 4,994 regular-season games and 603 playoff games, scoring 1,444 goals in the regular season and playoffs and putting up 3,209 points.

Duane won four Stanley Cups with the Islanders, two of which Brent was also there for, and Darryl won two Stanley Cups as coach of the Los Angeles Kings.

They also clashed countless times as opponents. All of the six were in the league together from 1981–82, when the twins jumped to the NHL after the conclusion of their junior season, until Darryl's retirement after the 1986–87 season.

Each Sutter had a different outlook on facing the others in the NHL.

"I hate it," Darryl said. "You find yourself watching your brother maybe more than you should."

"I still get a big thrill out of playing against my brothers," Ron said. "When I'm sitting on the bench, I'll watch them come up the ice, even when they don't have the puck. But of course, I bang them when I have to."

"You're very conscious that you have a job to do," Ron told the *New York Times* before a game against Brent. "You try to take him out, but you wouldn't take a run at him, or use

Brothers Brent and Duane Sutter (fourth and fifth from left) celebrate with New York Islanders teammates. (Paul Bereswill/Hockey Hall of Fame)

The Sutter family gathers with Darryl (left) on the family farm in Viking, Alberta, to celebrate one of his two Cup wins as coach of the Los Angeles Kings. (Howie Borrow/Hockey Hall of Fame)

your stick on him like you would on someone else."

The *Times* report went on to detail that, after the two squared off for the opening puck drop, Brent won the draw, "and as he wheeled away, Ron whacked his stick across his brother's back."

Duane recalled that, in one of his games against the Flyers, he blurted out a warning to his brother/opponent Rich, who was killing a penalty while his brother/teammate Brent closed in on the forecheck.

"Get it out, Richie," Duane yelled.

"It just popped out of me because I wanted Rich to do well in the NHL," Duane explained to the *Toronto Star*. "I was lucky that no one on our bench noted what I'd done or the needling would have been fierce."

One of the first occasions when two Sutters met came in 1980, when Brian nicked Duane with a high stick and bloodied him. But the two resolved their differences after the game and went for dinner.

When Flyers coach Mike Keenan traded Rich to the Canucks after three years with his twin, both players were in shock. Keenan had the misfortune of getting Grace on the phone first when he called the farmhouse in Viking. "Iron Mike" almost wilted from the barrage of abuse the Sutter matriarch unloaded on him.

In 1992, the six Sutters found themselves on different sides in the first round of the playoffs. Brian was the head coach of the Blues, and had the twins in his lineup. Darryl was the associate coach of the Blackhawks, Duane was a scout, and Brent had joined Chicago earlier in the season via a trade.

The Blackhawks won the series in six games.

THE FINNISH FLASH

The legend of Teemu Selanne's rookie-record 76-goal season in 1992–93 was equal parts production and personality.

"Maybe more the second thing," said forward Kris King, Selanne's teammate with the Winnipeg Jets.

Selanne, nicknamed the "Finnish Flash," made his NHL debut at age 22 and wasted no time rewriting the league's scoring records for first-year players. His 76 goals shattered the record of 53 set by Mike Bossy of the New York Islanders in 1977–78. He finished with 132 points, blowing past the previous mark of 109 by Peter Stastny of the Quebec Nordiques in 1980–81.

Big numbers, all of them, but they paled in comparison to the infinite autographs, photos and smiles. Winnipeg's love for, and from, Selanne was off the charts.

"He had time for everybody," King said. "It was never really about the goals for him, despite all his success on the ice. He just really loved to play the game."

The bond between Selanne and the fans accelerated as quickly as he swooped in on goalies with his blazing speed, to the point that he could barely comprehend the history he was making.

"That year was so unbelievable, I didn't realize what happened until years later," Selanne said. "It was just like a

dream. I was so hungry to prove myself. It was like a snowball going down a hill. I had more and more confidence and I just wanted to score and enjoy every day."

There was scoring and enjoyment galore.

Selanne's 76 goals tied him with Buffalo's Alexander Mogilny for the NHL lead, and his 132 points placed him fifth in league scoring. He scored in 53 games, had 52 even-strength goals and 24 on the power play. He had five hat-tricks, scored 20 goals in March (still the NHL record for goals in one month) and finished the season with a 17-game point streak (20 goals, 14 assists). Remarkably, he scored on 19.6 percent of his 387 shots on goal.

Selanne got off to a fast start, scoring 11 goals in his first 11 games. At the midway point of the 84-game season, he was up to 34.

The rookie was just warming up. Despite more attention and closer checking from opponents, Selanne scored 42 goals in 42 games during the second half.

When the season was over, he received all 50 first-place votes for the Calder Trophy, making him the unanimous winner.

Selanne broke Bossy's record when he scored his 54th goal, completing a hat trick against the Quebec Nordiques on March 2, 1993. It was his ninth goal in a four-game stretch, and he said the eruption at Winnipeg Arena when he scored that goal was probably the highest point of his season.

"The most special memory from that year," he said. "And the white noise in the playoffs. But the way the people treated me, it was almost hard to understand and believe how people were so excited."

Fans loved what he did on the ice, but they adored how he gave back off it; an autograph at the arena, a wave in the grocery store or joining the neighborhood kids for road hockey games in Winnipeg's River Heights.

"I think my parents, the way they raised me was to treat people well and they will also treat you well," Selanne said. "And that's what I always tried to remember.

"That's the easiest part of being an athlete," he said of signing autographs. "Everything else is hard. Signing a few autographs here and there to make people happy, I'm happy if somebody's happy."

Selanne played with four other teams before retiring but has returned to Winnipeg often, including two regular-season games with the Anaheim Ducks before he retired in 2014. He said he still finds the same warmth and enthusiasm.

"I left there a long, long time ago and coming back, what I got, it was overwhelming. It was unbelievable. It was really special. I really loved that."

Time has not diminished the love affair. King, who became captain of the Jets in 1995, said there's a good reason for that.

"He knew right away there was something special there between him and the fans," he said. "It was never phony. It was always legit. He always had the time, and they loved him right away because of who he was.

"It was never different inside the room than it was outside. And that was really impressive. He did all the right things because he meant it."

The feeling from the fans was mutual. It has never faded and has been unrelenting, all sparked by one season of magic.

54
100

Opposite: Teemu Selanne's 76 goals for the Winnipeg Jets in 1992-93 still stands as the rookie record. (Chris Relke/Hockey Hall of Fame)

55

DOUG JARVIS'S IRON-MAN STREAK

On his way to a record-setting iron-man streak of 964 consecutive games played, Doug Jarvis had some close calls. But he managed to play through injuries, flu, and illness, as well as countless bumps and bruises.

The closest his streak came to ending early happened on January 8, 1985. Then with the Washington Capitals, Jarvis was rocked late in a game against the Detroit Red Wings. He had corralled a loose puck and scored into an empty net just as Detroit defenceman Randy Ladouceur delivered a hard bodycheck, causing Jarvis to miss the remainder of the game. He recovered in time to join his teammates for a game in St. Louis against the Blues the next evening: game 762 of his incredible streak.

When Jarvis was drafted in the second round (24th overall) in 1975 by the Toronto Maple Leafs, the native of Brantford, Ontario, obviously didn't set out to become the NHL's all-time iron man.

After his junior days ended with the Peterborough Petes, Jarvis simply hoped to one day make it to the NHL. A few weeks after drafting him, the Maple Leafs traded Jarvis to the Montreal Canadiens straight up for minor-league defenceman Greg Hubick.

After watching the effectiveness of checking forwards

Don Luce and Craig Ramsay as Buffalo defeated his Canadiens in the 1975 semifinals, Montreal head coach Scotty Bowman wanted to put together a similar tandem for his club. He was looking for another defensive forward to play alongside Bob Gainey, and he received a tip from his friend Roger Neilson, coach of the OHL Peterborough Petes, about Jarvis's prowess in the faceoff circle and his defensive ability. Jarvis and Gainey had just happened to play together in Peterborough, too.

So Bowman urged Canadiens general manager Sam Pollock to draft Jarvis. Pollock, however, felt the five-foot-nine, 170-pound Jarvis was too small.

Nevertheless, Bowman eventually got his way when Pollock swung a trade that summer.

Jarvis's iron-man streak began innocently on opening night of the 1975–76 season—October 8, 1975—with a 9–0 Canadiens victory against the Los Angeles Kings at the Montreal Forum. He played in every Canadiens regular-season game over the next seven seasons and won a Stanley Cup in each of his first four seasons in Montreal.

After his only 20-goal season, in 1981–82, Jarvis was traded in the off-season to the Capitals along with Rod Langway, Brian Engblom, and Craig Laughlin for Rick Green and Ryan Walter. From the Capitals, it was on to the

Doug Jarvis of the Washington Capitals battles for position with Terry Johnson of the St. Louis Blues during a game on January 5, 1984. (O-Pee-Chee/Hockey Hall of Fame)

Hartford Whalers in a one-for-one deal for forward Jorgen Pettersson during the 1985–86 season.

Jarvis had departed the Capitals having played in 825 consecutive games. With the Whalers, he matched Garry Unger's record of 914, set in 1979, just before Christmas in a 2–0 win against the Boston Bruins. He passed Unger on Boxing Day of 1986 in a 1–1 tie at home—fittingly against his first NHL team, the Canadiens.

The next night, the Whalers and Canadiens met at the Montreal Forum, and Gainey helped make a centre-ice presentation to his former teammate to mark his 915 consecutive games.

Jarvis's mother, Millie, said that her son, who won the Selke Trophy as the NHL's top defensive forward in 1983–84, had always had a good attendance record.

"He hardly ever missed school," she told the *New York Times*. "Maybe half a day here or there or when he had the chicken pox and was contagious."

"I've had bumps, bruises and cuts, colds, too," Jarvis added. "Everybody who plays this game does. But I've been very fortunate to avoid injury. I feel fortunate because there are so many things that can happen to you in games and practices."

Jarvis wound up playing every game of his first 12 seasons. His streak came to an end two games into the 1987–88 season, his 13th. The Whalers started the year with back-to-back losses, and Hartford head coach Jack Evans decided to play Brent Peterson in place of Jarvis.

He was later demoted to the Whalers' AHL affiliate in Binghamton and took on a player/assistant coach role under head coach Larry Pleau. Jarvis knew then what his next career would be: coaching.

He won two more Stanley Cups as an assistant coach with the 1998–99 Dallas Stars and 2010–11 Boston Bruins.

"The streak ended when my [NHL] career did," Jarvis said. "I just didn't have it anymore and I knew it was time to retire."

Bob Gainey (left) honours his former teammate Doug Jarvis for passing Garry Unger's record of 914 consecutive regular-season games played. (Paul Bereswill/Hockey Hall of Fame)

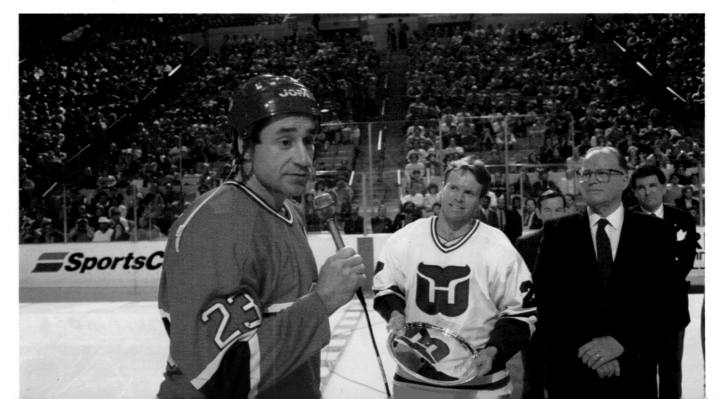

PHIL ESPOSITO GOES TO THE NEW YORK RANGERS

When the time came for Phil Esposito to say a final goodbye to his teammates Bobby Orr and Wayne Cashman, the toughest men on the Big Bad Bruins could not look each other in the face without crying.

There were plenty of water works in both Boston and New York on November 7, 1975, when two of the NHL's flagship teams traded marquee players. Esposito, the heartbeat of the Bruins, two-time Stanley Cup champion, and still a 40-goal scorer, was going to the hated Rangers for Brad Park, four-time runner-up (to Orr) for the Norris Trophy. Both had also played huge roles on Team Canada in the 1972 Summit Series.

The other two principals were big names as well: "Gentleman Jean" Ratelle, one of the most respected Rangers in franchise history, and Carol Vadnais, an effective rushing defenceman the Bruins had rescued from obscurity with the California Golden Seals.

The seeds of this deal had been planted by Bruins general manager Harry Sinden, who calculated that Orr's bad knees would not allow him to play at the top of his game

much longer. The team needed insurance—and why not get the next best thing to Orr?

Meanwhile, disgruntled Rangers GM Emile ("The Cat") Francis was still thinking about his team's loss to Esposito and the Bruins in the 1972 final. New York had won 40 games twice since, but not gone far in the playoffs. The 1975–76 season had not started well, either, with the Philadelphia Flyers, Montreal Canadiens, and now the crosstown rival New York Islanders threatening the Rangers' future.

"We were losing without resistance," Francis recalled of that autumn.

He needed a spark.

The situation with Orr's knees had not been revealed to Esposito, who was awakened with the stunning news at the team hotel during a West Coast trip by coach Don Cherry and Orr.

"If you tell me it's New York, I'm going to jump," Espo blurted out.

Cherry grimaced, turned, and said to Orr, "Bob, open the window."

The Rangers were also travelling on the day of the deal.

"Ron Stewart was the coach, and when he told me it was

When it came time to retire No. 7 in Boston, Esposito was welcomed back as a hero and Ray Bourque graciously switched to a new number, 77, at the ceremony.

Phil Esposito played parts of nine seasons with the Boston Bruins, winning the Art Ross Trophy as the league's top scorer five times. (Frank Prazak/Hockey Hall of Fame)

Boston, I was in complete shock," said Park. "I was the captain. I felt like I was the soul of the team."

Park could not fathom the reasoning behind the trade. He thought his place in Manhattan was secure and that Orr, still in Boston, was sure to get the prime ice time.

As word of the move leaked out, Park phoned home.

"I broke down during the call with my wife. After that, I came around to thinking one team doesn't want me and one team does. Eventually, I got mad at the team that traded me and I wanted to prove them wrong."

In New York, Rod Gilbert had No. 7, so Esposito took No. 77.

"I remember pulling on the sweater and thinking, 'What is this? Where's the spoked *B* and my No. 7? All I knew about New York was between Seventh and Eighth Avenues and 31st and 33rd Street—Madison Square Garden. We stayed at the hotel across the street and flew home on the shuttle after games.

"When I did learn the city, it was, oh my God, the greatest city and the greatest fans. We had some good years."

The bombastic Esposito was exactly the celebrity/athlete/leader the Rangers wanted. He scored 67 points in 62 games over the remainder of the season and would tally no fewer than 34 goals in each of the next four years. He

in Boston. Fans accorded him so much respect that he found it hard to motivate himself. But once he scored a few in the Garden, the natural order was restored. Years later, when it came time to retire No. 7 in Boston, Esposito was welcomed back as a hero and Ray Bourque graciously switched to a new number, 77, at the ceremony.

Park found his first days in Boston much more difficult.

"I was so hated in Boston before the trade," he said.

But once Orr had moved on to the Chicago Blackhawks, it was a different story.

"To this day, people tell me they hated me when I was with New York, but they loved me in Boston. It was a turning point in my career. I went to a very stable situation in Boston, while the Rangers went through a period of management changes.

"Plus, I got to play for Cherry. That was very entertaining. He knew how to motivate a veteran team. It was more motivation than strategy and Xs and Os, and we had success."

Park played eight seasons in Boston, never missing the playoffs, twice making the final. He was a first-team all-star on two occasions. Ratelle needed time to adjust without Gilbert, but also found productive years under Cherry.

It was less so for Vadnais as a Ranger. He retired in 1983, after a season with the first-year New Jersey Devils, at which point Park still had two productive seasons ahead of him with the Detroit Red Wings.

Defenceman Joe Zanussi, the little known fifth man in the trade, went from New York to Boston and had one goal in 68 games there.

was given the captaincy, and while the Rangers missed the playoffs his first two seasons, he would be a catalyst in their 1979 Cup drive, when they got all the way to the final against the Canadiens. His 20 points that playoff year was his best spring since Boston's '72 Cup run. He lasted another year and a half, retiring second in career points to Gordie Howe.

At first, Esposito was uncomfortable playing as a Ranger

Phil Esposito skates up the ice in his first season as a New York Ranger. Esposito would finish his playing career in New York. (Lewis Portnoy/ Hockey Hall of Fame)

57

THE DUCKS AND CANUCKS PLAY IN JAPAN

What was NHL hockey like in Japan?

Those present will never forget the rumble of players coming down the ice. Yes, the rumble, because the converted 30-by-60-metre Yoyogi Arena used for the two 1997 games between the then Mighty Ducks of Anaheim and the Vancouver Canucks sat atop an Olympic pool that reverberated in the deep end when the heavy bodies skated over the wooden base.

There were fears that the historic two-game series might not be played at all, after early-autumn Tokyo humidity threatened ice conditions and the two teams' practices chopped up the first effort at making a rink. The 15°C temperature at ice level was much higher than in a typical NHL rink.

But that's why the league brought along its resident ice man, Dan Craig of its hockey operations department. Craig taught the hosts about air-locking the building to keep it cool, and then two air-conditioning units were transported from a nearby Japanese military airbase and hooked into Yoyogi's big vents.

The players, meanwhile, learned to put up with the racket caused by the scaffolding over the 18-foot-deep pool,

> The 10,000-seat rink was filled with fans paying between 10,000 and 25,000 yen (roughly $10 and $25) for tickets, as an appetizer for the Nagano Olympics.

and the goalies adjusted to the sight of a high-dive tower at one end. And then there was the 10-hour time difference for the two West Coast teams to overcome.

The 10,000-seat rink was filled with fans paying between 10,000 and 25,000 yen (roughly $10 and $25) for tickets, as an appetizer for the Nagano Olympics a few months later and to get a close-up of players most had seen only in TV highlight reels.

The Ducks were without Paul Kariya, whose Japanese ancestry would have made the series all that more special and interesting, but the Canucks did bring Mark Messier, whose reputation and physical features fascinated the Japanese media. He received the biggest cheers during player introductions.

"Big guy, big shoulders, big head, big neck . . . it's not hard to see why he'd be popular here," middle-aged hockey fan Ted Takahashi said after chatting with Messier following practice.

"He's a man's man. Kariya is popular, yes, but we've known about Messier here for 10 or 15 years, since the Stanley Cups in the Oiler days."

Messier was photographed everywhere he went, including on a public date with a Japanese pop star.

"It's been incredible," said Devin Smith, Vancouver's media relations manager at the time. "Requests for time with him come all day. But he's very recognizable, a huge man with no hair walking the streets. He caused a real stir when he took the subway."

Messier said the exhausting week of travel to play two games was well worth the effort.

"I don't think there's anything negative about it," he said. "This is a way to show our game to a culture that hasn't seen it before. The game has been good to all of us. It's a pretty easy thing to do."

The series was split, with each team winning 3–2—which led one local newspaper to comment, "The NHL brought more excitement here than past games by the NFL, NBA and Major League Baseball."

In addition to the Olympics, the NHL sought a foothold in Japan and other Asian markets to keep pace with other North American sports. And the hosts were happy to see the real NHL in their front yard. Fans showed knowledge and enthusiasm for the game.

"This is the result of 10 years' work," said Shoichi Tomita, chief executive director of the Japanese Ice Hockey Federation. "The NHL, the sponsors, the dates, the Players' Association, and the International Ice Hockey Federation, all had to come together and finally did."

Brian Burke, then the NHL's director of hockey operations, struck a hopeful note.

"We rewarded loyal fans and hooked novices . . . I see us coming back," he said. "This is not just about selling T-shirts here. We want to be active in Japan. We have a hot sport."

Previous page: The Yoyogi Arena in Japan, site of the country's first NHL games. (Three Lions/Stringer/Getty Images)

58

THE OCTOPUS
(AND OTHER STRANGE THINGS)

Hockey fans have flung a myriad of objects onto the ice: beer cups, popcorn, programs, and hats. One irate supporter even tossed his prosthetic leg over the glass in protest of a referee's decision during a minor-league game in the 1990s.

The most unique tossing tradition, however, began on April 15, 1952, when a couple of Detroit Red Wings fans ventured out of their south-end seats at the Olympia and threw an octopus onto the ice surface.

Jerry and Peter Cusimano, who owned the Eastern Market in Detroit, were proud of their Red Wings that spring. The team was on the verge of becoming the first NHL team to go a perfect 8–0 in the Stanley Cup play-offs. So, during the second period, as the Wings were about to make history by sweeping the Montreal Canadiens in the final, the brothers celebrated Detroit's opening goal by tossing an eight-armed octopus onto the ice to symbolize the eight wins in Detroit's successful championship run.

The act caught linesmen George Hayes and Bill Morrison off guard. They left the dead octopus alone. Finally, it was Detroit defenceman Bob Goldham who skated over,

> The Red Wings have since adopted the octopus at a mascot. Two purple ones hung in the Joe Louis Arena rafters to symbolize the 16 wins it now takes to win a Stanley Cup.

picked up the cephalopod, and carried it to the sidelines.

But a tradition was born that continues to this day. In 1995, when the Red Wings advanced to the Western Conference final, Bob Dubisky and Larry Shotwell, coworkers at a local meat and fish shop, threw a 38-pound octopus onto the ice, and subsequently upped the size to a 50-pounder when Detroit advanced to its first Stanley Cup final in 39 years.

The Red Wings have since adopted the octopus at a mascot. Two purple ones hung in the Joe Louis Arena rafters to symbolize the 16 wins it now takes to win a Stanley Cup.

The octopus ritual has spawned some interesting responses from the fans of teams that have opposed Detroit in the postseason. A New Jersey Devils fan tossed a fish in the 1995 final. Supporters of the Nashville Predators threw catfish during a regular-season meeting versus Detroit in October 2003.

In 2006, when the Edmonton Oilers upset the Red Wings in the first round, a slab of Alberta beef landed on the ice in Edmonton. The following spring, a San Jose Sharks fan tossed a three-foot leopard shark over the glass.

About the same time as the octopus tradition was taking shape in Detroit, tossing hats on the ice when a player scored three goals in a game also came about.

In 1946, Chicago Blackhawks left wing Alex Kaleta visited Toronto haberdasher Sammy Taft on a road trip. When Kaleta said he couldn't afford a hat to go along with his new suit, Taft promised Kaleta he would throw in a free hat if the Blackhawk scored three goals against the Maple Leafs that night. Kaleta not only turned the trick, he scored four times.

It wasn't until a few years later, in the 1950s, that the New York Rangers' farm team in Guelph, Ontario—the Guelph Biltmore Mad Hatters—began presenting the same gift for a three-goal game. After all, the team was sponsored by the Guelph Biltmore Hat Company. Fans later caught on and tossed their hats onto the ice when a Mad Hatters player scored three times in a home game.

More than four decades later, fans of the Florida Panthers came up with their own homage to the local team, and began a plastic rat infestation at home games during the 1995–96 season.

Before the Panthers' home opener that year, Scott Mellanby had killed a rat with his stick as the rodent scampered across the floor of the Panthers' dressing room. He went out that night and used the same stick to score two goals in a 4–3 victory over the Calgary Flames, prompting Florida

Linesman Jerry Pateman picks up an octopus thrown on the ice during a game between the Detroit Red Wings and Tampa Bay Lightning. (Paul Bereswill/Hockey Hall of Fame)

Frank Bathgate played for the Guelph Biltmore Mad Hatters of the OHA Jr. League—the team sponsored by the Guelph Biltmore Hat Company that started the "hat trick" tradition. (Le Studio du Hockey/Hockey Hall of Fame)

goalie John Vanbiesbrouck to call Mellanby's feat a "rat trick."

After that, fans in South Florida began tossing plastic rats onto the ice after a Panthers goal, an undertaking that hit fever pitch in the team's unexpected run to the Stanley Cup final that season. Thousands of rats would litter the ice during playoff games.

The next season, the league instituted a rule that gave discretion to the referee to assess a delay-of-game penalty against the home team if, after a warning from the public address announcer, fans didn't stop throwing debris onto the ice.

Meanwhile, in Detroit, the octopus tradition thrived, making a celebrity out of Zamboni driver Al Sobotka as the Red Wings reeled off four Stanley Cup championships between 1997 and 2008.

When an octopus found its way onto the ice, Sobotka would walk out and retrieve it, and then swing the octopus over his head to pump up the Joe Louis crowd.

The NHL didn't take well to bits of the octopi landing on the ice from Sobotka's swinging action, so it directed the linesmen to dispose of any uninvited guests that hit the ice.

Instead the league allowed Sobotka to swing the octopi behind the glass in the Zamboni laneway.

WAYNE GRETZKY BECOMES THE NHL'S ALL-TIME LEADING SCORER

Wayne Gretzky's first thought, being the kind of sportsman he is, was that his last-minute back-hand goal had merely tied the score in a fairly meaningless October contest for the Los Angeles Kings.

But then the significance became clear. He had just become the National Hockey League's all-time leading scorer, with point No. 1,851. Among those in the crowd that night was Gordie Howe, unseated from the lofty position he'd held for three decades.

The torch was passed from Mr. Hockey to the Great One, and the greying Howe couldn't have been happier with who was replacing him. Both recalled being at a Kinsmen dinner in Brantford, Ontario, in 1971, attended by sports celebrities such as Howe, NFL quarterback Joe Theismann, and jockey Sandy Hawley. Gretzky, a local minor-hockey scoring phenom, was invited and, in a newly purchased suit, was introduced to his hockey idol.

Instead of a stilted picture together, Howe asked someone for a hockey stick, tucked the blade around Gretzky's neck, and pulled him in tight for what became an iconic portrait.

Flash forward to Edmonton's Northlands Coliseum on October 15, 1989.

Gretzky, in his 11th NHL season and second with the Kings, had assisted on a Bernie Nicholls goal in the first period, moving him into a tie with Howe at 1,850.

Howe and the NHL/media entourage that had followed his pursuit of the record for more than a week, sweated out nearly three full periods, wondering whether the moment would come in the arena where Gretzky had amassed the majority of his points and won four Stanley Cups, or a couple of days later at the Great Western Forum in Los Angeles, against the Boston Bruins.

Gretzky had estimated it would take him six games into the 1989–90 season to get the 14 points required to pass Howe. But "a chill" went through him when he first perused the schedule and saw that Game 6 would be against his old team, in his old city, from which he was trying to create a degree of separation as his career advanced.

His wife, Janet, still unfairly blamed by many Oiler fans for a perceived role in the 1988 blockbuster trade to the Kings, certainly hoped the big moment would come in L.A., as did owner Bruce McNall, looking for a full and loud house to celebrate the milestone.

Gretzky jokingly blamed the timing on Kings general

Kings captain Wayne Gretzky chases another record, against his former teammates in Edmonton. (David E. Klutho/Getty Images)

manager Rogie Vachon, the goalie who allowed Howe's last two NHL points on April 6, 1980. If Vachon had let Howe get in on two more goals that night, Gretzky reasoned, he would've needed more points back in L.A. to set the new mark.

But with Gretzky, timing was everything. His magical moments had always come on the most dramatic of stages. Much of Canada was tuned in that night. Not wanting to risk missing the moment, injured teammate Mike Krushelnyski paid his own plane fare from L.A. to Edmonton.

With a 4–3 score and just more than a minute remaining in the game, the Kings pulled goalie Mario Gosselin for a sixth attacker. After some line changing on both teams, Gretzky lined up for the draw in the Oiler zone as an extra winger, with Luc Robitaille, Nicholls, and Dave Taylor up front, and Larry Robinson and Steve Duchesne on the points.

The Oilers countered with some of Gretzky's best "boys on the bus" buddies from their Edmonton heyday: Mark Messier, Jari Kurri, Esa Tikkanen, Kevin Lowe, and Jeff Beukeboom.

Messier won the faceoff from Nicholls and the puck went into the corner, where Lowe had a chance to clear the zone. But Duchesne made a leaping hand block where the blue line met the glass. He collected the puck and fired it toward the net, where it hit Taylor's knee and bounced laterally along the crease to Gretzky, who for some reason had decided to park in front of the net, to goalie Bill Ranford's right, rather than in his usual "office" behind the opposition goal. A backhand, short-hop tap of the puck and the NHL had a new career points leader.

Gretzky jumped for joy into the arms of big Robinson and a line of Kings streaming off the bench to mob him. When Gretzky's head finally popped out of the pileup, the red carpet was already being rolled out for a league ceremony. President John Ziegler and vice-president Scotty Morrison were there, as was Wayne's dad, Walter. But of course, the honour of speaking first went to Howe.

"I've been looking forward to this day," he said. "I've spent the last 10 with Wayne and I thought I knew him before. But I think he's just grown another inch and a half in my mind, a great young man and a super hockey player, who shares in everything he does. And it's really nice for me to be sharing these honours with him.

"I think I'm as excited as Wayne's family, Mr. McNall, and the hockey club. And in all honesty, I think the guys sitting on the Edmonton bench are as much excited as the rest of us."

It was the 51st NHL record Gretzky had broken to that point. The crowd chanted his name as he took the microphone.

"Maybe it was only fitting," Gretzky said of where Howe's mark had fallen. "An award such as this takes a lot of teamwork and a lot of help. Both teams here today were a big part of these 1,800 points I've got in my career.

"I want to thank the Oiler players, who I developed great friendships with, for all their support and the organization for this ceremony. I would like to thank my current teammates, Mr. Vachon, Mr. McNall, Mr. Ziegler, and Mr. Morrison. It's a special game and everything I have in my life, I owe to the game of hockey. I want to thank you, the fans. It was a tremendous feeling."

He also introduced his parents, wife Janet, and baby daughter Paulina, adding, "Life isn't fun without family."

Messier presented him with a gold bracelet on behalf of the Oilers, the Kings gave him a crystal hologram, and the league gave him a silver tea service inscribed with the logos of all 21 NHL teams.

TV analyst Harry Neale marvelled at how Gretzky—again—had made history on the biggest stage.

"The job is done," Neale concluded. "Gretzky's stats speak very clearly for his superiority as an NHL superstar. But the real greatness in him is measured by his ability in making his teammates play better and utilize his skills in the best interests of the whole team.

"And isn't that the dictionary definition of Wayne Gretzky?"

No. 99 wasn't quite finished that evening. There was still overtime to be played, and coach Tom Webster turned to Gretzky again, as he got loose for yet another backhander and beat Ranford for the win.

60

THE RULES CHANGE

Between 1927 and 1930, the NHL enacted three significant rule changes that brought scoring up to speed. The first of these, introduced in 1927–28, gave players the green light to pass the puck forward in the defending and neutral zones. (The year before, the blue lines had been repositioned to enlarge the neutral zone.)

Before the advent of the new rule, players had rarely made it to double figures in assists. Howie Morenz of the Montreal Canadiens went from his previous season's seven helpers to 18 and won the 1927–28 scoring title with a record 51 points. Montreal scored a league-high 116 goals in the 44-game schedule.

Also codified for that season was a reduction in the width of goaltenders' pads, from 12 inches to 10. This change was also in the shooters' best interests, but it didn't much bother league-leading goaltender George Hainsworth of the Habs, as he kept his goals-against average to 1.05. That mark was better than Clint Benedict's 1.42 for the Montreal Maroons the season before.

The 1929–30 season also marked the first in which every club scored at least 100 goals, led by Boston's 179.

The rule was further amended a year later to allow forward passing in all zones, but not across either blue line. By Christmas 1929, scores were getting out of hand. The Maple Leafs, for example, notched 29 goals in their first nine games, while giving up 39. Their corresponding totals a year earlier were 18 and 17.

On December 21, the league made yet another change, ruling that no player could precede the play when entering the opposition zone—the forerunner to the modern offside rule.

The 1929–30 season also marked the first in which every club scored at least 100 goals, led by Boston's 179. Cooney Weiland of the Boston Bruins became the first player from an American-based team to lead the league in scoring, with 73 points.

The more wide-open, offensive game required players to do a lot more skating, leaving them fatigued. So, concurrent with these new rules came an increase in game-night rosters, from 12 players to 15, leading NHL teams a little closer to the tightly packed benches of today's 20-man teams.

61

THE HERITAGE CLASSIC

On a sunny but frigid day, a crowd of 57,167 snuggled into Edmonton's Commonwealth Stadium to brave the frosty temperatures for the NHL's first outdoor game, dubbed the Heritage Classic.

The hockey world was curious to take in what would become a trendsetting event on November 22, 2003. Not only was there a capacity crowd to watch the Montreal Canadiens defeat the hometown Oilers, 4–3, but a regular-season record 2.747 million viewers tuned in to CBC to watch "Shinny Night in Canada." By comparison, Gretzky's final NHL game on April 18, 1999, drew 2.161 million viewers on *Hockey Night in Canada*.

The outdoor game was the network's first high-definition hockey broadcast.

Earlier in the day, a team of Edmonton oldtimers such as Gretzky and Paul Coffey took on a team of Montreal legends that included Guy Lafleur and Larry Robinson. That game drew an off-the-charts 2.318 million viewers. Mark Messier, who at 42 was in his final NHL season with the New York Rangers, received permission to play alongside Gretzky and his former Stanley Cup teammates.

"It's kind of like the 1972 Series. You can never go back and try to do it again."

"It's not only the 57,000 who came to see the game, it's the 57,000 who came with enthusiasm. That's what's incredible about it," said Messier after his oldtimers beat Lafleur and company, 2–0, in a game that consisted of two 15-minute periods interrupted by a good old-fashioned shovelling of snow to clear the ice.

"I guess that's what makes Edmonton special."

"First of all, the whole weekend, the whole few days were just tremendous for everybody," Gretzky added. "I don't know if you can ever duplicate it.

"It's kind of like the 1972 Series. You can never go back and try to do it again."

The first one is always special. But the NHL decided to build on the first Heritage Classic with a New Year's Day game called the Winter Classic, as well as a Stadium Series and more Heritage Classics in Canada.

The original Heritage Classic was the brainchild of then–Oilers president Patrick LaForge. He had seen the success of the outdoor game between the University of Michigan and Michigan State, played in 2001 at Spartan Stadium in East Lansing, Michigan, and couldn't think of a

Jose Theodore tries to keep warm on a frosty November evening in Edmonton. (Dave Sandford/Stringer/Getty Images Sport)

better way for the Oilers to celebrate their 25th year in the NHL and the 20th anniversary of their first Stanley Cup championship.

"We were approaching our 25th season and we had a plan for celebrating, but it wasn't super," LaForge told the *Edmonton Journal.* "We were going to hijack the all-star game as part of our celebration."

For all the spectacle of the league's top players in a weekend-long exhibit of skill, LaForge imagined a game with more at stake, for fans and players. "So how do we bend it, make it more of a traditional event?

"On the flight home, we were noodling. I said I had picked up some knowledge in my beer [marketing] days about dreams of beer drinkers, and one of them was NHL players playing pond hockey," he said. "That just led us to our game, which was really an all-star game kicked off by the legends of the NHL, played outdoors, and really just a great community gathering. We just built on that."

The only thing that went wrong for the Oilers was that they lost to the Canadiens in the real game.

The temperature at the time of the opening puck drop was minus-18 Celsius (or zero degrees Fahrenheit) with a wind chill of minus-30 Celsius (minus-22 Fahrenheit). Players wore extra layers of long underwear, balaclavas under their helmets, and dealt with stiff, frozen equipment as well as chippy ice that caused the puck to bounce like a rubber ball.

In the hours leading up to game time, the intense cold meant it was a very real possibility that the game might need to be postponed.

But the game went on and the night was truly classic.

Canadiens goalie Jose Theodore made a memorable fashion statement, wearing a toque over the top of his mask. The Habs also kept warm on their bench with cups of piping-hot chicken soup.

After a goalless first period, Edmonton fell behind in the second on goals from Richard Zednik and Yanic Perreault. But Canadiens defenceman Sheldon Souray knocked the puck past his own goalie for a goal credited to speedy Oilers forward Jason Chimera to give the home side life.

In the third period, however, Perreault scored early for his second of the game. Edmonton's Jarret Stoll pushed his club to within one midway through the final 20 minutes, before Zednik and Oilers defenceman Steve Staios scored 29 seconds apart.

"If that's the last game they play outside, we wanted to be a part of history," Canadiens forward Joe Juneau said in a postgame scrum. "We wanted to be the team that won it."

62

CLARENCE CAMPBELL BECOMES PRESIDENT

Perhaps the greatest testament to Clarence Campbell's legacy is the record he set for longevity.

No league president or commissioner in North American professional sports has held their title longer than the native of Fleming, Saskatchewan.

Born in 1905, Campbell was a versatile athlete who starred in hockey and rugby in high school and at the University of Alberta, where he obtained a bachelor of arts degree at age 18 and a law degree when he was 20. He then studied as a Rhodes Scholar at Oxford, where he also played for the university's hockey team.

Campbell captained Oxford to victory in the 1929 Varsity Match against Cambridge, and his love of sports led him to become an official in hockey and lacrosse overseas. Campbell returned to Canada during the Great Depression and joined an Edmonton law firm. Along with two local business leaders, he designed and supervised the construction of Renfrew Park baseball stadium.

Campbell also refereed hockey games in western Canada, and was hired by NHL president Frank Calder in 1933. He officiated for six seasons before he transitioned to work in the league office in 1939.

But the outbreak of World War II beckoned. Campbell began as a private in 1941 and rose to the rank of lieutenant colonel. After the war, he served in the Canadian War Crimes Investigation Unit, tasked with collecting evidence in the murders of Canadian prisoners of war. Campbell was made a Member of the Order of the British Empire in 1945.

Calder died in 1943 after a series of heart attacks. Red Dutton, former general manager and coach of the by then defunct New York Americans, agreed to assume Calder's duties. Campbell returned to the NHL office in 1946 as the league's assistant president. Dutton resigned shortly after, and Campbell was named the third president of the NHL.

Campbell had his mettle tested early in his tenure when Boston centre Don Gallinger and New York Rangers centre Billy Taylor were involved in a gambling scandal in 1948. Toronto's Babe Pratt had been given a lenient sentence a few years earlier, but Campbell didn't like the trend he saw. To discourage future involvement with gambling, he banned both players for life.

The game grew under Campbell's leadership. He extended the regular season from 50 games to 60 (and later 70) and inaugurated the annual all-star game for the 1947–48 season.

Concerned with competitive balance among franchises, he initiated an intra-league draft two years later to promote parity.

The greatest test of Campbell's resolve came in 1955. He suspended Maurice "Rocket" Richard for the remainder of the regular season and the playoffs after the Montreal superstar struck an official in Boston on March 13. Campbell received death threats, but still appeared at the Forum four nights later when Detroit came to town.

Sitting in the stands, Campbell was verbally abused, had food thrown at him, and required security to keep fans from attacking him. A tear gas bomb was set off in the first intermission. The Forum was evacuated and the mayhem extended into the streets. The result was the Richard Riot.

Campbell guided the NHL through unprecedented growth. He was inducted into the Hockey Hall of Fame in 1966, the year before the league expanded, doubling in size after 25 years of the so-called Original Six. There were 18 teams in the NHL by the time he stepped down in 1977 after 31 years as president of the NHL.

Through it all, Campbell maintained his principles. After the rival World Hockey Association formed in 1972, Campbell refused to allow NHL players to participate in the 1972 Summit Series between Canada and the Soviet Union if players from the WHA—including the Golden Jet, Bobby Hull—were allowed to take part.

Clarence Campbell's name and achievements live on in the NHL via the Clarence S. Campbell Bowl, which is awarded each year to the Western Conference playoff champion.

Clarence S. Campbell (seated), third president of the NHL, with Toronto mayor Nathan Phillips. (Imperial Oil–Turofsky/Hockey Hall of Fame)

PAUL COFFEY BREAKS
BOBBY ORR'S RECORD

The pressure had piled up on Paul Coffey.

The Edmonton Oilers stalwart had three games remaining in the 1985–86 season in which to score two goals to eclipse Bobby Orr's single-season record of 46 goals by a defenceman. Orr had set the mark in 1974–75, his last full season with the Boston Bruins.

Eleven years later, Coffey had to overcome a slow start. Early in his sixth NHL season, he was hindered by a charley horse injury, even though he missed only one game. He also complained that he couldn't find a pair of skates that fit properly.

Coffey only had seven goals in his first 20 games, and it wasn't until the Oilers' 42nd game of the season that he scored his 19th and 20th goals. However, he put together three impressive goal-scoring streaks in the second half of the season, beginning with 14 goals in a 16-game stretch. In mid-February, Coffey scored seven goals in four games, and by early March he was perched on Orr's doorstep with an already-considerable 45.

He suited up for the Oilers' 78th game of the season, against the visiting Vancouver Canucks, hoping to at least tie Orr. And he did just that, stepping in front of Canucks forward Petri Skriko to intercept a pass late in the second period.

Coffey then fed that turnover to Wayne Gretzky at the side of the goal, but the puck bounded off Vancouver defenceman Doug Halward and past goalie Wendell Young, giving Coffey his record-tying 46th goal. The 24-year-old Coffey passed Orr with goal no. 47 in the third period, after hustling back to break up a scoring chance for Vancouver's Cam Neely. Coffey then took a pass in his own end from Jari Kurri and employed his remarkable skating stride to beat the Canucks defence and slide a shot underneath Young.

The Northland Coliseum crowd went nuts as Kurri retrieved the puck for his teammate. The Oilers went on to win the game, 8–4.

"On the first goal I was trying to pass to Wayne but it went in instead," Coffey remarked after the game. "To get a lucky one gave me a jump for the second one. It felt really good. I just tried to pick the corner."

Orr could not attend the game because he was playing in the pro-am at the Dinah Shore golf tournament in southern California. But he sent a congratulatory telegram to Coffey.

Paul Coffey crashes into Tim Hunter of the Calgary Flames at the Olympic Saddledome.
(Paul Bereswill/Hockey Hall of Fame)

"Please accept my congratulations for an outstanding accomplishment," Orr's message read. "You have been a credit to the game on and off the ice. I'm pleased a person of your calibre has succeeded me in the record book."

Coffey had arrived at the Oilers' 1985 training camp coming off a season that was spectacular in its own right. As a member of Team Canada, he had won his first of three Canada Cup titles. His play in the regular season had earned him the Norris Trophy, the first of three times he would win that award. And it had ended with the Oilers winning the second of back-to-back Stanley Cup championships. During the postseason, he'd set records for goals (12), assists (25), and points (37) by a defenceman.

So at the outset of 1985–86, Coffey wondered how could he top all of those achievements.

"My agent, Gus Badali, gave me a list of motivational things before the season, and two of them were to break Orr's goals and points records," Coffey said after the record-breaking game against the Canucks. "I thought it was impossible until about a month and a half ago, when people mentioned it and I began to feel the pressure."

Finally breaking Orr's goals record, he said, "was like having 1,000 pounds removed from my back."

Finally breaking Orr's goals record, he said, "was like having 1,000 pounds removed from my back."

Coffey would score one final time, in the Oilers' next game, a 9–3 loss in Calgary against the Flames. Scoring seven goals in the season's final seven games had increased his record output to 48 goals. He ended up with 138 points in 79 games, just one shy of Orr's all-time mark, set in 1970–71.

Over the course of his magical season, Coffey set a few additional records. He enjoyed the longest point-scoring streak for a defenceman—28 games, a remarkable run that ended on January 27 in Chicago and saw him score 16 times and register 55 points. His nine short-handed goals were also a single-season high for a defenceman, and he matched Tom Bladon's single-game points record for a defenceman.

Bladon had scored four goals and four assists in a game for the Philadelphia Flyers on December 11, 1977, against the Cleveland Barons. Coffey scored twice and assisted on six others in a 12–3 win at home against the Detroit Red Wings.

The Oilers would not win the Stanley Cup that spring, but Coffey and his Edmonton teammates rebounded to win the title in 1986–87. Coffey, inducted into the Hockey Hall of Fame in 2007, would win the Stanley Cup for a fourth and final time, with the 1990–91 Pittsburgh Penguins.

Charlie Huddy and Mark Messier hoist the Stanley Cup alongside Wayne Gretzky after the Edmonton Oilers beat the New York Islanders in Game 5 of the 1984 Stanley Cup Final. (Paul Bereswill/Hockey Hall of Fame)

64

OILERS END ISLANDERS' DYNASTY

All it took to end the New York Islanders' streak of four consecutive Stanley Cup wins were ice packs. Rest assured, it also took talent and strong goaltending. But above all else, those ice packs taught a young Wayne Gretzky about the blood, sweat, and tears necessary to win the Stanley Cup.

The Minnesota North Stars had ended Montreal's bid for a fifth straight Stanley Cup with a 3–2 win in Game 7 at the Forum on April 27, 1980. The door was open for a new team to start a dynasty, and the New York Islanders obligingly stepped through.

Long a team on the cusp of greatness, New York's stacked roster could counter any kind of game the opposition threw at them. If proof were needed that teams are built from the net out, the Islanders were Exhibit A. "Battlin' Billy" Smith and Glenn "Chico" Resch provided solid goaltending. All-Star Denis Potvin led a strong, mobile defence, and they possessed the best forward line in the NHL in Bryan Trottier, Mike Bossy, and Clark Gillies.

The Islanders had so far failed to deliver on their promise, so they made a key trade-deadline move, acquiring centre Robert "Butch" Goring from Los Angeles on March 10, 1980, for forward Billy Harris and defenceman Dave Lewis. Goring proved to be the magic ingredient the Islanders had been

lacking, and New York went on to win its first Stanley Cup by defeating Philadelphia in six games.

Three years later, the only obstacle between the Islanders and their fourth straight championship was Edmonton. The Oilers were not unlike the Islanders of the late 1970s: a young, talented team with championship expectations but little playoff success. Led by future Hockey Hall of Fame members Gretzky, Mark Messier, Jari Kurri, Glenn Anderson, Paul Coffey, and Grant Fuhr, Edmonton seemed destined to win a Stanley Cup at some point.

But not in the spring of 1983. New York dismantled the Oilers' high-powered offence and held them to just eight goals in a four-game sweep. The "boys on the bus" were taken to the woodshed by the battle-tested warriors from Long Island.

In an oft-told tale, Gretzky and some teammates were walking through the bowels of Nassau Coliseum after the game. When they passed the Islanders in the dressing room, they were astonished to discover very little celebrating. The weary Islanders sat with ice packs that covered the bruises and welts raised by blocked shots and puck battles. Gretzky said that witnessing that scene taught the young Oilers about the level of sacrifice necessary to win a Stanley Cup.

The two teams met again in the 1984 final, but this was a much different and more determined Edmonton squad.

Game 1 on Long Island was a match the Oilers would not have won the previous year. Edmonton upped its physicality and made a total commitment to team defence. Neither Billy Smith nor Grant Fuhr had allowed a goal after 40 minutes, and, indicative of the team focus, it was not one of Edmonton's star players who broke the ice. Early in the third period, Kevin McClelland beat Smith to give the Oilers a lead that Fuhr would never relinquish.

The Islanders evened the series two nights later with a 6–1 victory, but the point had been made. The Oilers played the unselfish style necessary to defeat a team that aimed for its fifth consecutive title, and had done so on the road.

The series shifted to Edmonton for the next three games, and the seismic shift in the series occurred in Game 3. After Gillies beat Fuhr to give New York a 2–1 lead early in the second period, Glen Sather's team outscored the Islanders, 18–4, over the next eight periods to end New York's four-year reign. The victory ignited a run of five Stanley Cups in seven seasons for the Oilers.

That's a lot of champagne. And ice packs.

GHOSTS OF THE MONTREAL FORUM

No one can prove they actually saw a ghost in the Montreal Forum, at least not one that cast a spell in favour of the Canadiens, although Dick Irvin Sr., the great coach and father of broadcaster Dick Irvin, would sometimes credit the "unseen hand" when talking to his son about an unlikely Forum occurrence.

But in winning 22 Stanley Cups between 1924 and 1993, more than any other NHL team, the Habs needed very little assistance from the spiritual world. They were that good in real life.

They were also the first team to win five Stanley Cups in a row, and the last team representing a Canadian city to drink from the Cup.

Their home at 2313 Ste. Catherine Street West was also the site of two championships celebrated by the Habs' original co-tenants, the Montreal Maroons.

It was at the Forum that Maurice Richard became the first NHL player to score 500 goals—and to trigger a riot that bears his name. It was the place where Howie Morenz lay in state, the first of many Montreal stars accorded the honour. It saw the longest game in NHL history: nine periods over parts of two days before the Red Wings beat the Maroons, 1–0.

Some still refer to the 3–3 tie between the Canadiens and the Central Red Army team, played on New Year's Eve 1975, as the best hockey game ever played. The worst, for the nation at least, was Team Canada's stunning 7–3 loss in the opener of the 1972 Summit Series, a defeat vindicated four years later by the overtime win over Czechoslovakia in the final of the inaugural Canada Cup.

The venerable Zamboni made its first Canadian appearance at the Forum, which was the first NHL rink to host a spring amateur draft. But nothing beat a snowy Saturday in winter, especially when an Original Six opponent was in town and there was a buzz in nearby restaurants and pubs that built steadily in the moments before the opening faceoff.

Amid shouting scalpers, the public could watch the Habs enter through the side entrance for their morning skate; visiting players ambling over from their hotel; and the *Hockey Night in Canada* crew having breakfast across the street at the Texan diner, beneath photos of glory-days players.

But there were also little bells and whistles once you were inside the building. The Cup banners and a long row of retired numbers belonging to Montreal Hall of Famers spoke for themselves.

"The character of the Forum is really the aura of

> "The character of the Forum is really the aura of success."

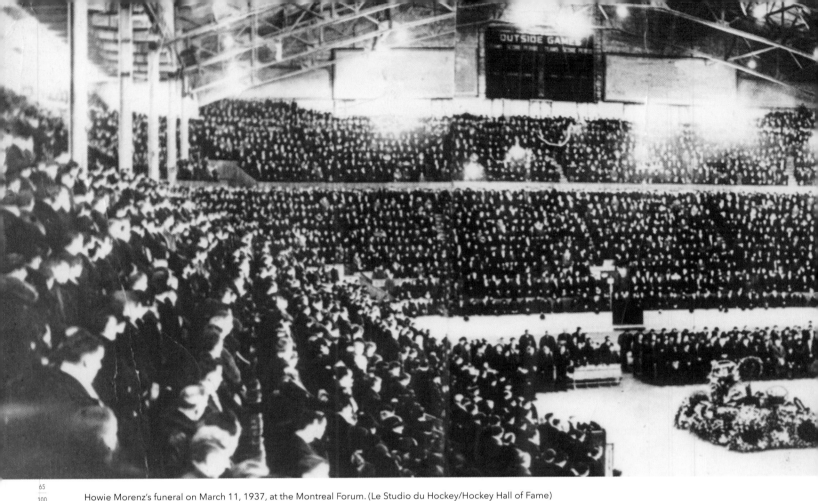

65
100

Howie Morenz's funeral on March 11, 1937, at the Montreal Forum. (Le Studio du Hockey/Hockey Hall of Fame)

success," said broadcaster Dick Irvin, whose association with the team dates back to when his father coached the team in the 1940s and '50s. "If you were 40 years old in Montreal [during the 1990s], chances are you grew up with the team winning a Cup almost every other year.

"What makes it an event is the French-Canadian fans. They're lively and they love the game. A lot is said [about their fickle behaviour], but they really don't care about winning and losing, they just want exciting hockey. Montreal home games have been called the best show in town."

That appetite for exciting hockey can be traced back to the early 1900s, before the NHL was created and the Forum was built. From Westmount Arena, which held 10,000 including standing room and boasted one of the first rinks to have rounded—rather than squared-off—corners, the Canadiens of the National Hockey Association emerged.

Westmount had artificial ice after 1914, and the Canadiens won the Cup two years later.

When NHL play began in 1917, the Habs shared a rink with the older Montreal Wanderers. But a fire destroyed the place, financially ruining the Wanderers and leaving the Canadiens to play out of the tiny Jubilee Arena, with space for less than 4,000. When it, too, suffered fire damage, they shifted to the new Mount Royal Arena, which had a little more room but lacked artificial ice.

The imminent arrival of another team in Montreal, one designed to cater to English fans (the Maroons), sped up the process of building new digs. Two proponents of a second team—Donat Raymond, a local sportsman and Liberal politician, and William Northey, who'd been involved in the construction of the Westmount Arena—approached Edward Beatty, the powerful president of the Canadian

Pacific Railway, to help recruit rich Montrealers to back an arena project.

The Forum (it was built in the classical style of the day before a 1968 renovation) was initially going to occupy a smaller footprint. A few investors were hesitant about its grand design, which took up a whole city block for a building that would house 12,500. But Northey assured them of the building's eventual value as an entertainment facility and sold them on the merits of a winning hockey team. It was built in 159 days for $1.5 million and was ready by November 1924. A little-publicized, hour-long exhibition between the Maroons and Canadiens broke it in, but the Canadiens played the first regular-season game in the Forum—against the Toronto St. Pats on November 29, a 7–1 Montreal win— and the Maroons lost their first official game there, 2–0, to the Hamilton Tigers.

The Habs, still awaiting a promised ice plant at Mount Royal as late as 1926, lost patience and became official co-tenants, taking full control after the Maroons suffered in the Depression years and folded in 1938.

It didn't take long for the Canadiens to make both French and English fans proud.

Morenz, the "Stratford Streak," was the team's star in the 1920s and early '30s, and the engine behind three Cups. When he died of complications from a career-ending broken leg in 1937, an estimated 50,000 people filed past his coffin in the Forum. Witnesses recall the eerie silence of the packed building.

There was no such quiet 18 years later, after superstar and francophone icon Maurice Richard was suspended for the balance of the 1954–55 season by NHL president Clarence Campbell for striking an official. Campbell, in a move that was either brave or foolhardy, came over from the nearby league office to attend the Canadiens' game against Detroit and was pelted by fans, whose tempers quickly boiled over. Tear gas went off, the game was cancelled, and angry fans (the Forum now held close to 16,000 after changes a few years earlier) took out their frustrations on storefront windows and cars in the streets until Richard himself appealed for calm.

After the 1950s dynasty, four more Cups followed in the '60s as the Forum was completely modernized. The team won another six in the 1970s as names such as Jean Beliveau, Guy Lafleur, and Larry Robinson delighted the crowds. In that decade, with Scotty Bowman behind the bench and a strong front office and ownership in place, few teams could top the Canadiens on the ice, at the draft table, or in trades.

The game-night experience, often starting with Roger Doucet belting out a bilingual "O Canada," was enhanced by "guaranteed win night" on most evenings, particularly in 1976–77, when Montreal won 33 of 40 regular-season home games. The sound of Claude Mouton's excited PA announcements and the lively organ music still ring in everyone's ears nearly a half-century later.

Great memories, unless you played for a team such as the Boston Bruins, who suffered the most at the hands of the Habs. Of 18 playoff series between 1946 and 1988, the Bruins lost every one, including three Cup finals. Don Cherry's team was close to an upset in the 1979 semifinals, leading 3–1 in the third period of Game 7 before a penalty for too many men on the ice, and an overtime gut buster,

took them down. No wonder the talk of mischievous spirits at work in the Forum rafters returned.

"There was all the talk of the jinx of the Forum and the ghosts of the Forum," said *Boston Globe* writer Fran Rosa, a winner of the Hockey Hall of Fame's Elmer Ferguson Award for hockey writing. "Harry Sinden and Cherry believed in them. The puck would always seem to take a weird bounce or something at a critical time."

Visiting fans from nearby cities, mostly Boston and Toronto, often procured tickets, making the Forum a colourful Saturday-night battlefield. Hard-nosed forward Chris Nilan, who played for both the Bruins and Habs, claimed there was once talk of the league scrapping Saturday matches between the two teams because of all the fights.

But no matter what ghosts roamed its rafters, the Forum came to a dignified end, with the surviving team captains passing a torch in a closing ceremony on March 11, 1996, a gesture emblematic of the motto in the Forum dressing room: To you from failing hands we throw the torch, be yours to hold it high (from "In Flanders Field," a poem by John McRae). The proceedings were meant to ensure the spirit of the old Forum would follow them to a new home at the Bell Centre. Richard's introduction resulted in a standing ovation of several minutes.

Dick Irvin and Richard Garneau were the English and French emcees for the ceremony after the 4–1 Montreal win. Irvin, who'd had bad throat trouble on a prior road trip, didn't think he'd be able to make it through the night. But he found his voice. Credit the unseen hand with helping one last time.

66

RED LINES, BLUE LINES

To cross a line at high speed and enter a modern era sounds like a premise for a science-fiction time-travel story.

Yet most hockey minds recognize the introduction of the centre red line, prior to the 1943–44 season, as the dividing line between the NHL's old and new eras.

Prior to that, puck carriers emerging from their own zone had to lug the puck over the blue line before they could relay it forward, which left them subject to stifling forechecking. Keep in mind, too, that it had been less than 15 years since forward passing of any kind had first been allowed in the league.

Frank Boucher, general manager of the New York Rangers, made the formal proposal at the league's 1943 general meetings to split the rink into 100-foot defensive zones divided by a centre line, giving the attacking team an extra 25 feet to work with. His proposal was intended to speed up the game by reducing the overabundance of off-side calls.

Unfortunately for Boucher, his Rangers didn't profit from the revolutionary idea. While the added passing territory saw four teams increase their output to more than 200 goals in the 1943–44 season (198 had been the record, set by

The layout of the hockey rink remains an ongoing conversation.

the Maple Leafs the previous season), the last-place Rangers scored just 162. Herb Cain of the Bruins became the first player in league history to break 80 points, because of the introduction of the centre line.

In the NHL's inaugural season, a centre-ice face-off dot and lines between the goal posts were the only markings on the ice. The blue lines were added for the NHL's second season, and they took on new importance late in 1929, when the first offside rule was adopted. It stopped players from preceding the puck into the offensive zone, and forever halted what would be referred to in later years as "goal sucking."

In a related move a few years earlier, the practice of randomly firing the puck down the ice from a team's own end in a bid to kill time or relieve forechecking pressure had resulted in the icing rule. Teams that iced the puck were penalized by the staging of a faceoff in their end of the rink.

For decades, the offside and icing rules remained unchanged, to the detriment of faster-skating teams with more dynamic offensive players. Because passes across two lines were not permitted, less-skilled teams could prevent plays from being made by clogging the neutral zone, a technique known as the "trap."

As part of a complete overhaul of the game after the 2004–05 lockout, the centre line became "invisible," allowing the "stretch pass," from as far back as behind the net all the way to the opposing blue line.

Concurrent with that change was the return of tag-up offsides, which allowed a player who had preceded the puck into the attacking zone, but hadn't yet touched it, to skate back to the neutral zone, thus negating the offside call. The idea was to increase the fluidity of the game by reducing the number of stoppages.

The layout of the hockey rink remains an ongoing conversation with the number and placement of markings having changed a few times over the years as the league experiments with such ideas as shrinking the neutral zone or adding space behind the nets, all in the name of creating more scoring as goaltenders and defences became harder to penetrate.

Linesman Ray Scapinello reminds Wayne Gretzky to stay onside at the Montreal blue line during Game 3 of the 1993 Stanley Cup Final. Canadiens centre Vincent Damphousse follows the L.A. rush. (Paul Bereswill/Hockey Hall of Fame)

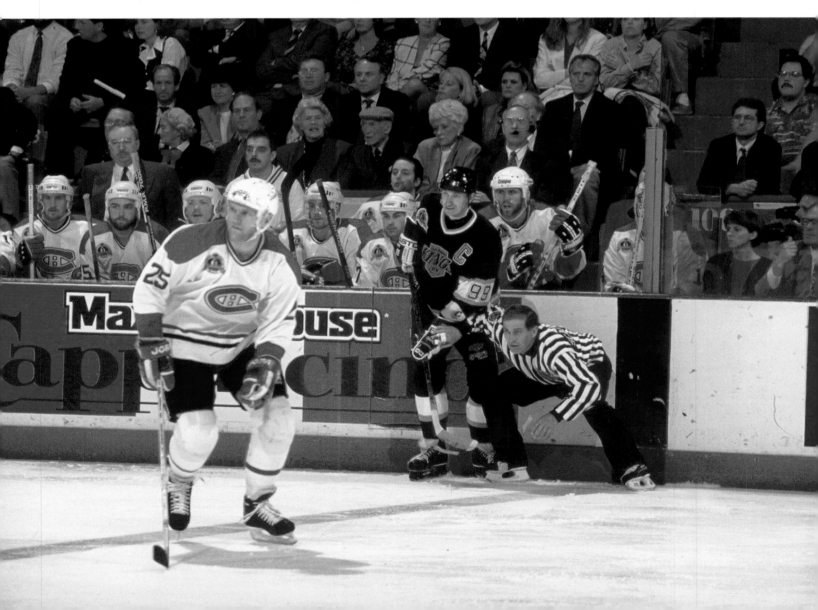

THE FIRST AND ONLY COMMISSIONER

On June 22, 2016, Gary Bettman entered a hotel ballroom and made a historic announcement.

The NHL Board of Governors unanimously had approved expansion to Las Vegas—awarding the city its first major league sports franchise.

"This expansion," Bettman added, "comes at a time when our game is more competitive than ever, ownership is stronger than ever, the player base is more talented than ever, and the future opportunities for the business are greater than ever."

That new franchise fee was $500 million, a landmark figure for a league that was doing just over $400 million in business, total, when Bettman took office February 1, 1993.

Now the longest tenured commissioner among North America's four major professional sports, Bettman took over a league with a broken business model, stabilized it at the harrowing cost of a lost 2004–05 season—the price deemed necessary to fix the economic problems—and now looks ahead to a future that features global opportunities in China and elsewhere, technological advancements such as player and puck tracking, and greater fan engagement.

League revenues now approach $4.5 billion annually. The average player salary, around $450,000 in 1992–93, now is roughly $3 million.

While there have been three labour disruptions since Bettman took over, each time when the games resumed the league became stronger, on and off the ice, and continued to grow

Bettman, a native of New York and a graduate of Cornell University and the New York University School of Law, had worked as a senior vice president and general counsel with the National Basketball Association before being hired by the NHL. He succeeded Gil Stein, who had taken office briefly after John Ziegler ended his 15-year tenure as president.

When Bettman was hired, network television access in the U.S. was profoundly limited, but now it has long-term, multi-billion-dollar broadcast agreements in Canada and the U.S. and its largest national viewing audience ever. There was one referee on the ice, virtually no video replay, shootouts didn't exist, and playing an outdoor NHL game—much less one that could draw 105,000 people on a snowy, frigid New Year's Day in Michigan—would have been as inconceivable as, say, an NHL team in Las Vegas.

While Las Vegas may be considered a non-traditional NHL market, the growth of the sport has proven that, over time, many of them can create their own histories and customs. At the end of the 2017 Stanley Cup Final, Bettman had presented the trophy for a 24th time—including presentations to the home team in Los Angeles

NHL Commissioner Gary Bettman speaks at the Hockey Hall of Fame Induction Ceremony on November 12, 2012. (Mathew Manor/Hockey Hall of Fame)

(twice), Anaheim, Raleigh, and Denver. Nashville, another non-traditional market, was a Cup finalist in 2017.

As important, new markets lead to new rinks and new opportunities. Toronto forward Auston Matthews, the top pick in the 2016 draft, was born in California, grew up in Scottsdale, Arizona, and was drawn to hockey by watching the Phoenix (now Arizona) Coyotes. Matthews was one of 12 U.S.–born players selected in

that first round, an NHL record and a further indication of the growth of the game at the grassroots level.

When the league celebrates its 100th birthday on November 26, 2017, NHL games and its stories will have reached more fans around the world than ever before on its assorted platforms.

"This is, to say the least, a fabulous time for the NHL," Bettman said that day in Las Vegas.

68

THE ROAR AT CHICAGO STADIUM

I f you never saw a hockey game at old Chicago Stadium, just stand beside a 747 jet engine at takeoff to get a feel for the experience.

And that was before the air horn from owner Bill Wirtz's yacht, blown after Blackhawks goals, was installed in the ear-splitting building.

As a famous homemade banner, unfurled during the deafening roar that accompanied the performance of the American anthem at the last regular-season home game in April 1994 reminded, "It Will Never Be the Same." Truer words . . .

While the Blackhawks of old weren't the force they've become this century—they won just one Stanley Cup between 1939 and the Stadium's closing—they didn't call their home the Madhouse on Madison for nothing. Just as Wrigley Field, the first Comiskey Park, and Soldier Field held a special place in the heart of this great American sports town, the Stadium, located on the gritty Near West Side, provided fans with the ideal backdrop for hockey.

With its low roof, the Barton organ built right into the wall, and steeply pitched seating that made it feel like the crowd was perched right over the ice, games could feel

In the 1989 playoffs, the volume at ice level was measured at 130 decibels, causing the plexiglass to vibrate.

like fervent political rallies. Sixty minutes of shots, body-checks, and fights—some on the ice, others in the stands—made it a memorable evening.

Unlike cities such as Toronto, where patrons arrived fashionably late, everyone was at the Stadium on time to applaud during "The Star-Spangled Banner." The tradition of "The Roar" began in earnest during big-game playoff series within the rock 'em, sock 'em Norris Division in the 1980s, especially in games against Original Six opponents Toronto and Detroit and geographic rivals the St. Louis Blues.

With Wayne Messmer singing and Frank Pellico at the keyboards, the din would start with "O say can you see," and by the time Messmer wrapped with "and the home of the brave," always accentuating the last word, his voice would be drowned out by the cheers.

"You felt like joining the army afterwards," said Calgary Flames executive Al MacNeil.

Of course, such theatrics intimidated the visitors, who had to climb a set of 21 stairs to ice level like they were prisoners being marched to their doom in the ancient Roman Colosseum. They had to stare across the blue line at 20 iconic

Blackhawk logos on the jerseys of the emboldened home team, all of whom knew the dimensions of their smaller rink well enough to get the most from its bounces and angles. The Hawks would feed off the fired-up crowd until puck drop.

In the 1989 playoffs, the volume at ice level was measured at 130 decibels, causing the plexiglass to vibrate.

"It was past the pain threshold," declared Chicago defenceman Trent Yawney.

Many an opposing coach said that surviving the first five minutes of a game in the Stadium atmosphere was vital to victory.

Ironically, the visionary behind the Stadium did not fulfill his dream to bring an NHL team to the city. Chicago businessman Paddy Harmon came to the 1926 NHL meetings determined to buy an expansion team, with fifty $1,000 bills in his suitcase. Huntington "Tack" Hardwick was granted the franchise but sold it a month later to Major Frederic McLaughlin, who named the new team for his infantry division from World War I, the Blackhawk Division.

Harmon decided he would get his piece of the action by building the team a grandiose home. Many dismissed his idea, but he raised $2.5 million and cajoled enough support to erect the Stadium with 16,600 seats by 1929. One of the features added was the massive pipe organ, with its six keyboards. Longtime player Al Melgard could not only create music, but add sound effects, such as a train.

Despite the lack of Cup banners, the Hawks did give the Stadium faithful much to savour and celebrate through the years. The fans loved Harold "Mush" March, Lionel Conacher, Doc Romnes, Bill Mosienko, and the Bentley Brothers. In the '60s, Bobby Hull thrilled with a raft of 50-goal seasons, three of them attained at the Stadium, where he also recorded his 1,000th point. Hull, the driven centre Stan Mikita, and goaltending iron man Glenn Hall led the Hawks to a championship in 1961.

Chicago remained a force into the early '70s, but could never quite unseat Montreal, Toronto, Boston, and Detroit.

NHL realignment in the 1980s found the Hawks in the rough-and-tumble "Chuck" Norris Division, with teams that were brawnier, but also better skilled thanks to the likes of Denis Savard, Doug Wilson, Jeremy Roenick, Chris Chelios, and Ed Belfour. Coaches such as "Iron Mike" Keenan no doubt inspired fans to turn up the volume, as well.

"I loved playing there, with the fans and the noise," said Minnesota North Stars bruiser Shane Churla. "Some guy once threw a trailer hitch at me. They're a different breed of fan, but that gets me going."

That emotion would come in handy on January 19, 1991. Chicago had been awarded the NHL's all-star game, long before anyone knew the otherwise quiet weekend on the sports calendar just ahead of the Super Bowl would be preceded by the first Gulf War. A nation desperate to send a message of public support to its troops and international allies let loose when the game was aired globally.

The Stars and Stripes were displayed everywhere that afternoon, along with fan-created banners bearing slogans like "No flag burners here." Standing beside Mark Messier on the blue line, Wayne Gretzky looked around as the anthem hit its crescendo and said, "This is unbelievable."

However, a few years later, the Stadium's end was near. Bill Wirtz needed to maximize profits for his Hawks as well as for the NBA's Chicago Bulls, of which he was a minority owner and who were then in the midst of a basketball dynasty led by Michael Jordan. More than 60 years old by 1994, the Stadium was showing its age, and despite its history and character, a bigger and better arena was being built across the street. The long goodbye culminated with the final regular-season home game on April 14, 1994.

The three Cup banners were lowered in preparation for the trip to the United Center, as were the four retired Hawks

Maybe no NHL arena was as intimidating to visiting players as the Chicago Stadium. (Le Studio du Hockey/Hockey Hall of Fame)

numbers of Hall, Mikita, Hull, and Tony Esposito, all of whom flew in for the ceremony.

"I won't be afraid to cry," said Mikita.

The anthem that night was another ear-buster, with an added element of drama because Messmer was in hospital with a bullet wound, the victim of a random shooting a few days earlier. Hawks play-by-play man Pat Foley read a message from Messmer that ended with "Goodbye old girl, I'll miss you." His pre-recorded anthem played amid sparklers and the frantic waving of "Remember the Roar" signs.

Unfortunately, the Leafs won, 6–4, with Toronto defenceman Jamie Macoun having the presence of mind to grab the last puck as a souvenir for his two-year-old son Colin. The win was a little revenge for Toronto, which had lost its first game at Maple Leaf Gardens, in 1931, to Chicago (Harold March scored the first goal at the Gardens and kept the puck).

Chicago met Toronto in the first round of the 1994 playoffs, but the last game in the Madhouse on Madison ended in a 1–0 defeat.

However, for those who witnessed one, the memory of a night at the Stadium lives on.

"If your heart wasn't pumping by the time you made it to the top of those steps, then you weren't alive," said former referee Bryan Lewis. "It was great to work there, because the crowd wouldn't let your mind get out of the game."

Blackhawks fans gather outside the Stadium in Chicago, ready to roar. (Le Studio du Hockey/Hockey Hall of Fame)

69

THE CUP RETURNS TO NEW YORK

The 1993–94 season was different, right from the beginning.

The New York Rangers went to London, England, for a couple of exhibition wins against the Toronto Maple Leafs.

A 12–0–2 run from late October to late November put the Rangers out front and in first place for good. The start had the loyal fan base believing this was the year the half-century Stanley Cup drought would end.

It had been 54 long years since Hall of Famer Bryan Hextall scored early in overtime at Maple Leaf Gardens to push the Rangers past the Toronto Maple Leafs in six games for their last Stanley Cup championship, in 1940.

There had been teases in the ensuing five decades. The Rangers made trips to the championship series in 1950, 1972, and 1979, but lost each time. There was frustration in seeing expansion teams such as the Philadelphia Flyers, New York Islanders, and Edmonton Oilers break through in the 1970s and '80s for a combined 10 titles.

So when the Rangers cruised through the 1993–94 regular season with a Presidents' Trophy–winning 52 victories and

Television cameras caught a fan in the stands at Madison Square Garden with a sign held high that read: "Now I Can Die in Peace."

then ended the postseason with dramatic seven-game wins in the Eastern Conference final and the Cup final, a lot of emotion poured out in Midtown Manhattan on June 14, 1994.

"The waiting is over," roared the Rangers' veteran play-by-play man Sam Rosen after Craig MacTavish won a last-second faceoff against Vancouver Canucks forward Pavel Bure to the right of New York goalie Mike Richter.

"The New York Rangers are the Stanley Cup champions," Rosen continued. "And this one will last a lifetime."

Television cameras caught a fan in the stands at Madison Square Garden with a sign held high that read: "Now I Can Die in Peace."

Grown men and women openly wept in the stands.

To get to that moment wasn't easy. After the Rangers missed the playoffs the previous spring, Mike Keenan was brought in as coach. Steve Larmer and Nick Kypreos were added in an early-season trade, while Brian Noonan, Stephane Matteau, Glenn Anderson, and MacTavish joined the team at the trade deadline.

Anderson and MacTavish were the latest players stockpiled from the Edmonton Oilers dynasty by Rangers general

manager Neil Smith. They joined Mark Messier, Adam Graves, Jeff Beukeboom, Kevin Lowe, and Esa Tikkanen.

Alexei Kovalev, Alexander Karpovtsev, Sergei Nemchinov, and Sergei Zubov also would play prominent roles and become the first Russians to have their names engraved on the Cup.

As smoothly as the regular season transpired, as well as the first-round sweep of the rival Islanders and the five-game victory against the Washington Capitals in the second round, the collars tightened for the Blueshirts in the conference final and championship series.

The New Jersey Devils had a 3–2 series lead in the East final. That's when captain Messier uttered his famous Game 6 guarantee of a victory. He went out and scored a hat trick in a 4–2 road win. Then Matteau scored in Game 7 double overtime to win the series.

The Rangers lost the Final opener, 3–2, in overtime at home but responded with three wins in a row. The Canucks, however, forced a seventh and deciding game, with a 6–3 win in Manhattan and a 4–1 victory in Vancouver.

Rangers defenceman Brian Leetch and Graves put their team in front, 2–0, with first-period goals. Canucks captain Trevor Linden scored a shorthanded goal early in the second period, but Messier restored his club's two-goal lead with a power-play marker later in the middle 20 minutes.

Linden pulled his team close again with a power-play goal early in the third period. As the celebration revved up, the final 90 seconds took forever to play out, as Vancouver players Jeff Brown and Bure drew icing calls from linesman Kevin Collins.

Closing games out had not been the Rangers' strength in this playoff run. They had blown final-minute leads

New York Rangers captain Mark Messier, Brian Leetch, and other teammates embrace after beating Vancouver 3-2 to win the series and take home the Cup. (Doug MacLellan/Hockey Hall of Fame)

213

NHL Commissioner Gary Bettman presents Mark Messier with the Stanley Cup. (Doug MacLellan/Hockey Hall of Fame)

twice in the conference final against the Devils, as well as in the series opener against Vancouver.

There only were 1.6 seconds left when MacTavish lined up against Bure in the Rangers zone. As MacTavish shovelled the puck into the corner, his teammates began jumping for joy.

There was one exception. Larmer had pinned Brown in the corner as the two met at the puck after the buzzer sounded. It was almost as if there was disbelief from Larmer that the drought was over. He took no chance.

"We're going to celebrate this like we've never celebrated anything in our lives," Messier screamed after winning his sixth Stanley Cup. "Once you get a taste of the Cup, you never want to lose it.

"I'm so numb, I don't know what to say. This is completely different—the pressure, the magnitude of being under the microscope, erasing all the ghosts."

Trying to exorcise those ghosts had caught the attention of the sporting world. Even though the New York Knicks were simultaneously involved in the NBA final against the Houston Rockets, sports fans watched every step of the Rangers' Stanley Cup chase.

Game 7 drew a record national-cable rating of 5.2—or 3.28 million—homes for ESPN, despite a blackout in the New York area to protect Madison Square Garden Network. The previous high was 5.0 for Game 7 of the 1987 final between the Flyers and Oilers.

The CBC broadcast in Canada pulled in 4.957 million viewers for the most-watched CBC sports program at that time.

"The Stanley Cup is what we all play for and the Cup here in New York is just amazing," Leetch said amid the dressing room celebration afterward. "This was the toughest game I've ever been a part of, just so tough to win.

"It wasn't the 54 years, it was just never having been through it before. Mark kept telling me the fourth game would be the toughest you'll ever have to win in your life, and it was.

JEAN BELIVEAU'S
POWER-PLAY HAT TRICK

I n the early days of the NHL, players served hard time for a minor penalty. They could not return to the ice until the entire two minutes had elapsed, even if the opposition scored a goal, or two or three, during the power play.

For teams that took too many penalties or weren't very good at penalty killing, that was a problem. Especially when the opposition was loaded with offensive firepower.

Which brings us to the game played on November 5, 1955, at the Montreal Forum.

Already having led the league in scoring during the early part of the decade with the likes of Maurice "Rocket" Richard, Bernie "Boom Boom" Geoffrion, and Bert Olmstead, the Montreal Canadiens were about to embark on a run of five consecutive Stanley Cup championships. But another significant player had just been added to the arsenal.

Jean Beliveau, a six-foot-three centre, had become a full-time Canadien in 1954–55, finishing third in scoring with 73 points in 70 games, and was bent on improving on that output.

He was frustrated in the first month of the '55–56 schedule, later claiming he "must have hit 15 posts," before coach Toe

> In the span of 44 seconds, Beliveau had a hat trick—all three goals on the same power play, a record that still stands.

Blake suggested he shoot at the net as a whole and stop zeroing in on a particular corner or a perceived goalie weakness.

With the Boston Bruins in town, he was about to put that advice to good use in a tour-de-force performance that would lead the NHL to change its rule governing the man advantage.

The Bruins took a 2–0 lead in the first period, but Cal Gardner drew a penalty with 10 seconds to play. Then, just 16 seconds into the second, Boston took another minor, this time on defenceman Hal Laycoe.

For the five-on-three power play, Beliveau was sent out with Richard and Olmstead on his wings and two other future Hall of Famers, Doug Harvey and Tom Johnson, on the blue line. It was feeding time.

It took only 26 seconds for Beliveau to score, receiving an Olmstead pass from the corner, and beating goalie Terry Sawchuk. At 1:06 of the period, Olmstead set up Beliveau again, and once more at 1:26. In the span of 44 seconds, Beliveau had a hat trick—all three goals on the same power play, a record that still stands. Late in the third, he added another goal—this one at even strength—to make the final score 4–2 for Montreal.

Incensed at referee Jerry Olinski for putting his team two men short, Boston coach Milt Schmidt harangued him and the Bruins threw objects onto the ice from their bench.

It was the first of many nights on which teams would fall victim to Montreal's predatory offence and a power play so loaded with firepower it sometimes featured 50-goal forward Geoffrion on the point.

That season, the Canadiens scored 222 goals in all, eight times with a second power-play goal on the same penalty. Beliveau won the 1955–56 scoring title with 47 goals and 88 points, nine more than Detroit's Gordie Howe.

But the other five teams had seen enough. League president Clarence Campbell was already considering a change to the power-play rule, and the clubs pressed for penalties to end after one goal.

The motion passed by a 5–1 vote, with dissenting Canadiens GM Frank Selke snapping at his colleagues, "Go out and get your own power play."

Joseph Hector "Toe" Blake watches from the bench in the Montreal Forum during his first season as an NHL coach in 1955-56. (Studio Alain Brouillard/Hockey Hall of Fame)

A portrait of Jean Beliveau as a member of the Montreal Canadiens during the 1953-54 NHL season. (Louis Jaques/Hockey Hall of Fame)

THE PHILADELPHIA FLYERS
WIN THE FIRST EXPANSION CUP

There was no official race to become the first expansion team to win a Stanley Cup.

But when the Los Angeles Kings, Minnesota North Stars, Oakland (later California Golden) Seals, Philadelphia Flyers, Pittsburgh Penguins, and St. Louis Blues entered the NHL in 1967, doubling the league's size from six to 12 teams, everyone was wondering how long it would take for one of these "second six" clubs to win their first championship.

The Blues skated to the front of the pack as soon as the expansion era opened its doors, with three straight visits to the Stanley Cup Final. They didn't win, but it was becoming apparent that one of their fellow expansion clubs just might. By the end of their sixth season, the Flyers had become legitimate contenders.

They had a world-class goaltender in Bernie Parent; leadership and determination in their young captain, Bobby Clarke from Flin Flon, Manitoba; team toughness from a handful of players led by Dave Schultz; and a peculiar but effective coach in Fred "The Fog" Shero.

> "There are a lot of great teams that didn't win the Stanley Cup because they lacked great coaching."

"We had all the ingredients in terms of what it took to win in the way the game was played back then," Clarke said. "We had a lot of talent, great goaltending, a strong middle, and toughness."

That aggressiveness prompted *Philadelphia Bulletin* reporter Jack Chevalier and editor Pete Cafone to tab the team as the Broad Street Bullies in January 1973.

They entered the playoffs that spring with a 50–16–12 record for 112 points, second only to the 113 points put up by Bobby Orr and the 52–17–9 Boston Bruins.

Parent, Gary Dornhoefer, Ed Van Impe, and Joe Watson had become Flyers via the 1967 expansion draft, and they were all still there on May 19 when Philadelphia became the first of the six expansion clubs to win the Stanley Cup.

Parent, who was traded to the Toronto Maple Leafs but returned to the Flyers after a stop in the WHA with the Philadelphia Blazers, won the Vezina Trophy in 1973–74. His peers voted Clarke winner of the Lester B. Pearson Award (now called the Ted Lindsay Award) as the most outstanding player. Shero won the Jack Adams Trophy as coach of the year.

"I don't think you can win a Stanley Cup without a great coach," Clarke said. "Fred was an introvert who knew how to get the most out of his players, to play their best at the right time, to have each of them pulling together on the rope in the right direction.

"There are a lot of great teams that didn't win the Stanley Cup because they lacked great coaching."

Parent was named to the league's first all-star team with Orr and his Boston teammates, Phil Esposito and Ken Hodge. The second team included Clarke and Philadelphia defenceman Barry Ashbee, along with Boston's Wayne Cashman.

For all the Flyers' skill, there was plenty of focus on the team's other tactics. They had seven players finish with more than 100 penalty minutes in the regular season: Schultz (348), Andre Dupont (216), Don Saleski (131), Bob Kelly (131), Dornhoefer (125), Van Impe (119), and Clarke (113).

But it bothers Clarke that the Flyers were criticized for their fighting ways and winning through intimidation.

"The way I see it, teams were tough back then," Clarke said. "Before we became tough, St. Louis was tougher than us and Boston certainly was tougher than us. The league was tough back then and we needed tough personnel to compete with them.

"People say we fought our way to the championship. But we had plenty of talent and we proved that with back-to-back Stanley Cups. Rick MacLeish scored 50 goals and Bill Flett scored 43 the year before we won our first Stanley Cup. Bill Barber became a 50-goal scorer. We added Reggie Leach and he scored 61."

In the spring of 1974, the Flyers opened with a first-round sweep of the Atlanta Flames. Philadelphia then staved off an upset-minded New York Rangers team in a seven-game semifinal.

This set up a clash between the Flyers and Bruins in a much-anticipated Final. The Bruins were considered the heavy favourites, having won the Stanley Cup in 1969–70 and 1971–72. Boston also had the home-ice advantage.

In the series opener, the game was tied, 2–2, when the Flyers had an open net late in the game. But Orr saved the day with a block and then took the puck into the other end of the rink to score the game winner.

The Flyers, however, rebounded two nights later with a 3–2 victory. Dupont scored with 52 seconds left in the third period to tie the game. Clarke then scored in overtime.

Coach of the Philadelphia Flyers, Fred Shero, guides his team to victory during the 1974-75 season. (Frank Prazak/Hockey Hall of Fame)

The captain's timely goal was believed to be the biggest of the series because the Flyers were tied as they headed home, where they had been dominant all season long. But Clarke dismisses the notion that his overtime winner was any more important than other key goals in the series.

"What if the Bruins come back to win the series?" Clarke reasoned. "It was bigger because we won, but not any bigger than other goals, like MacLeish's goal in the final game."

The Flyers returned home to win twice, but the Bruins forced a Game 6 when they beat Philadelphia, 5–1, at Boston Garden. MacLeish scored the lone goal in the first period of the series finale as Parent earned the shutout and Conn Smythe Trophy honours.

The Flyers finished the postseason a perfect 9–0 at the Spectrum. Added to their triumphant ways at home was their good-luck charm, singer Kate Smith. Back in December 1969, in place of the national anthem, the Flyers had begun playing a recording of Smith belting out Irving Berlin's "God Bless America."

The Flyers had a 19–1–1 record when they employed the Smith recording. She showed up to sing the song in person before Game 3 of the Stanley Cup final, and her near-perfect record stayed intact. She took the microphone again, prior to Game 6. Esposito tried to break the curse by presenting Smith with flowers, but the Flyers prevailed and made history.

"Ladies and gentlemen, the Flyers are going to win the Stanley Cup," screamed legendary Philadelphia play-by-play broadcaster Gene Hart in his call. "The Flyers win the Stanley Cup. The Flyers win the Stanley Cup. The Flyers have won the Stanley Cup."

Dave "the Hammer" Schultz, one of the Philadelphia Flyers' toughest players, is separated from his opponent by linesmen. (Graphic Artists/Hockey Hall of Fame)

72

WAYNE GRETZKY'S BIG YEAR

n November 1981, soap opera fan Wayne Gretzky was invited to make a cameo appearance on *The Young and the Restless.*

Portraying a thug, he was given one line that afternoon: "I'm Wayne. From the Edmonton operation."

No. 99 was definitely miscast in that role, but he certainly beat up the NHL record book in the 1981–82 season. Few would recognize it after Gretzky amassed 92 goals, 120 assists, and 212 points, all in 80 games. It had been barely a decade since the 100-point barrier was broken. Now came a kid barely out of his teens who reached triple figures in assists alone.

The same month as his "acting" debut, Gretzky scored seven goals in seven periods to launch his assault on the league's Mount Everest of quests: 50 goals in 50 games. It soon became clear he would not just succeed, but exceed. Gretzky had 31 goals in his first 26 games, then stalled briefly, going four games without a goal. Just before Christmas he turned it back on with an incredible 10 goals and 19 points in a four-game stretch that bookended the holiday. With 45 goals in 38 games, on December 30 the Philadelphia Flyers arrived at Northlands Coliseum, and Gretzky's march toward 50 turned into a sprint.

Edmonton fans hoped Gretzky might manage one or two against the Flyers, which would give him an excellent shot at scoring his 50th during the trio of home games that would open the new calendar year. With the finish line in sight, Gretzky had other ideas.

He fired two goals on Pete Peeters in the first period, and then added one each in the second and third to put him at 49 on the season, giving his Oilers a 6–3 lead that Philadelphia narrowed to 6–5 midway through the third period.

What happened next was hockey history— not to mention the impetus for a challenging trivia question: Who was the goalie who gave up Gretzky's 50th goal in his 39th game? The answer is no one—Peeters had been pulled for a sixth attacker. With only seconds left to play, Oilers netminder Grant Fuhr steered the puck to Glenn Anderson, who set Gretzky free to beat the sprawling Bill Barber, who was trying in vain to block the empty net.

"People often ask me about my favourite record," Gretzky said. "And I tell them that's the one. I know that records are made to be broken and that's one of the attractions of sport, but I think that one will be hardest to break."

Gretzky amassed 92 goals, 120 assists, and 212 points, all in 80 games.

Gretzky had 50 goals under his belt, and the season was only half done. After his 21st birthday on January 26, the next plateau was Phil Esposito's NHL record of 76 goals in a season. In late February, Edmonton scored seven times against each of Minnesota, Hartford, and Detroit. In all three games, Gretzky registered at least five points, including his record-tying 76th goal.

The league brought big Phil into Buffalo for the February 24 game to witness Gretzky breaking his record.

Esposito had played his last NHL game, for the New York Rangers, just the year before.

After 40 minutes against the Sabres, Gretzky had managed only two early assists. But the fans at Memorial Auditorium would not be disappointed. Gretzky stole the puck at the Buffalo blue line and put goal no. 77 past Don Edwards at 13:24 of the third period. Having broken both the Esposito record and the 3–3 tie, he added two more goals for emphasis.

Wayne Gretzky of the Edmonton Oilers celebrates his record-setting 77th NHL goal on February 24, 1982, at the Memorial Auditorium in Buffalo. (Bob Shaver/Hockey Hall of Fame)

Soon afterwards, Bobby Orr's single-season record of 102 assists also fell, as did Esposito's all-time high of 152 points. Gretzky became the first NHL player to break 200 points, and the 212th came in the last game of the season, as he assisted on Jari Kurri's power-play goal in a 2–1 win over Winnipeg.

Gretzky's 92-goal output has been approached only three times, all within the decade that followed. Gretzky himself scored 87 in 1983–84, while Mario Lemieux managed 85 in 1988–89, and Brett Hull split the difference with 86 in 1990–91.

Gretzky certainly reaped the rewards of his amazing year, starting with the Hart Trophy. It was his third of eight consecutive MVP nods and the first unanimous vote among the hockey writers, Orr's big years included. Gretzky landed 65 of 65 first-place votes.

He was also the runaway winner of the Lester B. Pearson Award (the players' pick as MVP, the first year he'd ever won it), and made it onto the cover of *Sports Illustrated* as Sportsman of the Year, a rare honour for a hockey player.

With Gretzky at the helm, Edmonton also became the first team to break the 400-goal barrier. His ability was head and shoulders above anyone in the league—or even on his own team. Known as the fun-loving "boys on the bus," the young Oilers' star power was still in its formative stages. Gretzky outpointed his nearest teammate, Glenn Anderson, by 107. Defenceman Paul Coffey, the so-called fourth forward, was 123 behind. Mark Messier? Try 124.

The 1981–82 regular season set the table for Gretzky's domination of the game. He would retire as the only man to score 1,000 goals, 2,000 assists, and 3,000 points (all including playoffs).

73

THE FIRST WINTER CLASSIC

Call it the perfect storm. Because it really was.

On January 1, 2008, at Ralph Wilson Stadium in Buffalo, home of the Bills of the National Football League, with 71,217 looking on and millions more watching on television, the NHL staged its first Winter Classic, a regular-season game played outdoors, and it couldn't have unfolded any better.

The temperature was just cold enough, at 33 degrees Fahrenheit, but not too cold, and before the game was over, heavy snow was falling while rising star Sidney Crosby scored a shootout goal to give the Pittsburgh Penguins a 2–1 win over the host Sabres.

From these beginnings, amid what someone described as a "snow globe" setting, the Winter Classic has grown into an annual tradition and then some. Through 2016–17, a total of 22 outdoor games have been staged, attracting 1,208,317 fans.

Played annually, almost always on New Year's Day, the Winter Classic has become the NHL's annual showcase event.

It has happened every year since its inception, except 2013, when there was another lockout.

After Buffalo, the road show moved to Chicago's Wrigley Field, Boston's Fenway Park, Heinz Field in Pittsburgh, and Philadelphia's Citizens Bank Park. The 2013 game was to be played at the "Big House" at the University of Michigan, but had to be rescheduled for the following year, when it drew a record crowd of 105,491 fans. The 2015 game was held at Nationals Park in Washington, D.C., and then it was on to Foxboro, Massachusetts—home of the NFL's New England Patriots—and on January 2, 2017, the Blues and Blackhawks met at Busch Stadium in St. Louis, one day after the Toronto Maple Leafs and Detroit Red Wings played the Centennial Classic outdoors at Exhibition Stadium in Toronto.

Each Winter Classic has had its own charm, but the first one was truly special, with its magical setting, the feeling that hockey was revisiting its roots, and an incredible game.

"When you see 70,000 people jammed into a stadium to watch hockey, it's a good sign," said Crosby. "The atmosphere and environment, I don't think you can beat that."

Both teams wore throwback uniforms—the Penguins in their late-1960s powder blue, while Sabres wore the blue, white, and gold they'd sported from the early '80s to the mid-'90s.

The Penguins scored on the first shift, 21 seconds into the game. Crosby went hard to the Sabres net, but was stopped

Each Winter Classic has had its own charm, but the first one was truly special.

225

by goalie Ryan Miller, wearing a toque on top of his mask. Colby Armstrong was able to tap in the rebound.

The Sabres tied the game two minutes into the second period, with defenceman Brian Campbell beating goalie Ty Conklin, who was excellent all day. Interestingly, Conklin had been the Sabres' backup goalie the previous season and was playing only because the Penguins' No. 1 goalie, Marc-Andre Fleury, had a sore ankle.

Conklin had also been the starter for the Edmonton Oilers in the Heritage Classic, played in the frigid outdoors in Edmonton in November 2003. But on that day the Oilers lost, 4–3, to the Montreal Canadiens in front of 57,167 fans.

Back in Buffalo, with the snow continuing to fall and the crowd full of energy, it was Crosby who gave the Penguins the win with his shootout goal. It couldn't have been scripted any better.

73
100

Pittsburgh Penguins captain Sidney Crosby slips the puck behind Buffalo Sabres goalie Ryan Miller, winning the shootout and the first Winter Classic, held at Ralph Wilson Stadium in Orchard Park, New York. (Kevin Cobello/Hockey Hall of Fame)

JACQUES PLANTE WEARS A MASK

Among other things, Joseph Jacques Omer Plante was renowned for his knitting.

He was also pretty good at stopping pucks and stringing together wins.

Through a marvellous Hall of Fame career that spanned 19 seasons, Plante will always be remembered as the first goalie to regularly wear a mask in NHL games.

In hindsight, it's hard to believe that 41 years of NHL hockey passed before a goaltender began routinely protecting his face.

Clint Benedict of the Montreal Maroons wore a rudimentary mask on February 20, 1930, to protect his broken nose. Roughly six weeks earlier, he had taken a shot from Montreal Canadiens star Howie Morenz. When he returned to play the Americans in New York, he wore a leather mask, but the protection was discarded a few games later because he had difficulty finding the puck at his feet.

Goaltenders who represented Japan in the 1936 Winter Olympic Games wore masks, and 18 years later, when the Kenora Thistles, champions of the Western Intermediate Hockey League in Canada, played a 10-game series of exhibition games in Japan, the goalies there were still wearing them.

According to the book *Saving Face: The Art and History of the Goalie Mask* by Jim Hynes and Gary Smith, the first netminder to wear a mask was Elizabeth Graham, who played goal for the 1927 Queen's University hockey team. Her father made her wear a fencing mask to protect her teeth.

However, no goaltender had ever worn a mask on a permanent basis in the NHL until November 1, 1959. It was not the only innovation the native of Shawinigan Falls, Quebec, pioneered in his long and storied career.

The oldest of 11 children, Plante suffered from asthma as a child, and as a result he gravitated toward playing goal. Though he was recruited by many teams, Plante waited until he finished high school before he signed with the Quebec Citadelles of the Quebec Junior Hockey League in 1947. Plante missed playing with another young star, Jean Beliveau, by one season.

The pair would star together soon enough, however.

Plante caught the eye of Montreal Canadiens general manager Frank Selke when the Citadelles upset the Montreal Junior Canadiens to win the 1948 Q JHL championship. Selke invited Plante to the Canadiens' NHL training camp, and he signed with *les Habitants* the following year.

> It's hard to believe 41 years of NHL hockey passed before a goaltender began routinely protecting his face.

When a shot from Rangers forward Andy Bathgate broke Jacques Plante's nose and cut him for seven stitches, the Montreal goaltender put on a mask he'd been trying in practice and returned to the game. (Bettman/Contributor/Getty Images)

Plante began his climb to the Canadiens, playing with the Montreal Royals, who then toiled in the Quebec Senior Hockey League. The 19-year-old broke in with another rookie, Verdun's Dollard St. Laurent, who played on the blue line. The pair would later go on to win four Stanley Cups together in Montreal in the 1950s.

Plante always displayed a cerebral approach to the game and was not afraid to defy conventional wisdom. In the minors he worked on several aspects of his trade that were previously unheard of for a goaltender. In the process, he was ready to revolutionize the game by the time he reached the NHL for good in 1954.

For one, Plante would go behind the net to stop the puck for his defencemen, which wasn't a play coaches desired. Eddie Shore, as coach in Springfield of the American Hockey League, went so far as to use a rope to tie his goaltender's neck to the crossbar so that he wouldn't leave his feet or crease in practice.

Plante also got involved in the play and became the first netminder to raise his arm to let his defencemen know that icing was about to be called.

He constantly refined his game and led the Canadiens to five consecutive Stanley Cups between 1956 and 1960, in the process winning the Vezina Trophy for five consecutive years. Both achievements are still records.

It was during the final season of that five-year run that Plante introduced his everlasting gift to hockey: he put on a mask in practice. A hockey fan named Bill Burchmore, who worked in the fibreglass business, had seen Plante get cut in a game and asked if he could make him a moulded mask.

During that historic game in New York, on November 1, 1959, Rangers forward Andy Bathgate unleashed a shot

Jacques Plante guards the net after losing his stick during the 1960 Stanley Cup Final. (Imperial Oil–Turofsky/Hockey Hall of Fame)

that broke Plante's nose and cut him for seven stitches. Miraculously, Plante was able to return to the game, but would only do so if he could wear the face mask.

Grudgingly, Canadiens coach Toe Blake gave his permission. He really didn't have any other choice, because teams didn't carry backup goalies. And Blake viewed the mask as a temporary fix to get Plante through that game. The goalie thought otherwise and wore the mask through an eventual 18-game unbeaten streak. The discussion between coach and player subsided considerably after that stretch.

Just as Plante would knit his own toques, he made his own masks, constantly upgrading the material to make the protection stronger and lighter. Shortly thereafter, he began to produce masks for other goaltenders.

Despite a sixth Vezina Trophy and the Hart Trophy as the league's most valuable player in 1962, Plante's relationship with Blake continued to erode. Montreal traded Plante to the Rangers, where he enjoyed limited success over two seasons while playing with a damaged right knee. He retired in 1965 after a sparkling 13-year career.

Plante's nickname, "Jake the Snake," had actually been a misnomer. In reality, he perfected a standup style that always kept him square to the shooter and in position to make saves and stop rebounds. He was also not afraid to come out of his crease to minimize the shooter's angle. It was a style that served him well after he came out of retirement in 1968.

By then, the NHL had expanded to 12 teams and the coach of the St. Louis Blues—Scotty Bowman, who grew up in the Montreal Canadiens system—offered Plante the opportunity to return to the league. Planted joined another future Hall of Famer, Glenn Hall, to give St. Louis a tandem that led them to their second and third straight appearances in the Stanley Cup final, in 1969 and '70.

Once again, the mask saved Plante from catastrophic results. In the 1970 final against Montreal, Plante took another shot to the face on a deflection and later claimed that the mask saved his life.

His NHL career continued when he was traded to the Maple Leafs in 1970, and the 41-year-old responded with a league-best goals-against average of 1.88 and earned second-team all-star recognition.

Plante played three seasons in Toronto before he was traded to Boston near the 1973 trade deadline. He finished his career the next year, playing with the Edmonton Oilers of the World Hockey Association.

In all, Plante played 19 seasons in the NHL and WHA, and finished with six Stanley Cups, seven Vezina Trophies, seven all-star selections, and a Hart Trophy. Plante became an Honoured Member of the Hockey Hall of Fame in 1978 and passed away in 1986.

From his rudimentary fibreglass original that clung to the face, masks and the protection they offer have improved greatly and even changed the way goalies stop the puck. The designs of the masks have evolved as well. Hockey is a rare professional sport in North America that allows a player the opportunity to individualize his equipment. It's a privilege extended only to goalies and only to their masks, which often sport elaborate artwork.

This practice began in 1967 with Gerry Cheevers's famous mask. The Boston goaltender had his trainer, John "Frosty" Forristall, use a marker to draw stitches on all the places Cheevers would have needed them had he not worn the protection.

As the NHL enters its second century, designs have saluted everything from action heroes to horror author Stephen King's rabid (and fortunately fictional) St. Bernard, Cujo.

The last NHL goalie to play without a mask was the Pittsburgh Penguins' Andy Brown, in 1974 (he played without a mask for a few more seasons in the WHA).

75

EXPANSION THROUGH THE 1990S

The NHL had gone a dozen years without adding any new franchises, no new blood following a decade of expansion, introducing several new teams in the late 1960s and '70s.

But starting in 1991, when the San Jose Sharks became the NHL's 22nd team, the league began a period of rapid growth. By 2000, the NHL would include 30 teams, a number that would remain the same for the next 17 years.

The Sharks were the first into that new wave of expansion, an addition that was stocked partially by an expansion draft and partially by players from the Minnesota North Stars, who would move to Dallas in 1993, leading eventually to one of the final expansion teams of the era, the Minnesota Wild.

The Sharks, who reached their first Stanley Cup Final in 2016, lost 58 games in their first season and an NHL–record 71 games in their second before becoming one of the league's most reliable playoff contenders, making the playoffs in 18 of the next 22 seasons.

In 1992, two more teams, the Ottawa Senators and the Tampa Bay Lightning, came on board. Their arrival marked old and new territory for the NHL. The original version of the Senators had played in the NHL from 1917 to 1934,

winning the Stanley Cup four times in the 1920s. The Lightning became the league's first team in Florida.

One year later, the NHL added the Florida Panthers (based in Miami) and the Mighty Ducks of Anaheim, two more teams in warm-weather markets. From 1991 through 1993, the league had expanded by five teams, bringing its total to 26.

After a five-year break, the next four teams arrived in rapid succession.

The Nashville Predators, who made the Stanley Cup Final for the first time in 2017, joined the league in 1998. The Atlanta Thrashers were added in 1999, and the Columbus Blue Jackets and Minnesota Wild became the 29th and 30th teams in 2000. The Thrashers relocated to become the new Winnipeg Jets in 2011.

Not only were the new teams in American cities, but the NHL continued a trend of locating franchises in non-traditional hockey markets, with the exception of the return to Minneapolis-St. Paul.

Though most of the expansion teams of the 1990s started off slowly, some found success far more swiftly than many expected. For instance, the Sharks reached the Stanley Cup Playoffs and won a series in their third season.

Joel Bouchard pursues the puck during the inaugural season of the Nashville Predators, January 28, 1999, in Buffalo. (Dave Sandford/Hockey Hall of Fame)

With a rat serving as their good-luck charm, the Panthers reached the Stanley Cup Final in their third season before being swept by the powerful Colorado Avalanche.

The Wild got to the Western Conference final in their third season before being swept by Anaheim.

Of the nine teams that joined the NHL in the 1990s, six have reached the Stanley Cup Final: the Sharks, Senators, Lightning, Panthers, Ducks, and Predators. Two of those six, the Lightning in 2004 and the Anaheim Ducks in 2007, have won the Stanley Cup.

Anaheim had to change its name from the Mighty Ducks (named after the movie by The Walt Disney Company, which owned the team before selling it in 2005) to the Ducks. Anaheim won the Cup in their first season with the new name.

The Senators nearly made another Stanley Cup Final in 2017, reaching Game 7 of the Eastern Conference final against the eventual champion Pittsburgh Penguins. If they had, it would have marked the third time a team in the 1990s expansion group reached a second Final. The Lightning have made two Finals, as have the Ducks.

In the fall of 2017, the NHL welcomed to the ice its 31st franchise, the Vegas Golden Knights.

Pat Jablosnki tends goal for the expansion Tampa Bay Lightning during their first game, October 7, 1992, at Expo Hall in Tampa, Florida. (O-Pee-Chee/Hockey Hall of Fame)

76

MARIO LEMIEUX TAKES CONTROL

There was no single player to whom Mario Lemieux could be compared. Rather, anyone trying to describe one of the greatest players ever to grace the NHL inevitably had to fall back on a combination of greats that preceded him.

Born in Montreal in 1965, Lemieux possessed the vision and hands of Gretzky in a body bigger than Beliveau's, with a shot as accurate as Bossy's and the moves of his idol, Guy Lafleur. All rolled into a six-foot-four, 200-pound frame.

Lemieux was an impressionable teenager when his hometown team reeled off four consecutive Stanley Cups between 1976 and 1979. The youngster obviously took notes as he watched.

Lemieux was chosen by Laval first overall in the 1981 Quebec Major Junior Hockey League Draft. He collected 114 goals and 280 points during his first two seasons, but exploded the following season. He led the Voisin to a berth in the 1984 Memorial Cup championship while amassing a total of 334 points in the regular season and playoffs. In the process, he broke the single-season points record of his idol, Lafleur. Lemieux finished his three-year junior career with 562 points in 200 regular season games

> Born with a flair for the dramatic, Lemieux became the first player ever to score goals in five different ways during a single game.

and added 98 points in 44 playoff matches.

Lemieux was in the middle of two controversies before he even entered the NHL. Late in the 1983–84 season, the Pittsburgh Penguins and New Jersey Devils were neck and neck to finish in the league basement. The Penguins did their best to finish last and earn the right to draft this generational talent with the first-overall pick—to some people's minds, they did more than their best.

Then Lemieux defied convention and NHL tradition when Pittsburgh did select him in the NHL draft, held in his hometown on June 9, 1984. His refusal to don a Penguins sweater and shake the hand of general manager Eddie Johnston ignited a controversy (the two sides had already started contract negotiations, and they weren't going well).

But the kid from Montreal did not disappoint. Six days after his 19th birthday, he stole the spotlight in his first NHL game, and during the 16 seasons he played he shared it only with Wayne Gretzky. Only a pair of personal work stoppages, caused by a bad back and Hodgkin's lymphoma, ever slowed him down.

On his first big-league shift, Lemieux stripped the puck from perennial all-star Ray Bourque and beat goalie Pete

Pittsburgh Penguins captain Mario Lemieux celebrates after scoring against the Bostin Bruins during the 1991 Wales Conference final, on the way to the Penguins' first of two consecutive Stanley Cups. (Paul Bereswill/Hockey Hall of Fame)

Peeters with his first shot. That was a harbinger of things to come. He finished his rookie season with 100 points in 73 games and won the Calder Trophy as the league's top rookie.

It seems absurd to say Lemieux came of age *after* he had recorded a 141-point season, but his performance in the 1987 Canada Cup brought all his skills to the forefront. He led the hard-fought tournament with 11 goals in 9 games and saved his best for last.

The best-of-three final between Canada and the Soviet Union was a championship for the ages. Both countries won 6–5 decisions to set the stage for the winner-take-all final game at Hamilton's Copps Coliseum. With the score tied at five, and 1:26 left in the third period, Gretzky fed the puck to Lemieux, who scored the goal that gave Canada the series and catapulted him to another level of hockey history.

He recorded 168 points in 1987–88 and followed that up

with 199 points in 1988–89. Most important, in 1989 Pittsburgh made its first playoff appearance in Lemieux's five seasons with the club.

Born with a flair for the dramatic, Lemieux became the first player ever to score goals in five different ways during a single game. On New Year's Eve 1988, Lemieux toyed with the New Jersey Devils, potting an even-strength goal, a power-play marker, a shorthanded tally, a penalty-shot score, and an empty-netter.

At first blush, the lanky centreman had a good year statistically in 1989–90: 123 points in 59 games, including a 46-game point streak. But Lemieux's back became progressively worse—and it, not the opposition, ended the point streak. Ultimately, a herniated disc required surgery that was performed in the summer of 1990. But an infection led to a rare bone disease that sidelined Pittsburgh's captain for the first 50 games of the 1990–91 season.

No. 66 returned with a vengeance. Strengthened by trades that fortified Pittsburgh with such talents as Ron Francis, Ulf Samuelsson, Joe Mullen, and Larry Murphy, the Penguins marched to their first Stanley Cup. Despite constant back pain, Lemieux recorded 44 points in the post-season, second only to Wayne Gretzky's 47 in 1985, and was awarded the Conn Smythe Trophy.

Lemieux's penchant for the memorable play was in evidence in Game 2, when he stickhandled through two Minnesota North Stars and beat goaltender Jon Casey for a highlight-reel goal that will live in history.

That troubled back limited Lemieux to 64 games in 1991–92, but he still claimed his third Art Ross Trophy with 131 points. He also endured a broken hand in the playoffs, but still led Pittsburgh to its second consecutive title while earning his second Conn Smythe Trophy.

Lemieux had overcome many obstacles in his career, but nothing could prepare him for the diagnosis he received in January 1993, when he learned he had Hodgkin's lymphoma,

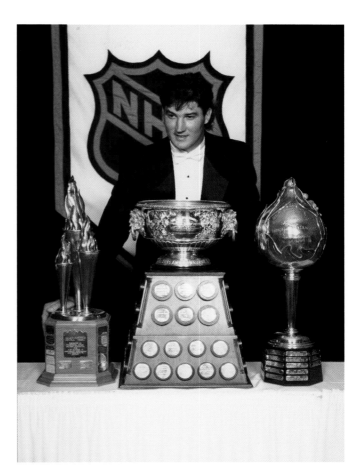

Mario Lemieux at the 1993 NHL Awards ceremony. (Doug MacLellan/Hockey Hall of Fame)

a form of blood cancer. He missed two months of the season while undergoing aggressive radiation treatment. His return to action in Philadelphia on the same day that he received his last treatment in Pittsburgh displayed the passion that was always masked by his shy, understated manner.

Exhaustion and continued back agony forced him to miss 60 games in 1993–94, and all of the following season. Lemieux returned for 1995–96 and once again claimed the Hart and Art Ross Trophies. He led the league in scoring the following season as well, but by then his body had experienced enough. He retired at the age of 32 with a resumé that included the Calder Trophy, the Bill Masterston Trophy for perseverance, sportsmanship, and dedication to the game, two Stanley Cups, two Conn Smythe Trophies, three Hart Trophies, four Lester B. Pearson Awards—now called the Ted Lindsay Award, awarded to the game's most outstanding player as chosen by his peers—and six Art Ross Trophies.

But if Mario Lemieux's career was a three-act play, the true denouement arrived in 2000. Financial troubles had forced the Penguins to declare bankruptcy in 1998. Over time, Lemieux parlayed money he was owed by the club into controlling interest of the organization, and he returned to the ice at the ripe age of 35, in part to help the team, but also because his young son, Austin, born in 1996, had never seen him play.

It was as if he had never left: 76 points in an injury-plagued 43 games. A hip condition was the latest addition to the long list of ailments, and between 2000–01 and 2005–06,

Lemieux managed to play only 170 of a possible 410 games, but still recorded 229 points.

The highlight for Lemieux in his final hockey hurrah occurred at the 2002 Winter Olympic Games in Salt Lake City. He was chosen as captain of Team Canada by general manager Wayne Gretzky, and together they orchestrated a gold medal. Lemieux had six points in five games, but it was what he didn't do with the puck that demonstrated his omnipresent flair for the dramatic.

Down 1–0 to the United States in the first period of the gold medal game, Lemieux allowed a Chris Pronger pass to go between his legs to Paul Kariya, who beat Mike Richter to spur Canada to a 5–2 victory. That decision displayed Lemieux's brilliant vision and spatial awareness.

The play was incomparable. Much like the player who made it happen.

Mario Lemieux with the Stanley Cup in 1992, celebrating in the dressing room of the Chicago Stadium after his Penguins beat the Blackhawks to win their second Stanley Cup. (Paul Bereswill/Hockey Hall of Fame)

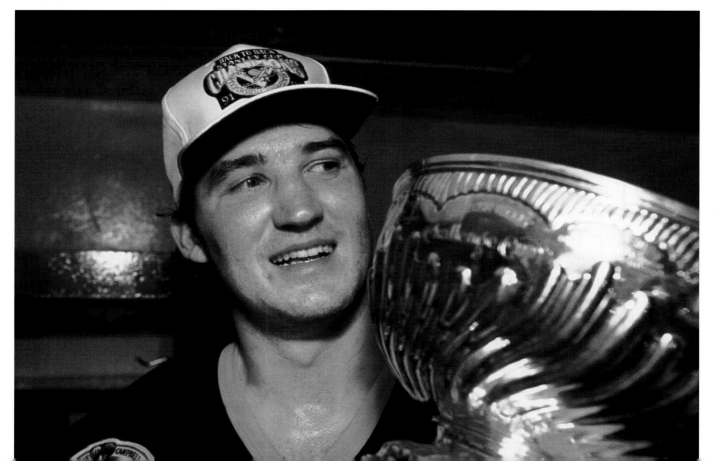

SCOTTY BOWMAN'S NINTH CUP

Scotty Bowman could have retired after coaching the Detroit Red Wings to back-to-back Stanley Cup championships in 1996–97 and 1997–98.

After all, he was 64 years old, and his eighth Stanley Cup as a coach matched the record held by his coaching idol, Toe Blake.

But Bowman wanted a ninth, so he could stand alone. That record-breaking moment came four years later.

As the final seconds ticked down on the Red Wings' five-game victory over the Carolina Hurricanes in the 2002 Stanley Cup final, Bowman left his usual place behind the Detroit bench, took off his dress shoes, and laced up a pair of skates to take one final victory lap.

Bowman had made the decision to retire during the scheduling break for the 2002 Winter Olympics in Salt Lake City, Utah. He told a few friends, including his longtime associate coach Barry Smith and his East Amherst, New York neighbour Harry Neale about his decision, but not even his wife, Suella, knew this was his last hurrah.

"I told my wife 10 minutes ago," the 68-year-old Bowman said on the ice at Joe Louis Arena. "She was kind of hoping

Bowman once said his two greatest days in hockey were his first Stanley Cup win in 1973 and his final win behind the bench.

I would retire. I just felt that it was time."

Bowman didn't want to tell anyone about his decision because he didn't want it to be a distraction down the stretch as the Red Wings chased another championship.

"I never told any [of the players] because I didn't feel that's what they wanted to hear anyways," he explained.

Bowman began coaching in his early 20s, after his playing career was cut short because of an injury suffered while playing with the Montreal Junior Canadiens.

The native of Verdun, Quebec took his first coaching job with a Junior B team, but he also had to work for a paint company to supplement his income.

On his lunch hour, he would slip into the Montreal Forum and study Blake as he conducted practice. It was a short time later that Sam Pollock took Bowman to Ottawa to help him run the Junior Canadiens when the team moved to the nation's capital. They won the 1957–58 Memorial Cup championship. Bowman was then assigned to run the Peterborough Petes.

He was eventually hired to coach the St. Louis Blues, who advanced to three consecutive Stanley Cup finals between 1968 and 1970.

Scotty Bowman was a head coach in the NHL for 30 years. (Graphic Artists/Hockey Hall of Fame)

He returned home to replace Al MacNeil as coach of the Canadiens in 1971. Bowman won his first Stanley Cup in his second season in Montreal and finished the decade with a string of four consecutive championships.

After that remarkable run, he departed to run the Buffalo Sabres as general manager, but failed to win a title there. The Pittsburgh Penguins then hired Bowman as their director of player personnel, but he found himself behind the bench again in 1991–92 after Penguins coach Bob Johnson was diagnosed with brain cancer.

Johnson had steered the Penguins to a Stanley Cup championship the previous season and Bowman followed suit for his sixth title.

He then moved to Detroit. The Red Wings ended a 42-year Stanley Cup drought under Bowman in 1996–97 with a sweep of the Philadelphia Flyers, followed by another four-game win over the Washington Capitals the next spring.

"I thought about retiring in 1998, and then came back for four more years," Bowman said. "I was fortunate I had

Head coach Scotty Bowman wore his skates to hoist the Stanley Cup for a record ninth and final time, after leading the Detroit Red Wings to a 2002 championship. (Elsa/Getty Images/NHLI)

three more chances to win another Cup, and I know it's time to go now."

After ending their lengthy Stanley Cup drought in 1997, Bowman believed the Red Wings won the following year because of a "win one for Vladdy" mentality. Hard-rock Detroit defenceman Vladimir Konstantinov had lost his career due to injuries suffered in a limousine accident the previous June.

The Colorado Avalanche eliminated the Red Wings in the 1999 and 2000 playoffs, and the Los Angeles Kings upset Detroit in the first round in 2001. But the following year, pursuing their coach's record ninth victory, the Red Wings were inspired to win for Stanley Cup–less veterans Steve Duchesne, Dominik Hasek, Fredrik Olausson, and Luc Robitaille, as well as pushing Bowman to his record.

"I have had a career that I never thought I would have had," Bowman said in his postgame press conference. "And it means a lot to leave on a winning note."

In total, Bowman steered teams to 16 Finals in his 32 years as a head coach in the NHL. He won a record 223 playoff games and 1,244 regular-season outings.

He has been part of 14 Stanley Cup–winning teams, including five as an executive—one each with the Penguins and Red Wings, as well as three working alongside his general manager son Stan with the Chicago Blackhawks. Only Jean Beliveau, with 17, has won more Stanley Cup rings.

"I have been pretty fortunate," he said. "I have to thank a lot of people, but the two I would thank the most are my wife, who I met in St. Louis when I was a young coach, and the other person I would thank immensely is Sam Pollock.

"He gave me my first job when I was 22 years of age. He had a lot of confidence in me, brought me to Ottawa, and brought me back to Montreal and started a run of a lot of Stanley Cups there—five of them. He was the general manager on four of them. Somebody has to take a chance on you, and he's the one that took the chance on me."

Bowman once said his two greatest days in hockey were his first Stanley Cup win in 1973 and his final win behind the bench.

"The fact that I had made up my mind not to coach the following year, I'm very fortunate because most coaches lose their last game and get fired. To be able to go out on a winning note was very special for me. It was just a nice way to do it, without any regrets or doubts.

"When we won it, it was a close game. I had the trainer all set up. I told him if we win, I'm going to put the skates on for the Cup. It was the first time that had happened.

"At that moment, when I had the Cup, to skate around was great. I wasn't able to do that as a player. But at that moment I felt good obviously because we had won, but I also felt good because I could finally say it was my last game and I was going out a winner."

THE PHILADELPHIA FLYERS'
UNBEATEN STREAK

Pat Quinn didn't see a record 35-game undefeated streak coming. Not by a long shot.

In fact, only two games into the 1979–80 schedule, the Philadelphia Flyers' head coach wasn't sure which way his team was headed.

Quinn was in his first full season behind the Flyers bench when a 5–2 win against the New York Islanders in the home opener was followed two nights later by a 9–2 drubbing at the hands of the Atlanta Flames on the road.

Quinn and the Flyers were five months removed from a devastating second-round, five-game defeat to the New York Rangers. It was an upset made worse by the fact the Rangers were coached by Fred Shero, the guru who had led the Flyers to back-to-back Stanley Cup championships in their mid-70s glory days.

Under Quinn, the Flyers were a team in transition. They still had Bobby Clarke, Bill Barber, Rick MacLeish, and Reggie Leach from the Stanley Cup days, but they were also relying on Ken Linseman, who was 21 and in his first full season with the Flyers, and 20-year-old rookie Brian Propp.

The goaltending tandem was made up of rookie Pete Peeters and veteran Phil Myre, while unknowns Norm Barnes, Frank Bathe, and Mike Busniuk made up half of the Flyers' blue-line corps.

Before the season began, the Flyers had announced that Clarke would be a player/assistant coach and Mel Bridgman would replace Clarke as captain.

"I had lots on my mind that night," Quinn recalled to the *Philadelphia Inquirer* on the 10th anniversary of the streak. "It was my first full season and I was doubting myself. Was I using the right goalie? Was I using the right lines?

"You get to thinking like that, and soon you start wondering if you're ever going to win another game."

Of course, the Flyers won more than a few games over the next three months. On October 14, the night after the Atlanta debacle, they defeated the Toronto Maple Leafs, 4–3, at the Spectrum, and the astonishing streak was on.

They won a couple more games before an entertaining 6–6 tie against the visiting Montreal Canadiens, who had won four Stanley Cups in a row, to prolong the streak.

The next thing the Flyers knew, they had reeled off nine consecutive victories over the Rangers, Detroit Red Wings, St. Louis Blues, Canadiens, Buffalo Sabres, Quebec Nordiques, Islanders, Vancouver Canucks, and Edmonton

Oilers. All of a sudden, that loss in Atlanta was a distant memory and the Flyers were 12–0–1 in their last 13 games.

"I knew a lot of people around the league and I can't tell you how many times people came up to me that year and said, 'How the heck are you guys doing this? With mirrors?'" Quinn said.

"They'd look and see defencemen with names like Norm Barnes, Mike Busniuk, and Frank Bathe and a winger like Al Hill, and they just couldn't understand how we were able to play so well."

The truth was, the Flyers were a decent team in a groove. The nine-game win streak ended, but the undefeated streak

Philadelphia captain Bobby Clarke led the 1979-80 Flyers on a record-setting 35-game unbeaten streak. (Lewis Portnoy/Hockey Hall of Fame)

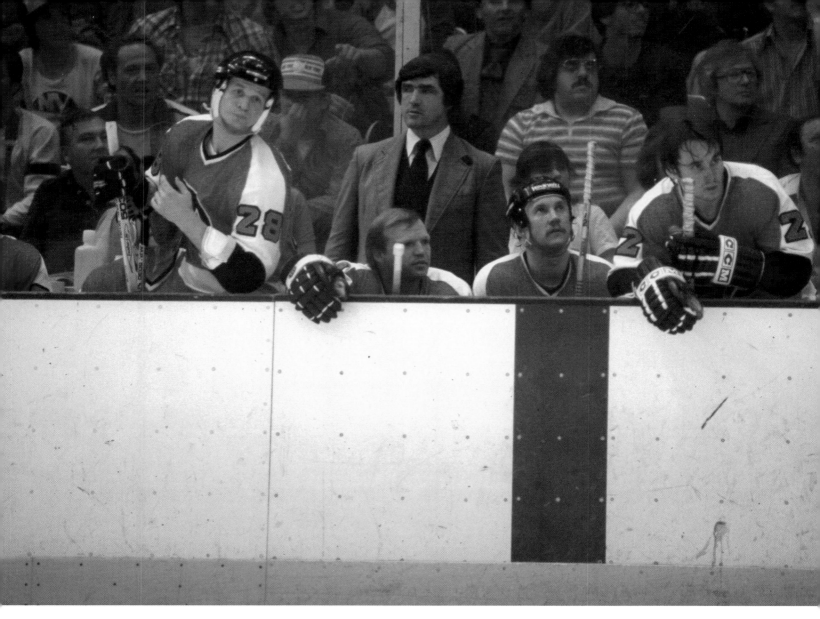

Flyers coach Pat Quinn saw his team through a record-setting 35-game unbeaten streak at the beginning of the 1979-80 season. (Jack Mecca/Hockey Hall of Fame)

continued when the Flyers allowed a 3–0 lead in St. Louis to turn into a 3–3 tie.

"We didn't think much about the streak early on because, to be honest with you, we had so many questions about that team," Quinn said. "But after about 15 games we all started to realize that this was something special.

"On the bench, the guys were starting to stand up for the entire third periods of close games. They were beginning to get excited. They just didn't want to see it end."

Three consecutive draws—against the Maple Leafs on

the road and Detroit and Boston at home—to start December had the Flyers at 16–0–6 and thinking about the Canadiens' record of 28 games without a defeat (22 wins and 6 ties), set in 1977–78.

Three more wins and three more ties, and the Flyers had matched the Habs' record. On December 22, they arrived in Boston for a Saturday matinee and a chance to set a new one. The Flyers beat the Bruins, 5–2, with Clarke scoring early to notch career point no. 900.

"The only time I really felt the tension was in Boston,"

Clarke said. "Damn, we came through that day."

Clarke and Barber scored in the first period and Linseman added another in the second to build a 3–0 lead. After the final buzzer sounded, even the Bruins faithful gave the visiting Flyers a standing ovation for their accomplishment.

But the Flyers were not done. They managed a win and draw in a home-and-home set with the Hartford Whalers, and road victories against Winnipeg, Colorado, the New York Rangers, and Buffalo, before the streak ended on January 7 with a 7–1 loss against the North Stars in Minnesota.

"It was a once-in-a-lifetime thing," Quinn said. "I don't know, maybe I was part of something that will stand forever in history."

Peters went 14–0–4 and Myre was 11–0–6 during the streak. Of the 10 draws, only twice did the Flyers have to rally to tie the game. They went 14–0–6 at home and 11–0–4 on the road and defeated every team in the 21-team league with the exception of the Washington Capitals.

After the streak, the Flyers finished with a 22–11–10 run for a 48–12–20 record, good for 116 points and first place overall. But they lost to the Islanders in a six-game Stanley Cup Final. In Game 6, Duane Sutter scored at 14:58 of the first period to put New York ahead, 2–1.

The Islanders won that game, 6–5, in overtime on a series-clincher from Bob Nystrom.

"I think everyone who played on that team remembers that streak as something special," Barber said. "I think we all realize it was just one of those things that will never be equalled."

ALL IN: HOCKEY IN VEGAS

The Vegas Golden Knights became the NHL's 31st team at the start of the 2017–18 season, but long before the first puck was dropped they already had ignited enough hockey heat in the desert to, well, melt a sheet of ice.

They quickly sold out of their allotment of 13,000 season tickets. Some 3,000 youngsters signed up for a Golden Knights program called Sticks for Kids, which provided every participant with a stick and a ball and hockey instruction, albeit of the street variety.

Fans certainly were taking notice of the first major professional sports team to call Las Vegas home. Viva Las Vegas, indeed.

The NHL's expansion to Las Vegas—the first addition to the league since the expansion Minnesota Wild began play 17 years before—was several years in the making for owner Bill Foley, who first met with the league's board of governors in December 2013.

Foley, who made his money as a mortgage financier and winery tycoon, started getting season-ticket commitments for the team, a sure way to gauge interest in the potential new franchise, which would play at the spectacular new 17,368–seat T-Mobile Arena.

Foley, who paid a record $500 million U.S. for the franchise, hired George McPhee to be his general manager, to build his hockey department and team. McPhee, a former GM of the Washington Capitals, met with Bob Clarke and Doug Risebrough, who were GMs of the expansion Florida Panthers and Minnesota Wild respectively, to pick their brains about what made both those franchises successful early.

Over the years, the NHL has changed its expansion draft rules and it was widely believed they were the best ever for Vegas, giving them the best chance to ice a strong team sooner than later.

"They've done their best to make this the best expansion draft ever," said McPhee.

Of course, success will only help to grow interest in the team, which was already taking off quickly, beyond just the Golden Knights.

Though there were only five rinks in Nevada as of June, 2017—including the two sheets the Golden Knights were looking to complete two months later—Scott Zucker saw an ice age soon coming, just as it had in other markets where the temperature is more likely to be in the 90s than the 20s.

"You can feel the buzz building," said Zucker, president of the Nevada Amateur Hockey Association (NAHA). "My guess is you're going to see an explosion in the number of youth players all over Nevada."

A project director for Station Casinos, Zucker knows his way around construction, and the rink, being the father of five hockey-playing kids, including middle son Jason, a forward with the Minnesota Wild.

Jason Zucker was the first Nevada-raised player ever selected in the NHL Draft when the Wild picked him in the second round (no. 59) in 2010. If history holds true, more will follow.

"The Knights will create a domino effect and pique the curiosity of kids at a younger age, which will cause them to start playing younger, which will make them better players in the long run," Jason Zucker said.

Indeed, from Anaheim to Arizona, Nashville to Raleigh, Miami to Tampa, the pattern is as clear, according to Dave Ogrean, former executive director of USA Hockey.

"If you plant a pro franchise, especially an NHL franchise, in a place where hockey hasn't been, interest is going to grow in concentric circles," Ogrean said. "The NHL comes. Interest grows. People want to play. Rinks get built. It all trickles down, and all works together."

To Ogrean, the transformational moment for the growth of youth hockey in the United States came when Wayne Gretzky was traded from the Edmonton Oilers to the Los Angeles Kings on August 9, 1988.

Zucker said there were 455 kids under 18 playing hockey in Nevada as of June 2017 and said that number could approach 2,000 by 2022.

It may have been unimaginable to think, back in the days of the Original Six, or even years after that, that hockey would ever be played hard by the Strip.

True, the NHL had been staging its annual awards show in Las Vegas since 2009. But now it has brought an even bigger show.

"What hockey will do for Las Vegas is give it an identity that is unto itself, as opposed to the Strip . . . an identity it has never had," said Foley. "It's going to be fun being part of it."

With great fanfare, the Vegas Golden Knights present their name and logo on November 22, 2016, outside T-Mobile Arena. (Icon Sportswire/Getty Images)

THE PRONGER-SHANAHAN TRADE

After the 1993 entry draft, first-overall pick Alexandre Daigle infamously said, "I'm glad I got drafted first because no one remembers No. 2."

Chris Pronger would beg to differ, and did so on many occasions as he won the Hart Trophy, Norris Trophy, and Stanley Cup, and forged a Hall of Fame career. Daigle, meanwhile, bounced around six different teams and never scored a playoff goal.

Pierre Turgeon had been more gracious toward Brendan Shanahan when the latter followed him to the draft podium a few years earlier in 1987. But it was Shanahan's New Jersey Devils who wowed the NHL in the playoffs months later, not Turgeon's Buffalo Sabres. And that's Shanahan's name on the Stanley Cup three times—and, like Pronger, he won Olympic gold.

In the summer of 1995, these second picks were swapped in one of the biggest one-for-one trades in league history. The two bruisers, who would combine to rack up more than 4,000 penalty minutes, were supposed to be mainstays on their respective teams at the time: the rugged power forward Shanahan with the St. Louis Blues; the

> Pronger represented Canada seven times and won two Olympic gold medals. Later, with his world championship in 1997 and a Stanley Cup in 2007 with Anaheim, he joined the exclusive Triple Gold Club.

Pronger fulfilling his destiny as "the next Larry Robinson" in Hartford, in the opinion of GM Jim Rutherford.

But there was restlessness behind the scenes in both cities. Shanahan was not seeing eye to eye with his coach, and when that man is "Iron Mike" Keenan, differences don't usually end with a hug. Keenan found fault with Shanahan's work ethic, one of the greatest assets the winger thought he possessed. When Keenan sent Shanahan's linemate Craig Janney out of town a few months before the trade, many saw the writing on the boards.

The six-foot-six Pronger had been so coveted by Rutherford two years earlier that he'd traded Sergei Makarov and three draft picks, including Hartford's first, to move up a few slots to second overall.

But as attendance slipped, the "win today" mentality was overtaking the Whalers' front office. Rutherford told reporters he needed a star now, not a star in waiting who was demonstrating slow maturity.

After unsuccessfully pursuing Teemu Selanne of the Winnipeg Jets (a move that would've brought Pronger close to his hometown of Dryden in Northern Ontario),

Previous page: St. Louis fans quickly learned to love Chris Pronger, winner of both the Hart and Norris Trophies in 1999–2000. (Dave Sandford/Hockey Hall of Fame)

Above: One of the game's great power forwards, Brendan Shanahan never failed to make his mark as a team leader. (Paul Bereswill/Hockey Hall of Fame)

Rutherford dialled Keenan's number around the 1995 NHL trade deadline.

"At that time, they said there was no way they would move Brendan," Rutherford said after the deal was made. "I was approached at the draft in Edmonton by Keenan, wondering if I would move Chris. The answer was no.

"Out of the blue, talks heated up. Mike said he might move Shanahan, but Pronger had to be part of the deal.

"Everyone in this organization was unanimous in favour of this trade. I don't have the same disappointment in Pronger that maybe some of the fans and media do. I think Chris is right on track and I'm maybe one of his biggest supporters. I believe he's going to be a very, very good player. But I also believe that what we needed to do to improve our team was add an impact player."

Keenan said it was just as hard on him to cash out on Shanahan. His signing by the Blues as a restricted free agent in 1991 had cost the franchise when St. Louis was ordered to send defenceman Scott Stevens to New Jersey as compensation. Keenan picked up on the Larry Robinson theme, reminding the trade's critics that Robinson did not start blossoming with the Canadiens until his early 20s.

Shanahan had been extremely popular in St. Louis, and it took a while for Pronger to win over the fans. When he did, it became one of the great love affairs in the sports-mad city.

In 1999–2000, Pronger won the Hart and Norris Trophies. He was only the second player in Blues history to receive either award, after Brett Hull and Al MacInnis, respectively. Only one other NHL defenceman, Bobby Orr, had ever captured both trophies in the same year.

During his nine years in St. Louis, Pronger reached at least 35 points seven times, topped by a career-best 62 in his MVP season, and racked up at least 100 penalty minutes five times.

"He had an uncanny ability to put up some good numbers when he was playing 30 minutes a game and playing back," fellow Hall of Fame inductee Phil Housley said. "But he could also sneak in the play, knowing when to pop into those holes.

"He was such a great passer. Everything was on the tape, even from his own net, and that was a great way to start [a rush]. If you could break down forechecks and be a little dirty in your end, that's a pretty darn good defenceman."

Pronger represented Canada seven times and won two Olympic gold medals. Later, with his world championship in 1997 and a Stanley Cup in 2007 with Anaheim, he joined the exclusive Triple Gold Club.

Shanahan's one full season in Hartford, during which he was given the captaincy, resulted in 44 goals. But the Whalers had become an unstable franchise and Shanahan requested a trade. That came two games into the 1996–97 season, in another fairly significant deal that sent him to Detroit for Keith Primeau and Paul Coffey.

Shanahan would help put the perennially Stanley Cup–cursed Wings in the role of champions in three of the next six seasons.

Years later, in one of the strangest of ironies, the two roughhouse players were both working for the NHL, Shanahan as vice president of hockey and business development, beginning in 2009. He later modernized the role of senior VP in charge of handing down supplemental discipline, using slick videos to explain the suspensions he'd meted out, and sometimes his decisions not to.

Pronger played until injuries sidelined him early in the 2011–12 season. He served as the league's Director of Player Safety and most recently joined the Florida Panthers' front office.

81

MADISON SQUARE GARDEN

Madison Square Garden lives up to its reputation as the world's most famous arena, certainly among the most exciting to watch hockey, as part of the New York City experience.

"When I played there, the place was electric," said retired Rangers defenceman Chris Kotsopoulos. "The fans were very vocal and you knew you were at home. It was the second loudest building after old Chicago Stadium."

Stanley Cups have been few and far between for the Rangers, but big games seem all that much bigger at MSG.

There was Stephane Matteau's double-OT winner in the '94 Eastern Conference final against the Devils—after captain Mark Messier had guaranteed the Rangers would win Game 6 across the river in the Meadowlands. Messier, defying the "curse," also grabbed hold of the Prince of Wales Trophy to show the win-starved fans.

That win in New Jersey set up, a couple of weeks later, another Game 7, this one at the Garden to bring back the Rangers' first Stanley Cup in 54 years. Messier scored in the game against Vancouver, and in a hail of red, white, and blue streamers, lifted the Cup.

There have been low points and losses, but no one

The current MSG is actually the fourth venue with that name.

seemed too concerned after the Pittsburgh Penguins won, 2–1, in overtime on April 18, 1999. In one of the most touching scenes at MSG, Wayne Gretzky had played his last game. There were scoreboard messages from Gordie Howe and basketball's Michael Jordan, and Gretzky took his post-game victory lap with the Ranger team behind him.

Naturally, New York's leather-lunged supporters didn't let him go quietly, and an hour after the game, Gretzky still had his sweater on, shaking hands, doing interviews.

"It's a great place to play because of the fans," said Rangers Hall of Fame defenceman Brian Leetch near the end of his own 17-year career. "You almost expect to have 100 of them around your car every night."

Conscious of The Big Apple's stature, the Rangers have introduced special guests during games: a collection of models, movie stars, musicians, and famous athletes from in and out of town. A popular game-night feature had former mayor Ed Koch, who'd become a judge on the TV Show *The People's Court*, recruited for scoreboard videos when the visiting team was penalized. "Two minutes—tripping!" Koch would shout in his official robes, then whack his gavel while the crowd roared.

Many people coming for the first time are fixated on the banners for retired Rangers such as Messier, Leetch, and Rod Gilbert, as well as those marking Cup wins, titles for the New York Knicks, and longtime MSG performers such as Billy Joel.

But opposing players dread the experience of being singled out by some of the most caustic fans in the league. During his playing days—and for decades after he retired—Islanders captain Denis Potvin would hear his name denigrated.

"The crowd would be yelling at him out on the blue line during the national anthem; booing, waving signs, unfurling banners," laughed Leetch. "Potvin was just standing there and I thought, 'This guy is something special to be taking all of this abuse.'"

After having the "1940" chant burning their ears during the six-decade Cup drought and the New York Islanders' four-year dynasty, the Rangers finally won back bragging rights in 1994. They proceeded to sting their crosstown rivals with "1983—last Cup you'll ever see." When the long-suffering Maple Leafs are in town, the derogatory "1967" chant picks up, too.

The current MSG is actually the fourth venue with that name. In the late 1800s, a roofless hippodrome existed in nearby Madison Square, which sits at the crossing of Broadway, 23rd St., and 5th Ave. But lack of covering saw it razed for an 8,000-seat arena. The latter was not a huge moneymaker and came down in 1925 to make space for a skyscraper, just before the Rangers were born.

The MSG name carried over to a new building at 8th Ave. and 50th St., where the first NHL tenants were the New York Americans, purchased by Prohibition rum-runner Bill Dwyer in 1925 when they'd been the financially-ravaged Hamilton Tigers. Dwyer beat well-known local boxing promoter George "Tex" Rickard to the punch to move the team from Canada, but Rickard had organized the businessmen who built and owned the new MSG, and wanted his own club as main attraction in the 18,000-seat rink.

The league welcomed two New York teams and granted Rickard an expansion club, which the media christened Tex's Rangers. Brothers Bill and Bun Cook were among its early all-stars, along with Frank Boucher, Babe Siebert, and Ching Johnson.

The Americans eventually folded during the austerity of World War II, while the Rangers fell on hard times after the 1940 Cup. Through the 1950s and '60s, they missed the playoffs 18 times in a six-team league. By the mid-1960s, a proliferation of other sports teams in New York, not to mention NHL expansion and a desire to lure in more major entertainment acts, led MSG chairman Irving M. Felt to seek a bigger home. He made the clever decision to quietly buy development rights above Penn Station between 7th and 8th Ave., so when his new rink was approved, there would be handy transit below thousands of fans.

The new MSG opened in 1968, and with it came a great era of Rangers: Jean Ratelle, Rod Gilbert, Vic Hadfield, Harry Howell, Ed Giacomin, Brad Park, and later Phil Esposito after a big trade with Boston. The Rangers appeared in the '72 final, the same year Hadfield became the first 50-goal Ranger at MSG, and again in '79. But there was always the quest for a better and more profitable venue. In 1991, MSG underwent a $200 million (U.S.) renovation adding 89 private boxes.

As the new century dawned, there were thoughts of erecting yet another MSG, perhaps across the street at 8th Ave. and 33rd St., using the giant Corinthian colonnade of the U.S. Postal Building as a grand entrance. But the Rangers and Knicks stayed put, deciding on the most ambitious renovation yet, a $1 billion, three-year plan that updated technology, creature comforts, and an aging infrastructure.

It remains one of the few pro-sports homes without a sponsor's name in its title.

However, the last set of changes ended some Garden traditions, such as upper-level metal seats that reverberated when the gallery gods rattled them during celebratory wins, late-game rallies, or player salutes.

Also removed was the cozy corner-rinkside press box. In an era when press areas were an afterthought and often located too high above the ice, MSG kept space for media just a few feet from the glass and the visiting team's bench. Reporters were thus afforded a rare chance to experience the games close up.

MSG and the Rangers celebrated the rich and famous, but it was also a shrine for ordinary New Yorkers. One of its frequent guests was NYPD officer Steven McDonald. Left paralyzed from the neck down by a felon's bullet in 1986, the lifelong Ranger fan forgave the shooter, and became the city's symbol for tolerance and a game-night fixture near the Rangers' dressing room. The team named an Extra Effort Award for him, and when he died in 2017, a tribute ceremony featuring many Ranger greats inspired multiple standing ovations.

Rangers star Vic Hadfield becomes Madison Square Garden's first resident 50-goal scorer, in 1971-72. (O-Pee-Chee/Hockey Hall of Fame)

GRETZKY'S HAT TRICK AGAINST TORONTO

As he prepared to depart his hotel for Game 7 of the 1993 Western Conference final at Maple Leaf Gardens, the ever-gracious Wayne Gretzky chatted to a security guard in the elevator.

The guard remarked how quiet it was at that moment, but predicted that his night on the premises would be a long one, starting around 10:30 p.m.

He was implying that a Maple Leafs win over the Los Angeles Kings—and the team's first trip to the Stanley Cup final since 1967—would have the whole of downtown in a frenzy. Toronto had already won two previous Game 7s that spring, each of which touched off massive celebrations.

"I wouldn't worry about 10:30," Gretzky assured the guard, "because my job starts at 7:30."

The bigger the stage, the better Gretzky played.

As remarkable as the Leafs' journey had been that year—an incredible revival under coach Pat Burns, GM Cliff Fletcher, and the tireless Doug Gilmour—Gretzky was about to shoot holes into the notion of an all-Canadian Toronto–Montreal Final.

The entire country was tuned in to the sweltering

> "I wouldn't worry about 10:30," Gretzky assured the guard, "because my job starts at 7:30."

Gardens on May 29: Leafs lovers, haters, and the many fans Gretzky had won across North America for raising the Kings from West Coast obscurity.

The Leafs had a feeling of destiny about them, determined to shake off the events of Game 6 in L.A.

Gretzky had accidentally clipped Gilmour with a high stick in overtime, opening an eight-stitch cut that, under rules of the day, should have resulted in a major penalty. But a huddle between referee Kerry Fraser and his linesmen determined that none of them had seen the contact. Gretzky was allowed to continue, and he soon scored the power-play game winner.

The sharp criticism he and the officials received over the next 48 hours as the teams flew back east grated on the Great One. So by the time the last strains of "O Canada" were heard, he was as fired up as he would be for the Stanley Cup Final.

Gretzky began taking the air out of Carlton Street with a shorthanded goal off a two-on-one breakaway, then set up trailer Tomas Sandstrom for another before the first period ended. It was hard, but not impossible, for the Leafs to find

Right: Doug Gilmour was a heart-and-soul leader who took his share of cuts and bruises during the 1992-93 season. (Doug MacLellan/Hockey Hall of Fame)

Previous page: Los Angeles Kings captain Wayne Gretzky skates near Doug Gilmour of the Toronto Maple Leafs in the 1993 semi-final series playoff game at Maple Leaf Gardens in Toronto. (Graig Abel/Getty Images)

their legs and confidence with the Gardens crowd urging them onward. Sure enough, they made it 2–2, only to have L.A. coach Barry Melrose call a time out to disrupt their momentum. Soon after, a Gretzky slapper beat Felix Potvin in the Leaf net.

In the third period, Gilmour responded to Gretzky's challenge with a sweet pass to Toronto captain Wendel Clark. Gretzky briefly gave way to Mike Donnelly's heroics, as the journeyman left winger put the Kings ahead on a rather weak goal with less than four minutes remaining.

Then came Gretzky's coup de grâce, as he fought off Toronto defenceman Todd Gill behind the net and banked a backhander off the skate of Gill's partner, Dave Ellett, for his third goal of the game.

The Kings squeezed out a 5–4 win, and Gretzky, not Gilmour, would be leading his team to the Cup Final.

"Before the game, I was crazy nervous," Kings owner Bruce McNall recalled. "We were obviously big underdogs and Gilmour was playing terrifically. I was a nervous wreck and Wayne came up to me and said, 'Bruce, just

relax. I got this. You know who I am; you know what I can do. Relax, okay?'"

Another boost for Gretzky was that his parents were in the crowd, two years after his father Walter's brush with death from a brain aneurysm. If there was one thing Gretzky loved more than playing a big game in an Original Six rink, it was having his family present for it.

"Of course, Gretzky goes out there and gets a hat trick," McNall marvelled. "He said it was the greatest game he's ever played, and it was certainly the biggest win the Kings ever had."

Truth is, Gretzky said it was the greatest *NHL playoff game* he ever played. In his view, the second game of the 1987 Canada Cup final was his career highlight. Canada defeated the Soviets, 6–5, in double overtime in that game. Gretzky finished the night with five assists.

"That [Canada Cup] series was probably the best hockey I've ever played," he said. "That game was the greatest game I ever played in my life."

Game 7 versus the Leafs was a pretty good No. 2.

83

THE MAX BENTLEY TRADE

n its 100 years of existence, Toronto's NHL franchise has won 13 Stanley Cups. But the team most observers consider its "greatest" earned that distinction in part because of a seven-player swap that helped define the term "blockbuster trade."

On November 2, 1947—the same day Howard Hughes took to the skies with the world's largest aircraft, the "Spruce Goose"—Toronto acquired Max Bentley from the Chicago Blackhawks. Bentley was the centrepiece of Chicago's Pony Line, with his brother Doug and Bill Mosienko, and had won the Hart Trophy the previous year.

The impetus for the deal was simple. The Leafs, who'd won the Cup the previous year, thought they were capable of more, as all their stars returned from service in World War II. They were also making preparations for the retirement of Syl Apps in the next couple of years. Chicago, despite the Pony Line's success and the 20-goal seasons of Max and Doug in 1946–47, had no depth beyond the top unit.

In those days, players didn't have much control of their fate as far as trades were concerned. But Max, with more than 200 points in 160 games after becoming a full-timer,

Toronto sports columnist Dick Beddoes, reflecting on the era, wondered whether Wayne Gretzky could've cracked the Leafs at centre that season.

was in a different class. After general manager Bill Tobin gave him the choice of staying or moving on, with a chance to win a Cup as well as to help the Hawks, Bentley green-lighted a trade.

He and forward Cy Thomas went to the Leafs for left winger Gaye Stewart (a first-team all-star), centre Gus Bodnar (rookie of the year in 1944), and Bud Poile (a four-year Leaf winger). They comprised the Leafs' third line, known as the "Flying Forts" because all three came from Fort William, Ontario (part of today's Thunder Bay).

Also in the deal were Bob "Golden Boy" Goldham, who was one of the most technically sound Leafs on defence, and fellow blue-liner Ernie Dickens, who'd been a rising star before military service but lost his place in the lineup to Bill Barilko.

The big names in the trade surprised the hockey world. New NHL president Clarence Campbell called it the biggest deal ever made. Leafs manager Conn Smythe called it a gamble worth the risk.

Bentley's story was remarkable. His father Bill, born in Yorkshire, England, became a speed skater in the wilds of North Dakota and later crossed the border to Delisle,

Saskatchewan, to take up farming. It was a livelihood that six Bentley brothers would embrace as much as their love of hockey, but only four of them, led by the two youngest, Max and Doug, took their skills much beyond the barnyard. Bill and his wife had seven daughters who also played.

Eldest sons Jack and Roy watched the cattle and crops, while the next two in line, Wyatt and Reggie, did well in junior, Reggie making the Blackhawks for 11 games. But Max and Doug, their hands strengthened by countless days spent milking cows and playing ball hockey, were able to give the NHL their full commitment.

As a Leaf, Bentley had to get used to something of a lesser role, with Apps and Teeder Kennedy lighting it up, but his masterful stickhandling set him apart. Bringing with him six points in six games before the trade, he wound up eventually tied with Poile with 54, just behind the fourth-place Stewart among the league's top 10 scorers in 1947–48. But the playoffs were a romp for first-place Toronto, which lost just one of nine postseason games and swept Detroit in the final. Chicago, despite its newfound wealth, was once more relegated to last spot.

Apps, Kennedy, and Bentley, who was by then famous as the "Dipsy-Doodle Dandy from Delisle," each racked up at least 20 goals in the regular season, and the latter two reached double figures in points in the playoffs. Max, whose height (five-foot-eight) was certainly no detriment, was placed on the point on the power play, an unusual move at that time. Toronto sports columnist Dick Beddoes, reflecting on the era, wondered whether Wayne Gretzky could've cracked the Leafs at centre that season.

The Leafs were able to fill the gaps left behind by their traded players and chased a third consecutive Cup in 1949. Left winger Harry Watson, another important part of the offence, nudged out Bentley for top scorer after Apps retired. Chicago was only seven points behind fourth-place Toronto, with Doug Bentley almost winning the scoring title. But again, Max was a strong performer as the Leafs lost just once in the playoffs and became the first NHL team to capture three Cups in a row.

A fourth title would have to wait until 1951, but even that had Bentley's fingerprints on it. With the Leafs facing defeat in Game 5 of the final against Montreal, a series in which all matches went to overtime, Bentley's puck magic with the goalie pulled helped set up Tod Sloan for a late tying goal, which set the stage for the legendary overtime goal by Barilko.

As Max thrived in Toronto (in 2016, he was named the 21st-greatest Leaf of all time), the club approached the Hawks about acquiring Doug as well. But Chicago, which had never recovered from the loss of Max, wouldn't part with his sibling.

The Bentleys were eventually reunited in New York in 1953, after Doug was acquired and the Rangers purchased Max outright for one season. Each was already en route to the Hall of Fame, but in 1947 the Leafs clearly got the better of the deal.

Brothers Doug and Max Bentley in 1947 after Max was traded to the Toronto Maple Leafs. (Imperial Oil–Turofsky/Hockey Hall of Fame)

84

BRODEUR'S RECORD

Of all the words of praise that were heaped upon goaltender Martin Brodeur during his illustrious career, perhaps none were loftier than those given by a former teammate.

"Some of his records," said former New Jersey Devils forward and later coach John MacLean, "are Gretzky-like. They are going to be hard to break."

High praise, indeed. Because what Gretzky was to scoring, Brodeur was to preventing scoring. Meaning none have ever been better than either man at their respective crafts. Brodeur, a native of Montreal, owns the NHL record in virtually every significant goaltending category.

He is number one in wins with 691.

He is number one in shutouts with 125.

He is number one in games played with 1,266.

A first-round pick of the New Jersey Devils in 1990, it was three years later that Brodeur became a regular in the NHL. During that 1993–94 season, he recorded three shutouts and won the Calder Trophy as the league's top rookie. He also got the Devils to within a victory of an appearance in the Stanley Cup Final, losing the conference final to the New York Rangers in seven games.

It was a great start of a brilliant career.

In the shortened 1995 season, Brodeur helped lead the Devils to their first Stanley Cup victory, sweeping the Detroit Red Wings in the final.

Brodeur and the Devils would win the Cup again in 2000, and lost in seven games to the Colorado Avalanche the following spring.

In 2002–03, Brodeur won the first of four Vezina trophies and another Stanley Cup. Along the way, he also won the Jennings Trophy—awarded to the goaltender(s) on the team allowing the fewest goals against—five times.

In total, he won the Stanley Cup three times, and twice lost in the final.

He also won a gold medal with Canada at the 2002 Winter Olympics in Salt Lake City, ending Canada's 50-year gold medal chase.

Brodeur was the definition of a workhorse. Twelve times he played 70 or more games in a season. His goals-against average was under 2.50 in 18 of 20 seasons, including 1996–97 when it was 1.88, the lowest the league had seen in 25 seasons.

Brodeur played 205 playoff games, winning 113 of them, ranking second all-time to Patrick Roy. He also had a record 24 playoff shutouts.

The New Jersey netminder didn't always receive the praise he deserved because, most seasons, his Devils teammates were known for their incredibly tight defensive play. But the Devils would never have been as good defensively without their stand-out goaltender. You couldn't have one without the other.

At a time when most goaltenders were big and tall and playing the butterfly style, Brodeur played a more hybrid style. He was also a gifted puckhandler, often described as being like a third defenceman with his ability to move the puck. Three times he converted that skill into a goal at the opposite end of the ice, scoring twice in the regular season and once in the playoffs.

The craft of stopping pucks was in Brodeur's genes. His father, Denis, won a bronze medal between the pipes with Canada at the 1956 Olympics. After retiring, he became one of the top hockey photographers in Canada. By the time Denis retired himself, in 2015, his son had given him plenty of memories worth capturing.

New Jersey Devils netminder Martin Brodeur set numerous NHL records, including career regular-season wins (691) and shutouts (125). (Mathew Manor/Hockey Hall of Fame)

85

MAPLE LEAF GARDENS

I can be argued that the most famous building in the history of the National Hockey League was Maple Leaf Gardens in Toronto.

Thanks to the introduction of radio broadcasts in 1931 and *Hockey Night in Canada* telecasts that began in 1952, Maple Leaf Gardens was known across Canada, from sea to shining sea. It was a Saturday night ritual for families to gather around the radio and listen as Foster Hewitt in his famous gondola provided the play-by-play. Unless you rooted for Montreal.

The Leafs—and their predecessors the St. Patricks and Arenas—had started out by playing their home games at the Mutual Street Arena, which accommodated about 7,500 fans for hockey. However, new multipurpose arenas began to dot the National Hockey League landscape by 1930: the Forum in Montreal, the Olympia in Detroit, Chicago Stadium, Boston Garden, and New York's Madison Square Garden.

By this time, the irascible Conn Smythe, who had been a noteworthy amateur player, had put together the investment team that bought the Maple Leafs franchise. He was also the team's coach and general manager. A decorated World War I hero, Smythe had been held as a prisoner of war for 14 months. He was not about to let the Great Depression stand in the way of his bid to get a new, larger arena built. An accomplished entrepreneur in his own right, Smythe raised capital and even paid construction workers partially in Maple Leaf Gardens stock to reduce financing costs in those economically challenged times.

Built in an incredible five-and-a-half-month span, the new home of the Maple Leafs was erected at the corner of Church and Carlton Streets, with a seating capacity of roughly 13,000.

In time, it came to be known as the Carlton Street Cashbox.

The arena opened on November 12, 1931, and hosted a lifetime of hockey memories. Harold "Mush" March scored for Chicago just 2:30 into that first game. Charlie Conacher scored the first Leafs goal at the Gardens, but Chicago would go on to win, 2–1, before 13,542 fans.

The Leafs went on to win the Stanley Cup in the Gardens' inaugural season, sweeping the Rangers in a three-game final, and they would win it 10 more times over the next 35 years.

The first All-Star game took place at Maple Leaf Gardens in 1934. The event was played as a benefit to aid Maple Leafs

> He was not about to let a Great Depression stand in the way of his bid to get a new, larger arena built.

forward Ace Bailey, who had fractured his skull and almost died after a hit by Boston's Eddie Shore a few months earlier.

Other iconic moments included Bill Barilko's overtime goal in Game 5 of the 1951 Stanley Cup final that "won the Leafs the Cup, " to quote the Tragically Hip song "Fifty Mission Cap," which Barilko's goal inspired. George Armstrong's 1967 empty-net goal to give Toronto its fourth Stanley Cup of the 1960s provided another highlight.

Doug Gilmour and Wendel Clark orchestrated stirring memories in the 1990s, while Pat Quinn and Mats Sundin provided fans with similar heroics less than a decade later.

The Gardens hosted a pantheon of all-stars and Hall of Fame players who displayed legendary skill on the ice: Charlie Conacher, Busher Jackson, Joe Primeau, Teeder Kennedy, Darryl Sittler, Gilmour, Sundin, and Turk Broda.

The teams that won four Stanley Cups in the 1960s iced a mix of 13 future Hall of Famers: Armstrong, Andy Bathgate, Johnny Bower, Dick Duff, Tim Horton, Red Kelly, Dave Keon, Frank Mahovlich, Bert Olmstead, Marcel Pronovost, Bob Pulford, Terry Sawchuk, and Allan Stanley (Al Arbour made it 14, though he was inducted as a builder). Sixty-three Maple Leafs are Honoured Members of the Hockey Hall of Fame, the most of any team. Sixteen more executives are Honoured Members in the builder category.

Maple Leaf Gardens was also home to the Toronto Marlboros of the Ontario Hockey Association, a Maple Leafs farm club that won seven Memorial Cups and produced many of the great Leafs who were later enshrined in the Hockey Hall of Fame.

In a bizarre turn, Maple Leaf Gardens also became home of the Toronto Toros of the World Hockey Association. The league was formed in 1972 to rival the National Hockey League, and its teams signed some of the NHL's biggest stars—including the Maple Leafs' Paul Henderson. After a year in Ottawa, the Toros played the 1973–74 season at Varsity Arena, then spent two seasons at the Gardens before moving to Birmingham, Alabama, in 1976.

Hockey wasn't the only sport that had fans on the edge of their seats at 60 Carlton Street. Wrestling was a mainstay from the opening of the building. The top attraction in the 1940s was a local kid, "Whipper" Billy Watson, who captured the fans' imagination. They flocked to the Gardens to see wrestling for decades.

Before there was a National Basketball Association, there was its precursor, the Basketball Association of America. The first game in that league's history was contested at Maple Leaf Gardens on November 1, 1946, when the New York Knickerbockers edged the Toronto Huskies, 68–66. The Huskies disbanded after one season, and the Gardens would not see a regular basketball tenant again until 1995, when the Toronto Raptors entered the NBA.

Indoor track and field was an annual attraction, while indoor soccer had a few kicks at the can. Boxers such as George Foreman and Larry Holmes entertained sold-out crowds. Hometown favourite George Chuvalo challenged Muhammad Ali for his heavyweight title on March 29, 1966, and went the distance with the champion in their 15-round bout, but Ali retained his crown. After the match, Ali famously called Chuvalo the toughest man he ever fought.

Canadian prime ministers William Lyon Mackenzie King and Pierre Elliott Trudeau addressed throngs at the Gardens, as did the former prime minister of the United Kingdom, Sir Winston Churchill. Evangelist Billy Graham was an annual speaker. Entertainers from Dean Martin and Jerry Lewis to Bob Hope appeared at the landmark.

Some of the greatest musical artists in history performed on the Gardens stage: Duke Ellington, Frank Sinatra, Elvis Presley, the Beatles, and countless other star attractions made sure a visit to Maple Leaf Gardens was a mandatory stop on their tours.

But by the mid–1990s, Maple Leaf Gardens began to feel antiquated compared to the lucrative arenas recently

built in Chicago, Boston, and Montreal. The team's owner-ship group now operated under the banner Maple Leaf Sports and Entertainment, and its 1998 purchase of the NBA's Toronto Raptors included Air Canada Centre, which was already under construction. That transaction sealed the Gardens' fate.

Sixty-eight years of history ended when the Chicago Blackhawks skated away with a 6–2 victory in the Leafs' final home game at the Gardens, on February 13, 1999. A star-studded procession closed the building and led a parade to the club's new home on Bay Street.

Maple Leaf Gardens sat dormant for five years until it was purchased by a major grocery chain in 2004. The build-ing remained unused for another five years until Ryerson University co-operated with the retailer to develop a large grocery store at the former ice level and an array of athletic facilities for Ryerson students on upper levels, including a rink with seating for almost 2,800.

The most famous building in Toronto, and perhaps the hockey world, is now an institution. As hockey fans have always known.

Defying the economics of the Great Depression, Conn Smythe built
Maple Leaf Gardens at the corner of Carlton and Church Streets,
where it served as home to his Toronto franchise from 1931 to 1999.
(Graphic Artists/Hockey Hall of Fame)

86

RON HEXTALL SCORES

Ron Hextall made quite a first impression.

In the Philadelphia Flyers' 1986–87 season opener, the rookie surrendered a Jari Kurri goal on the first shot he faced, but then shut the door with a 21-save performance in a 2–1 win against the Edmonton Oilers in front of an appreciative home crowd at the Spectrum.

Hextall did not win the Calder Trophy that year; the honour went instead to Los Angeles Kings sniper Luc Robitaille. But the Flyers star did win the Vezina Trophy as the most outstanding goalie as voted by the NHL general managers.

He then steered the Flyers to the Stanley Cup Final, only to suffer a devastating 3–1 loss in Game 7 in Edmonton. He was so good in the postseason that Hextall became only the fifth player to win the Conn Smythe Trophy, as the playoff MVP, in a losing cause.

His brilliant first NHL season earned him an invitation to back up Grant Fuhr on the Canada Cup championship–winning Canadian team in September 1987.

Hextall's second season, however, was delayed. He had been suspended for eight games for a nasty slash to the back of the knees of Oilers forward Kent Nilsson in Game 4 of the 1987 Stanley Cup Final.

> "It was a great feeling when I saw it roll in. It was not the biggest thrill, but it comes close."

So by the time Hextall played his first game in his sophomore NHL season, he had plenty of pent-up motivation to make an impact. He made 40 saves in a 2–2 draw on the road against the New York Rangers, but Hextall and the Flyers struggled in the early going of that season and the Philadelphia goalie was 2–8–2 after his first 12 games.

The team's fortunes began to turn around in late November, as Hextall embarked on a 12–0–1 run. He put an exclamation point on the unbeaten streak when he became the first NHL goalie to score a goal, in a 5–2 win at home against the Boston Bruins on December 8, 1987.

Billy Smith of the New York Islanders had been credited with a goal on November 28, 1979, when he was the last Islanders player to touch the puck before Colorado Rockies defenceman Rob Ramage accidentally passed it into his own empty net during a delayed-penalty call. But no goalie had ever shot the puck the length of the ice to score until Hextall.

With the Flyers ahead by two goals, the Bruins had goalie Reggie Lemelin on the bench for an extra attacker. Boston defenceman Gord Kluzak dumped the puck into the Philadelphia end.

Hextall had plenty of time to gather it in and flip it high into the air toward the Bruins goal. The puck landed around the Boston blue line, just out of the reach of Ray Bourque, and safely found a home just inside the right post with 72 seconds remaining.

"It was a perfect opportunity for me, with us being up two goals at the time," said Hextall. "I looked up and saw the open ice. I was hoping to get the puck close.

"It was a great feeling when I saw it roll in. It was not the biggest thrill, but it comes close."

His teammates emptied the Philadelphia bench to congratulate him. The Flyers awarded him a 1988 Mercury Cougar, painted in the team's black and orange colours, at the next game.

That Hextall became the first goalie to shoot and score a goal was not a shocker. He was regarded at the time as the best puckhandler among netminders and was so adept at directing the puck to his teammates that he operated like a third defenceman for the Flyers.

Hextall grew up in Brandon, Manitoba, and was a

Ron Hextall, known for his tremendous puckhandling skills, shoots the puck during Game 3 of the 1987 Stanley Cup Final. (Paul Bereswill/Hockey Hall of Fame)

third-generation NHLer behind his grandfather, Hockey Hall of Famer Bryan Hextall, his uncle Dennis, and his father, Bryan Jr.

All three were forwards who had shooting advice to pass on to Ron, who worked on his passing and shooting skills from a young age. He also played the goalie position more like a power forward, racking up a record 584 penalty minutes in 608 NHL regular-season games and 115 more in 93 playoff games.

Hextall, who would lose in his only other Stanley Cup final, in 1997 to the Detroit Red Wings, also became the first goalie to score in a playoff game when he did it against the Washington Capitals in an 8–5 win in 1989.

He went on to win a Stanley Cup as the Los Angeles Kings' assistant general manager in 2011–12 and then returned home to become the Flyers' GM.

"I don't mean to sound cocky, but I knew I could do it," Hextall said on that December 1987 evening. "It was a matter of when."

Ron Hextall makes a save during Game 4 of the 1987 Stanley Cup Final at the Spectrum. (Paul Bereswill/Hockey Hall of Fame)

87

GOING THE EXTRA MINUTES: OVERTIME

n the spring of 1983 the NHL general managers and owners agreed the game needed a bit of a change, something to make it more exciting and entertaining for its fans.

Borrowing from the old line that everything old is new again, the league took a page from its past in an attempt to improve the future.

For many years, regular-season games that were tied after regulation time were followed by a 10-minute overtime period. But this feature was dropped in November 1942 because of the schedule reductions World War II had forced on train travel. If the games went too late, many fans would be stuck with no way to get home.

After a 41-year hiatus, the league decided to bring back a five-minute sudden-death overtime period. If a team won in overtime they would receive two points. The losing team would receive zero points. If they remained tied after 65 minutes, both teams received a point.

In 1999, the league decided to make another change to the overtime format in an attempt to add to the excitement. Teams now played with four skaters a side, one fewer than normal. It provided more room on the ice and more scoring chances. It allowed fast and skilled players to shine. Teams that won in four-on-four overtime received the usual two points, but the losing team was awarded a point. Teams felt they deserved a guaranteed point if the game remained tied after regulation.

A few years later, for the 2005–06 season, the league introduced a shootout for games that remained tied after overtime. And for the 2015–16 season, the NHL removed another skater from the ice in overtime: teams now play three on three. The intent, as before, was to enhance the entertainment value, and also to try to have fewer games settled by the shootout. But with a nod to tradition and the value of team play, the league also determined that, for tiebreaker purposes in the standings, only regulation and overtime wins would count, and not shootout wins.

> If the games went too late, many fans would be stuck with no way to get home.

88

ULF STERNER'S CALL-UP

Ulf Sterner had all the attributes teams look for in an NHL player: size, speed, and skill.

A native of Deje, Sweden, Sterner was the first Swede and European-raised player in the NHL. He also enjoyed a long career in Sweden and distinguished himself on the international stage as a lightning-fast centre who fooled defenders with his deft puckhandling ability. His claim to fame was that he was the first player to execute the "stick-to-skate-to-stick" manoeuvre to control the puck and fool defenders.

The six-foot-two Sterner exploded onto the Swedish hockey scene when he made the roster of a second-division team, Forshaga IF, at the age of 15. He cracked Sweden's national squad two years later. He scored in his debut and would register 90 points in 86 international games during a career that saw him help *Tre Kronor* to one gold, five silver, and one bronze medal in nine world championships.

Sterner scored key goals for Sweden and led them to the 1962 world championship over Canada, before the Soviet Union claimed the title for the next nine years.

Sterner's play intrigued the New York Rangers, and they signed him to a five-game tryout after he led Sweden to a silver medal at the 1964 Winter Olympic Games in Innsbruck, Austria.

At age 23, Sterner accepted the tryout offer and agreed to start in the minors, first with the St. Paul Rangers of the Central Hockey League. He had 21 points in 16 games before he was promoted to the American Hockey League's Baltimore Clippers in the 1964–65 season.

Sterner added another 44 points in 52 games on a Clippers squad that featured future NHL players such as Jean Ratelle, Bob Plager, Ken Schinkel, and Bryan Hextall. His teammate in goal was Jacques Plante.

Sterner made his NHL debut for the Rangers on January 27, 1965, against Boston. He was held scoreless in four NHL games and returned to Sweden for the rest of his career.

Sterner scored 239 points in 172 games over 13 seasons in Sweden's first division. He also registered 12 points in a dozen games in the 1960 and 1964 Winter Olympics. He retired in 1978 and became an accomplished coach in Germany from 1986 to 1989.

Although Sterner never achieved great success in the NHL, his pioneering attempt at a hockey career in the world's best league opened the door for others to follow him, and inspired some NHL teams to begin scouting in Europe.

As it turned out, among those others was a memorable pair of Swedes, Borje Salming and Inge Hammarstrom, who both signed with the Toronto Maple Leafs in 1973.

Ulf Sterner, the NHL's first European-raised player. (Hockey Hall of Fame)

OUTDOORS IN LOS ANGELES

When the NHL awarded a team to Los Angeles during the first wave of modern expansion in 1967, it was confident there were enough laid-back Californians curious enough to come in from the gorgeous weather and watch an exciting sport.

But even league executives would never have foreseen the game, the technology, and the power of marketing advancing far enough to allow two southern California–based teams to actually play outdoors, especially in one of the iconic sporting locales in the country, Dodger Stadium.

"It's pretty cool being here and standing on, for me, where Sandy Koufax was pitching, and Don Drysdale was pitching, and Maury Wills [was stealing bases]," said Anaheim Ducks head coach Bruce Boudreau.

With legendary Dodgers baseball broadcaster Vin Scully joining Kings play-by-play man Bob Miller in the booth, L.A. hosted Anaheim on January 24, 2014. With temperatures around 63 degrees Fahrenheit (or 17 Celsius), the two teams paraded past palm trees and marched onto a rink created on the infield between first and third base, with home plate lining up with centre ice.

Wayne Gretzky performed the opening faceoff in front of a sold-out crowd of 54,099.

"This is an opportunity to show people in North America how great a hockey city this is," Gretzky, the former L.A. King, said.

Many of those attending had connections to the Dodgers, including the baseball team's general manager, Ned Colletti (who was once a hockey writer in Philadelphia); former manager Tommy Lasorda; broadcaster and ex-pitcher Fernando Valenzuela; and first baseman Nomar Garciaparra.

"Wayne was a big part of bringing hockey and awareness of hockey out here," said Garciaparra. "That was a big thing. But to play a game outside? No one had that in their head when they brought Gretzky here, let alone at Dodger Stadium."

Colletti, a huge hockey fan, settled in for the game, remarking how nice it was to come to Chavez Ravine and not care who won.

The celebs were everywhere: Jon Hamm, Pat Sajak, Alyssa Milano, Tom Arnold. The rock group Kiss introduced both teams with a wild pyrotechnic show.

"We felt like rock stars," Ducks defenceman Ben Lovejoy said. "We're not. We're simple hockey players. But for one night, that was so cool."

Unlike a couple of the Winter Classics in the north, where cold temperatures, strong winds, and blowing snow became factors, keeping ice level in California at a reasonable temperature was the only real challenge. Soft spots led to some unpredictable bounces, but rival coaches Darryl Sutter of the Kings and Boudreau were quick to say the conditions were the same for both teams.

Two of the Ducks who had been acclimatized to California the longest, Corey Perry and Ryan Getzlaf, combined on the first Anaheim goal at the 2:45 mark. Matt Beleskey added another a few minutes later.

Intermission and pre-game festivities featured very traditional local pastimes: a beach volleyball court was set up in the outfield, while fans in summer clothes meandered about, did yoga poses, threw Frisbees, or tossed a ball. But unlike baseball, there was a clock in this game, and time ran out for a Kings comeback.

Andrew Cogliano scored an empty-netter, and in a true reflection of how far hockey had come all over the world, Anaheim's Swiss-born goalie, Jonas Hiller, stopped Slovenian Anze Kopitar on a penalty shot under the California night sky, one of 36 saves he made to earn the shutout.

The 87-year-old Lasorda was impressed with everything: the game, the show, and the fans.

"We've had the Beatles here," Lasorda said. "And now we have ice hockey here. I never thought I'd see it."

The L.A. Kings and Anaheim Ducks square off beneath the California evening skies in the state's first outdoor NHL game. (Gregory Shamus/Contributor/National Hockey League/Getty Images)

90

DETROIT'S CUP DROUGHT ENDS

When Gordie Howe led the Detroit Red Wings to their Stanley Cup victory in 1955, it marked the team's fourth championship in six years.

Unfortunately for hockey fans in Motor City, it also marked the beginning of a futile streak that lasted 42.

Howe had a playoff for the ages that year, with 20 points in 11 games, setting a playoff scoring record.

Detroit remained competitive through the 1960s, but drifted into the abyss in the 1970s. Their performance turned fans so sour (and rival fans so bold) that the Red Wings were derided as the "Dead Things."

But their fortunes changed for the better when Mike Ilitch bought the team from Bruce Norris in 1982. A Detroit native, Ilitch had a passion for the team and the city. In an attempt to boost attendance, he gave away a car at every Red Wings home game.

He resisted the temptation to chase short-term fixes, instead having his management team focus on drafting and development. The rebuilding effort paid early dividends when the team drafted a kid named Steve Yzerman in 1983.

There were growing pains, but a decade later, the Red

Bowman matched the Grind Line straight up against the Legion of Doom and held them to two even-strength goals in a four-game series sweep.

Wings had developed into a strong organization that was close to a championship.

When Scotty Bowman took over as coach in 1993, he convinced the high-scoring Yzerman to play a two-way game. He told the Red Wings' captain that his point totals would suffer, but the team would have a better chance for success.

Yzerman bought in, and two years later Detroit advanced to the Stanley Cup Final. The bitter taste of New Jersey's sweep of that series provided the Wings with the fuel and resolve to try again.

After winning an NHL-record 62 games in 1995–96, Detroit lost the Western Conference final to the Colorado Avalanche. In a bid to add more physical presence to their lineup, the Red Wings acquired Brendan Shanahan from Hartford early in the 1996–97 season. The transaction rounded out a quintet that would eventually enter the Hockey Hall of Fame: Shanahan, Yzerman, Nicklas Lidstrom, Sergei Fedorov, and Igor Larionov.

Detroit made two other key moves that season, when they acquired forward Tomas Sandstrom from Pittsburgh in January 1997 and gave up future considerations to Toronto

Left: Sergei Fedorov and Eric Lindros battle for the puck during the 1997 Stanley Cup Final at Joe Louis Arena. (Doug MacLellan/Hockey Hall of Fame)

Previous page: Steve Yzerman hoists the Stanley Cup after Game 4 on June 7, 1997, at Joe Louis Arena. (Doug MacLellan/Hockey Hall of Fame)

90
100

Pete Babando and Harry Lumley of the Detroit Red Wings celebrate with the Stanley Cup in 1950. (Hockey Hall of Fame)

on trade deadline day for another future Hall of Famer, defenceman Larry Murphy. The Red Wings were now stacked and ready for the playoffs.

The creation of a new line helped Detroit as well. In the 1995 Final, Bowman had witnessed first-hand the havoc that New Jersey's Crash Line had produced. Bobby Holik, Randy McKay, and Mike Peluso disrupted and disturbed the Red Wings, while also chipping in with key goals. During the 1996–97 season, Bowman united Kris Draper with Kirk Maltby and Joey Kocur to create their own Grind Line.

The retooling helped Detroit turn the tables on Colorado in their Western Conference final rematch. The Wings prevailed in six games to advance and meet Philadelphia in the 1997 Stanley Cup Final.

The favoured Flyers were led by the Legion of Doom line of Eric Lindros, John LeClair, and Mikael Renberg.

Bowman matched the Grind Line straight up against the Legion of Doom and held them to two even-strength goals in a four-game series sweep. Detroit's 2–1 victory in Game 4 touched off a wild celebration.

Detroit was so dominant in the series that Philadelphia led for a total of just two minutes. Goaltender Mike Vernon held the potent Flyer offence to six goals in four games and was named the winner of the Conn Smythe Trophy as most valuable player in the playoffs.

With the long-awaited championship, the Dead Things were no more, and Motor City had picked up a new nickname that signalled Detroit's rekindled love affair with its Red Wings: Hockeytown.

WHA EXPANSION

The World Hockey Association always seemed like it could collapse at any second.

But the WHA had quite a run, from 1972 through 1979, with a cast of stars such as Bobby Hull and Gordie Howe leading a collection of star-crossed players and fly-by-night franchises.

By the end of the decade, however, the WHA was down to a handful of teams and was losing ground to the NHL, which was willing to offer up some expansion opportunities.

Some dealmakers in the NHL had hoped to absorb as many as 12 WHA clubs early in the new league's existence, if the WHA would drop the slew of lawsuits that had sprung from its creation and fork over $4 million per team in expansion fees.

That plan was defeated on both sides. More modest attempts to expand or merge were made in the ensuing years, but the appointment of John Ziegler as NHL president in 1977 was seen as a turning point. It was no longer a matter of *if* there would be a deal, but *when*.

The WHA actually believed that its 1977 championship, won by the Quebec Nordiques, would be the last Avco Cup

In Winnipeg, fans anxious to join the NHL, and angry at the Leafs, Canadiens, and Canucks for shutting them out, had begun organizing a boycott of Molson Brewery products.

awarded, amid talk that Edmonton, Winnipeg, Quebec, Houston, New England, and Cincinnati were about to join the NHL and form a new division in the league.

The sticking point, not surprisingly, was Toronto's Harold Ballard. At first ignoring and underestimating the legitimacy of the WHA, he lost many of his stars—including Dave Keon, Paul Henderson, and Norm Ullman—to the rival league, and then saw the WHA's Toronto franchise, the Toros, have some early success.

The Toros were even threatening to build a new arena, but when they were forced to play out of Maple Leaf Gardens, Ballard charged them high rent and made them pay to build a dressing room and use the rink's TV lights. He even took the soft padding off the players' bench.

The merger deal required the approval of three-quarters of the NHL's teams. To defeat it, Ballard needed only five "no" votes—his own, plus four others. His tireless lobbying of the other owners, combined with a report by the NHL finance committee that expressed doubt the WHA teams would be profitable, succeeded in getting the 1977–78 merger scrapped.

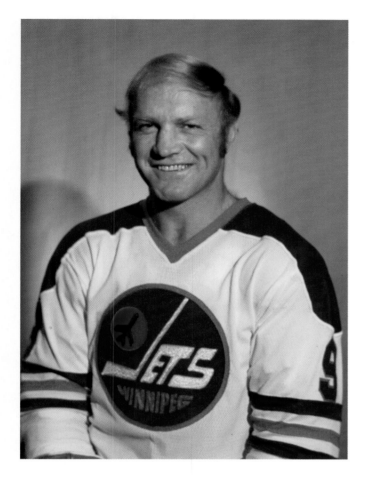

Opposite: Wayne Gretzky as a member of the Indianapolis Racers during the 1978-79 WHA season. (Graphic Artists/Hockey Hall of Fame)

Left: Bobby Hull as a member of the WHA's Winnipeg Jets. (Graphic Artists/Hockey Hall of Fame)

That led to a bold retaliatory strike by the WHA: the signing of underage juniors, topped by Indianapolis star Wayne Gretzky and the famous Baby Bulls, a stable of young stars signed by the Birmingham Bulls after the former Toros departed Toronto for Alabama.

The next season, with the NHL having encountered its own headaches with financially troubled clubs in Colorado, Cleveland, and Long Island, there appeared to be a deal on the table to merge the leagues. But up against time constraints for the coming season, those talks failed as well. Montreal, Toronto, Vancouver, Boston, and Los Angeles remained strongly opposed to the merger, and by March 1979, Houston was no longer in the discussion, Cincinnati was fading fast, and Birmingham was struggling.

Despite a proposal to get the Canadian NHL teams on board by keeping TV money away from Winnipeg and Edmonton, the five holdouts again blocked expansion at meetings held in Key Largo, Florida. But before the next day dawned, Washington Capitals alternate governor Peter O'Malley organized his own smaller huddle on Chicago owner Bill Wirtz's yacht. Inviting only Frank Griffiths from Vancouver from among the dissenters, and leaving out pro-merger governors that Griffiths didn't like, O'Malley let the Vancouver owner air all his expansion concerns.

The other governors listened and suggested ways the Canucks could be placated, including a balanced schedule to make sure popular teams such as Toronto and Montreal still made it to the West Coast on a regular basis.

A uniquely Canadian angle to all this was playing out as well. In Winnipeg, fans anxious to join the NHL, and angry at the Leafs, Canadiens, and Canucks for shutting them out, had begun organizing a boycott of Molson Brewery products. The principal sponsors of *Hockey Night in Canada* did not take this lightly and urged that a deal be done. In Ottawa, the House of Commons called on the NHL to be magnanimous and take in the new Canadian teams.

The next vote saw expansion for 1979–80 approved. Montreal relented, though Toronto, Boston (Paul Mooney), and Los Angeles (Jack Kent Cooke) opposed it until the very end. Griffiths's "yes" vote for Vancouver tipped the balance.

The Winnipeg Jets, Edmonton Oilers, Quebec Nordiques, and Hartford (ex–New England) Whalers came aboard for $6 million each (an increase of $2 million from earlier negotiations). The four newcomers were allowed to protect two skaters and two goalies, allowing NHL teams to reclaim any players they'd lost to the four WHA clubs, and the NHL teams were allowed to protect 15 players and two goalies. The WHA teams also agreed to go to the end of the line in the 1979 amateur entry draft.

"It was a pretty good deal for the NHL," said Howard Baldwin of the Whalers. "It's like you've got this ulcer that's driving you crazy and all of a sudden this ulcer is giving you money and players."

The new teams were spread among four divisions in a new 21-team NHL. Edmonton won the Stanley Cup within a few years. Quebec moved to Colorado in 1996 and won, and Hartford, which moved to Carolina, won in 2006.

To date, of the four only the Jets, who relocated to Arizona in 1996, have yet to triumph.

WHA Toronto Toros captain Frank Mahovlich. (Graphic Artists/ Hockey Hall of Fame)

L'AFFAIRE LINDROS

Eric Lindros made life difficult for the NHL when he decided not to play for the Quebec Nordiques after they made him the first-overall selection in the 1991 entry draft.

Nordiques president and co-owner Marcel Aubut then made life even more difficult for the league a year later when he traded Lindros to two teams—the Philadelphia Flyers and New York Rangers—on the same day.

That day happened to be draft day, in Montreal.

Lindros had been through a similar scenario as a 16-year-old Junior B sensation. He had skill and size and would later be anointed "The Next One" for his surefire superstar potential. He was clearly ticketed to be the first-overall selection in the 1989 Ontario Hockey League draft.

But Lindros made it clear he would not report to and play for the team that had the No. 1 pick, the Sault Ste. Marie Greyhounds, citing educational concerns and the fact the Northern Ontario city was too far from his Toronto home.

Greyhounds co-owner Phil Esposito drafted Lindros anyway, prompting the Big E to take his talents to Detroit, where he would begin the 1989–90 season in the North American Hockey League with the Detroit Compuware Ambassadors.

The OHL did not allow its member clubs to trade first-round selections back then, but the league changed its bylaws because it wanted Lindros in the league. In mid-December, the Greyhounds worked out a trade with the Oshawa Generals.

With Lindros, the Generals won the Memorial Cup that season, and the trade also helped transform the struggling Greyhounds into back-to-back league champions in 1990–91 and 1991–92, as well as Memorial Cup champions at home in 1992–93.

A few weeks after the Greyhounds celebrated their Memorial Cup championship, Lindros—by now a Philadelphia Flyer—finished fourth in the NHL's Calder Trophy voting behind winner Teemu Selanne, Joe Juneau, and goalie Felix Potvin.

Lindros could have been an NHL rookie a year sooner, but just as he had refused to play for the Greyhounds, he had also told the Quebec Nordiques he would not play for them, because his family did not like Aubut and there were concerns that he would not reach his full marketing potential in a small market like Quebec City.

The saga was given the moniker *l'Affaire Lindros*. Aubut and his general manager/coach Pierre Page spent the year trying to persuade Lindros to give Quebec City a shot, even offering him a 10-year, $55 million contract. Lindros and his

Philadelphia Flyers captain Eric Lindros faces off against Kevin Todd during the 1992-93 NHL season. (O-Pee-Chee/Hockey Hall of Fame)

Drafted first overall by the Quebec Nordiques in 1991, Eric Lindros didn't play an NHL game until after his trade to the Philadelphia Flyers. (S Levy/Contributor/Getty Images)

agent, Rick Curran, countered with a short-term, two-year offer that the Nordiques declined.

Instead, Lindros donned four different sweaters in 1991–92: he played for Canada in the Canada Cup, the world junior championship, and the 1992 Olympic Games, as well as playing 13 games for the Oshawa Generals.

Leading up to the 1992 NHL draft in Montreal, Page had worked out lists of players and assets from Rangers GM Neil Smith and his Flyers counterpart, Russ Farwell, and presented both potential trades to Aubut for a final decision.

But Aubut then agreed to both trades on the morning of Saturday, June 20, 1992, leaving the NHL to employ prominent Toronto labour lawyer Larry Bertuzzi to figure out which team Lindros should belong to.

The Rangers had offered forwards Tony Amonte and Sergei Nemchinov, defenceman James Patrick, prospect Alexei Kovalev, draft picks, a choice of goalies Mike Richter or John Vanbiesbrouck, and $20 million.

The Flyers' bid consisted of goalie Ron Hextall, defencemen Steve Duchesne and Kerry Huffman, forwards Mike Ricci and Peter Forsberg, their No. 1 draft choice in 1993, and $15 million.

After 11 days of deliberation, Bertuzzi deemed that Aubut had called the Flyers at 10:30 a.m. to agree to a trade and the Rangers at 11:50 a.m. The key piece of evidence was that Flyers owner Ed Snider had been given Lindros's phone number so that the Flyers could determine whether or not he was okay with playing in Philadelphia.

Aubut did not agree with Bertuzzi's decision, because he felt the Rangers' offer was better, but then proclaimed at a press conference a day later, "This marks the first day of a brilliant future for the Quebec Nordiques."

Smith also did not dispute Bertuzzi's decision, while the six-foot-four, 225-pound Lindros was overjoyed.

"Bags are packed," he said. "I'm just happy to get out of there."

The only wrinkle for Bertuzzi to iron out was the fact that the draft had come and gone, so the Nordiques had missed their chance to use the Flyers' first-round pick. Instead, the Nordiques received Philadelphia's first-round selection in the '94 draft—goalie Jocelyn Thibault—and forward Chris Simon.

A couple of weeks after Bertuzzi's decision, Lindros signed a six-year deal worth more than $15 million, a contract that paid less than the Nordiques' offer, but nonetheless a deal that changed the salary landscape across the NHL.

The double-dealing mix-up also resulted in the NHL instituting an event known as the trade call, whereby teams that have agreed to a deal must submit it to the league's Central Registry to be scrutinized.

Funny how things worked out for the three teams. The Rangers did not land Lindros, but did win their first Stanley Cup in 54 years in 1993–94. The Nordiques moved to Denver in 1995 to become the Colorado Avalanche. The Avs won the Stanley Cup in 1995–96 and again in 2000–01.

Lindros and the Flyers, however, never won the league championship. The closest they came was in 1996–97, when they were swept by the Detroit Red Wings in the final.

But even without a Cup, Lindros did have an impressive career, winning the Hart Trophy in 1994–95 and an Olympic gold medal with Team Canada in 2002, and he was inducted into the Hockey Hall of Fame in 2016.

With his combination of size and skill, Philadelphia Flyers captain Eric Lindros had many occasions to celebrate during his NHL career. (Dave Sandford/Hockey Hall of Fame)

93

THE COFFEY TRADE

Like a jagged crack in the smooth ice at Northlands Coliseum, the Paul Coffey trade was the first sign the high-flying Edmonton Oilers would one day need to be broken up.

When the mega-deal went down on November 24, 1987, the Oilers were in pursuit of their fourth Stanley Cup in five years, with Wayne Gretzky, Mark Messier, Jari Kurri, Glenn Anderson, and Grant Fuhr still in their prime.

But Coffey had crossed a line in the eyes of Glen Sather, chaperone of the "boys on the bus."

Sather had managed his stable of stars quite adroitly since the young Oilers had come of age, dethroned the New York Islanders as Cup champions, and proceeded toward a dynasty of their own. Gretzky was their unquestioned maestro, with plenty of help from wingers, second-liners, bodyguards, and other character players, but Coffey was just as feared and respected by NHL opponents. He could carry the mail, jump into the play, and, just as vitally, use his wheels to get back to his end if warranted.

Unlike some Oilers, Coffey's early NHL development took some time. He was the fourth defenceman to be selected among the top six picks in the 1980 NHL draft (Dave

Coffey mostly adhered to the Oilers' golden rules: "Be on time, don't embarrass the coach, and work hard."

Babych, Larry Murphy, and Darren Veitch went ahead of him), and the freewheeling ways he exhibited with the Kitchener Rangers made him exciting and dangerous offensively, but he had some struggles defensively, as young defencemen often do. He was stung by criticism from the media. But in his second season he improved dramatically.

But no one doubted he could skate like the wind, and Sather was quick to realize his potential as a virtual fourth forward in the Edmonton attack, especially when given open ice. "Do what you do best" was Sather's advice, and so Coffey took the puck and made history.

In 1983–84, the Oilers' first Cup campaign, Coffey passed Messier, Anderson, and Kurri and finished second to Gretzky in league scoring with 40 goals and 126 points. The next year, his numbers fell a bit, to 37 and 121, but he then piled up 37 playoff points and finished a plus-26.

More records fell, most notably Bobby Orr's mark for most goals in a season, which was topped by Coffey's 48 in 1985–86. That was the same season Coffey won his second Norris Trophy as top defenceman and had an eight-point game against Detroit, matching Gretzky's best night.

Coffey mostly adhered to the Oilers' golden rules:

Left: Paul Coffey and Edmonton Oilers team owner Peter Pocklington are interviewed after an 8-3 win over the Philadelphia Flyers in Game 5 of the 1985 Stanley Cup finals. (Paul Bereswill/Hockey Hall of Fame)

Opposite: Paul Coffey won his fourth Stanley Cup with the Mario Lemieux-led Pittsburgh Penguins in 1990-91. (O-Pee-Chee/Hockey Hall of Fame)

"Be on time, don't embarrass the coach, and work hard."

With the Oilers rising to prominence as a group and playing in one of the league's smaller markets, it was easier to maintain order, especially when they were winning.

The NHL's financial landscape was quickly changing, however. After Edmonton's third Cup in '87 and a role with Team Canada in that year's Canada Cup, Coffey was looking for a raise. He was on the same pay scale as Ray Bourque, who'd just won the Norris and played for the Boston Bruins. But in the days when Canadian teams paid in Canadian dollars, Coffey was taking a hit on the exchange rate and thought he deserved a break.

When Sather reached an accord with Messier but wouldn't renegotiate Coffey's deal, which had two years left to run, Coffey stayed away from training camp. Sather saw giving in to Coffey as a dangerous precedent and let him languish for weeks, further wounding Coffey's pride.

The stalemate was finally broken when the Pittsburgh Penguins decided they needed offensive help on the back end to complement young star Mario Lemieux. They also received big hitters Dave Hunter and Wayne Van Dorp in a deal that involved seven players in all.

Sather would miss Coffey, but letting him sit all year would certainly yield no return. Sather got the player he had his eye on, former No. 2 pick Craig Simpson, as well as checking centre Dave Hannan and defenceman Chris Joseph.

By this time the Oilers were already dealing with another headache on the contract front: that of backup goalie Andy Moog. But the biggest loss they would suffer was to come less than a year after Coffey was traded: the ugly divorce with Gretzky. Within a couple of years, Anderson, Fuhr, Messier, and Kurri would all be traded.

The Oilers still had enough magic to win the 1990 Cup and reach the Campbell Conference final for a couple more years, but the league's power base had begun moving south with Gretzky toward his Los Angeles Kings, and east to Pittsburgh, where Coffey recorded two more 100-point seasons, joining Lemieux in parading the Cup around Steeltown in 1991.

Coffey would eventually hook up with Gretzky and some other ex-Oilers in L.A., one of nine different teams Coffey played on—a record number of moves for a Hall of Famer. As of summer 2017, Coffey remained 13th in all-time NHL scoring with 1,531 points, second only to Bourque's 1,579 among defencemen. Bourque, Coffey, and Larry Murphy were all enshrined in the Hall in 2004.

94

JOHN ZIEGLER'S PRESIDENCY

Talk about having big shoes to fill.

When John Ziegler accepted the role of president of the National Hockey League in 1977, he replaced a legend in Clarence Campbell, a military officer who had served his country with distinction before taking the job in 1946. Campbell held the post for 31 years until his health began to suffer in 1977. The league required a successor.

John A. Ziegler Jr. was well-known to the NHL. The Grosse Pointe, Michigan native obtained his law degree from the University of Michigan and became a senior partner in a prestigious Detroit firm, later branching out on his own, doing work for the Detroit Red Wings for almost two decades, serving as an alternate governor from 1970-77.

During that time, Ziegler served on numerous league committees and began to gain the attention and respect of many club owners.

The 43-year old had just replaced Chicago Blackhawks owner Bill Wirtz as chairman of the league's board of governors in 1976, when he was tapped to replace Campbell a year later.

Upon taking office, one of the first challenges Ziegler faced was arranging a merger with the rival World Hockey Association and absorbing four of its teams into the NHL.

Not all the NHL owners were in favour of the move, but Ziegler deftly managed to reach a consensus amongst the league's governors.

The agreement with the WHA to absorb the Quebec Nordiques, Winnipeg Jets, Edmonton Oilers and New England Whalers for the start of the 1979-80 season, with $6 million entry fees, proved to be one of Ziegler's greatest accomplishments over his 15-year term as the NHL's fourth president.

Ziegler was instrumental in keeping the Cleveland Barons from folding, instead arranging for the merger of Cleveland and Minnesota in 1978-79.

During his tenure, the League grew from 18 to 24 teams.

And the stature of the League also grew on the international stage, with the advent of the Super Series, a series of exhibition games between NHL and Soviet teams, which included the famed 1975 New Year's Eve game between Montreal Canadiens and Red Army. There was also the 1979 Challenge Cup, three games between the Soviets and NHL all-stars, and later Rendez-Vous '87 in Quebec City.

Under Ziegler top European talent flowed into the NHL, expanding from two percent of players in 1977 to 11 percent in 1992. The American talent pool also grew, from two percent in 1977 to 18 percent in 1992.

The NHL All-Star Weekend and the TV Awards show also originated while Ziegler was president. Attendance grew

NHL president John Ziegler talks to the press in 1988. (Paul Bereswill/Hockey Hall of Fame)

and so did the business, thanks in part to Ziegler's good relationship with the NHL Players' Association under executive director Alan Eagleson.

In 1992, with the NHLPA under new leadership, Ziegler helped to bring an end to a 10-day player strike late in the season. Having been already elected to the Hockey Hall of Fame as a builder (in 1987), Ziegler stepped down as president before the end of the year.

95

THE KID WINS THE CUP

Sidney Crosby was playing junior hockey with the Rimouski Oceanic of the Quebec Major Junior Hockey League, when the Great One, Wayne Gretzky, was asked if he could imagine a player who might one day break some of his legendary NHL scoring records.

"Yes," said Gretzky. "Sidney Crosby. He's the best player I've seen since Mario [Lemieux]."

Heady praise, indeed, about the Next One.

That was 2003. Years later Gretzky's records may not be broken, but the Great One wasn't wrong about Crosby, who has been to his generation what Gretzky was to his and Lemieux to his. A generational player. A superstar.

Indeed, Crosby even did it for the same franchise as Lemieux, the Pittsburgh Penguins' part-owner and former star. He kept it alive and gave it a new pulse.

Lemieux, of course, was the Penguins' first-overall pick in the controversial 1984 entry draft. Controversial because many people believed that the Penguins didn't try to avoid finishing last in order to get the first pick, a turn of events that eventually led to the advent of the draft lottery.

But Lemieux turned the franchise around and made it a two-time Stanley Cup winner, and then saved it from bankruptcy when he assumed partial ownership.

Crosby was the first pick in the 2005 draft, after the Penguins won the first draft lottery coming out of the lockout season.

At first, Lemieux was briefly a teammate but also a mentor. The 18-year-old Crosby lived in a guest house with the Lemieux family. Like Lemieux before him, Crosby rejuvenated the franchise with his rare talent and helped restore the Penguins to glory. In 2009, at the tender age of 21, he became the youngest captain ever to win the Stanley Cup. He won two more, in 2016 and 2017, in many ways against longer odds.

There is no denying that Crosby is the greatest player of his era, just an inch ahead of the likes of Alex Ovechkin, Jonathan Toews, and Carey Price. All are superstars, but they aren't Sid. Between Cups, he won Olympic gold medals in 2010 and 2014, a Hart Trophy and scoring title in 2014, a World Championship in 2015, Conn Smythe Trophies in 2016 and 2017, and Rocket Richard Trophies in 2010 and 2017, all wrapped around prolonged absences due to injury. (Add to those achievements a World Cup and MVP honours in the summer of 2016, fresh off that second Stanley Cup.)

In 2009, at the tender age of 21, he became the youngest captain ever to win the Stanley Cup.

Penguins captain Sidney Crosby looks for an opportunity at the BB&T Center in Sunrise, Florida. (Ward Benjamin/Hockey Hall of Fame)

As Gretzky put it, Crosby has the ability No. 99 himself had, that Bobby Orr had, that Mario Lemieux had, to make everyone around him that much better.

In his rookie season, Crosby amassed 102 points and finished as the runner-up to Ovechkin for the Calder Trophy as top rookie. The next season, he had 120 points, won the scoring title, and was named the league's most valuable player. Knowing "The Kid" had all the ingredients, the Penguins asked him to set the table for his team and named Crosby captain in 2007–08 at 20 years of age, at the time making him the youngest to wear the *C* in league history. He helped lead the team to the 2008 Stanley Cup Final. The Penguins lost to the Detroit Red Wings in six games, but Crosby tied for the playoff scoring lead with 27 points.

The next season, the Penguins and Red Wings reversed roles, and Pittsburgh won the Cup in seven games. He led all playoff scorers with 15 goals and finished second in points with 31. He then led the NHL with 51 goals in 2009–10 and also scored what has been called the "Golden Goal" in overtime of the gold medal game at the 2010 Winter Olympics in Vancouver.

Sidney Crosby celebrates Pittsburgh's 2016 Cup win with former Penguins captain and now owner Mario Lemieux and wife Nathalie Asselin. (Craig Campbell/Hockey Hall of Fame)

But on January 1, 2011, playing in the Winter Classic in Pittsburgh, Crosby absorbed a hit from Washington Capitals forward David Steckel that seemed to start a series of health issues and prolonged departures from the game.

In the next two seasons, he played just 58 regular-season games and another 20 in the playoffs. But in 2014 he bounced back in a big way, leading the league with 104 points. Two years after that, despite a horrible start to the season, during which he was doubting himself, Crosby and the Penguins turned their fortunes around in December and won another Stanley Cup in the spring.

For those wondering why he wears the number 87, it's simple. He was born on August 7, 1987. The eighth month, seventh day, 87th year.

In 2011, he signed a 12-year contract extension worth $104.4 million (U.S.) with the Penguins that started in the 2013–14 season, making his average annual salary, fittingly enough, $8.7 million, though he will actually average $10.6 million over the first nine years of the deal, taking him to age 35.

In 2016, Crosby was asked about the next generation, the

With a record-breaking four goals in his NHL debut, Toronto Maple Leaf Auston Matthews is one of today's young stars hoping to be to their generation what Sidney Crosby has been to his own. (Rusty Barton/Hockey Hall of Fame)

With his first 100-point season in 2016-17, Edmonton Oilers sophomore and captain Connor McDavid will have ample opportunity to compare himself to the most accomplished player in today's game. (Rusty Barton/Hockey Hall of Fame)

likes of the Edmonton Oilers' young star Connor McDavid and the Toronto Maple Leafs' Auston Matthews, among others.

On *Sports Illustrated*'s website, The Cauldron, Crosby wrote: "As if outrunning the downside of my career wasn't motivation enough, the new guys coming into the league will surely have my attention, too. These are the young and hungry guys. The guys that want to be where you are.

"They're fast. They're strong. And with all the young talent throughout the league, it just makes you want to get better yourself. That's such a fun part of the game to me. I love having to adjust and adapt my game year to year to find ways to be my best."

And that explains why he is the best of his generation.

96

1967 EXPANSION

Ed Snider had sold flowers, vinyl records, and Christmas trees, and by 1966 he had parlayed all that into a 7 per cent ownership stake in the Philadelphia Eagles football team.

A casual hockey fan, he watched only the occasional game on TV, as there was no team in the City of Brotherly Love. That started to change after a conversation with Bill Putnam, who handled the Eagles' business with the J.P. Morgan bank. Putnam mentioned he'd be leaving the football club soon for a new opportunity in Los Angeles.

"What's going on out there?" Snider asked, and Putnam told him that as many as six franchises could soon be available in the National Hockey League. Putnam was getting in on the ground floor with owner Jack Kent Cooke, who was making one of the bids for the L.A. franchise.

"There was nothing in the papers in Philadelphia about NHL expansion," Snider said. "As far as the papers here were concerned, the NHL did not exist."

Putnam liked Cooke's chances to get a team for L.A., since he already owned the NBA's Los Angeles Lakers, a piece of the NFL's Washington Redskins, and other sports properties.

That intrigued Snider, as Philadelphia was a city with a northern climate and working-class sports fans. He, too, had a piece of an established team. Why not explore further? When Putnam told Snider that Baltimore was vying for one of the teams, that settled it. Snider's civic pride kicked in and he began to put a group together.

"'I think we'd be better than Baltimore,'" he told Putnam. "I went up to New York to see [Rangers boss] William Jennings, the head of the expansion committee."

The NHL had been a six-team league since the 1942–43 season. An early expansion bid, in 1945–46, had come from Frank Sinatra, who had promised to send a $10,000 deposit cheque and had been willing to build a 20,000-seat arena in Los Angeles. Sinatra's bid stalled, but after decades of a closed shop that went no further west than Chicago, the NHL started to get expansion fever midway through the swinging '60s.

Jennings of the Rangers was the true hawk for expansion, and others came on board when word started circulating that the big American television networks thought the NHL was too regional, but would pay to broadcast games if they had a larger pool of teams across the U.S., and especially

Thirteen groups from eight cities gathered at the board of governors meeting at the St. Regis Hotel in New York, early in February 1966, to make their bids.

if it included L.A., the ratings-rich southern California market. Thus, a team in L.A. was given the highest priority if and when expansion was approved, in particular because Cooke had plans to build the Fabulous Forum.

On March 11, 1965, the NHL announced it would consider applications. Thirteen groups from eight cities gathered at the board of governors meeting at the St. Regis Hotel in New York, early in February 1966, to make their bids. There were multiple groups from Los Angeles and Pittsburgh, and one each from Vancouver, Philadelphia, Minneapolis-St. Paul, Buffalo, Baltimore, San Francisco–Oakland, and Louisville.

There was also keen interest expressed from Cleveland and St. Louis, and some from Seattle, Portland, and Hamilton.

The expansion fee would be $2 million, and the prospective teams required an arena that could hold at least 12,500.

Most thought NHL president Clarence Campbell would proceed cautiously with expansion, starting with a gradual increase—perhaps two teams a year. When the announcement was made on February 9, 1966 that the league was doubling to 12 teams, shock waves were felt among hockey fans. There was outrage from some, who feared the league would become diluted. Some had to get out maps to see where these new teams would be located.

Yet the so-called Original Six had come to accept the expansion for many reasons, not the least of which was money: the franchise fees and the lure of big TV money.

Now they had to iron out the details of which cities made sense and how to stock the clubs. Having just one team in California made little sense from a travel perspective. The league had taken note of how the Los Angeles Dodgers and San Francisco Giants had built a coastal rivalry. Thus, Oakland was in with the Kings.

Minnesota's problem was its smaller market size, but a strong group of nine investors kept lobbying the governors,

warning them not to overlook America's most fervent hockey fans.

Pittsburgh had political and monetary clout and, unlike other teams, a strong pro-hockey tradition that included the Pittsburgh Hornets, once a farm team of the Leafs. Another plus was its fairly new building, the igloo-shaped Civic Arena, and city support to make the team part of an urban renewal plan.

Snider and his group had no grand rink to offer the league, but in planning the footprint of Veterans Stadium they realized a piece of land near Broad Street was available where they could shoehorn in a rink. With a few phone calls and help from city hall, Snider rushed through approval for what would become the Spectrum. That cinched the bid. The franchise was actually awarded to Putnam, who'd had a falling-out with Cooke.

Each new franchise had to write its $2 million cheque directly to an existing team. Philadelphia wrote theirs to the Maple Leafs.

The true dark horse was St. Louis, which was awarded a conditional franchise pending the ownership group obtaining an arena.

St. Louis had a rink, an aging white elephant called simply the Arena, a property owned by Blackhawks owner James Norris. After struggling in Chicago through the 1950s and then hitting the jackpot in the early '60s with a Cup winner and a stable of stars, Norris was the least willing to share any of his wealth and players with new teams.

An expansion vote had to be unanimous among the six governors, and Norris had been shaping up as an obstacle, until he realized that putting a team in St. Louis would give him a way to unload the Arena. Norris made the inclusion of a franchise by the banks of the Mississippi River the price of his vote; the idea was appealing because it would give the league another team in the Midwest to break up plane trips to and from the West Coast. The Salomon family, owners of

Cleveland Barons Bob Murdoch during a game at the St. Louis
Arena in 1977. (Steven Goldstein/Hockey Hall of Fame)

a local insurance company, stepped up as owners, but they paid a steep price. Between the expansion fee, the purchase of the arena, and upgrades to the rink, the cost was more than $7 million.

In June 1967, following the league's 50th season, the old and the new gathered in Montreal for the expansion draft. The existing teams were allowed to protect 11 skaters and one goalie.

"The day we got the franchise, we hired our general manager [Bud Poile] and coach [Keith Allen]," Snider said. "I think we did an incredible job [at the draft]. Seven of those guys played on the Stanley Cup champions [in 1974]. Usually, the players you get in expansion are mostly gone in a few years. The guys we got played a major role in our winning the Cup. We got Bernie Parent back, Doug Favell as our backup, Gary Dornhoefer, Joe Watson, Ed Van Impe.

"It was really a tremendous, tremendous expansion. That gave us the foundation, and when we brought in kids, they all adhered to our program."

As part of the expansion agreement, the new teams played in their own division, with a playoff structure that ensured an expansion club would advance to the Stanley Cup Final in each of the next three years.

St. Louis was that team all three years, and was swept in four games all three years—twice by Montreal, once by Boston.

Needless to say, many noses were left out of joint in the cities turned down for the Great Expansion. The inclusion of St. Louis and Philadelphia bumped Baltimore. Buffalo, convinced it was a lock, was bitter, as was the Vancouver delegation, which was quick to blame Toronto and Montreal for blocking it in order to avoid giving up a share of Canadian television-rights fees.

But the latter two cities would be added a few years later, and many of the bidders eventually joined the NHL in subsequent expansions that have since brought the league's membership to 31 teams.

Opposite: California Golden Seals goalie Giles Meloche and Len Frig during a game at St. Louis Arena in 1975. (Lewis Portnoy/Hockey Hall of Fame)

MESSIER GUARANTEES THE WIN

The headlines said it all.

"Mess Sez We'll Win," screamed the *New York Daily News* on the morning of May 25, 1994.

"Captain Courageous' bold prediction: WE'LL WIN TONIGHT" was the headline in the *New York Post*.

It was a day earlier, after a practice prior to the sixth game of the Eastern Conference final, when Mark Messier delivered his promise.

His New York Rangers were on the brink of elimination, trailing the New Jersey Devils, 3–2, in the series, with the weight of a Stanley Cup drought dating back to 1940 weighing heavily on their shoulders.

Players typically avoid making bold predictions or promises in public. No one wants to give the opposition any "bulletin board" additional motivation.

But Messier was a different breed.

He was a five-time Stanley Cup champion at the time, and was intent on being the messiah that helped lead the Rangers to their first Cup win in 54 years.

Whenever they played in New Jersey, or against their other local rival, the New York Islanders, hostile fans would start up the derisive chant "1940," referencing that last Cup win and the long drought since.

But Messier knew exactly what he was doing when he told reporters, "We're going to go in there and win Game 6. That was the focus this morning and it's the way we feel right now. We've done that all year, we've won all the games we've had to win. I know we're going to go in and win Game 6 and bring it back for Game 7."

He hadn't been asked for a promise, but he gave one. The captain wanted his teammates to know he believed they could overcome. He wanted to rally the team. And he put himself front and centre to take the heat.

Years later, Messier admitted he might have underestimated the stir his comments would create off the ice.

"I would've liked to crawl back into bed and had it disappear originally," Messier told the *Post*.

But his intentions were clear.

"I felt that it would be a great way to let my players know that I believed we could go in there and win Game 6 because we had beaten them six times during the regular season."

The game did not begin well for the Rangers, who trailed, 2–0, late in the second period. But then Messier did what great leaders do: he led by example.

Years later, Messier admitted he might have underestimated the stir his comments would create off the ice.

Determination and leadership, with the skill and strength to back it up:
Mark Messier was the captain New York Rangers fans had been waiting for.
(Paul Bereswill/Hockey Hall of Fame)

After Rangers coach Mike Keenan called a time out midway through the second period, he also adjusted his lines, putting Alex Kovalev alongside Messier and Adam Graves. It worked.

Messier set up Kovalev for a goal just before the period was over, with 1:41 left, giving the Rangers a little momentum heading into the third period.

The Rangers started to force the play offensively and Messier tied the game three minutes into the third period, then gave them the lead with 7:48 left in the game. He sealed the 4–2 win with an empty-net goal, forcing the seventh game back at Madison Square Garden he had promised.

As great as Messier was, all the Rangers agreed the game would have been lost much earlier had it not been for the outstanding goaltending of Mike Richter, who kept the game close and gave his team a chance to win and Messier a chance to be the hero.

Game 7 was a classic, with winger Stephane Matteau scoring in double overtime to give the Rangers a 2–1 victory.

"I think I was so focusing on trying to direct my attention to the team, and by doing so I forgot, or I miscalculated . . . that other people would be reading the article I intended for the players to read," Messier told the *Post* 20 years later. "Somehow I tried to find a way to instill that confidence back into the team. And you know, I guess the rest is history."

"What transpired in the papers and the guarantee didn't put any more pressure on me than I had already put on myself to try and find a way to win that game," Messier told *The Hockey News*. "Once the game started, luckily enough for me, I had a lot of experience playing in those types of situations and the one thing that experience teaches you is that you can't get too far ahead of yourself. You have to stay in the moment and try and execute a game plan from the start of the game to the end."

And so the Rangers advanced to the Stanley Cup final, which turned into an epic battle with the Vancouver Canucks.

After losing the series opener at home, the Rangers went on to win the next three games and had a chance to end the Curse of 1940 at home in Game 5. But the Canucks rallied to win the next two games, making the Rangers and their faithful sweat it out till the bitter end.

But the Rangers prevailed, 3–2, at home to end their 54-year drought.

98

GOALIE INNOVATIONS

Many hockey fans know the term "standing on his head" to describe an outstanding game by a goaltender.

Few realize, however, that the phrase actually had to do with a welcome rule change at the dawn of NHL play, allowing goalies to make saves by dropping to the ice. The early rules required goalies to stay on their feet at all times, forcing them to use mostly their sticks and skates to block pucks.

Non-compliance resulted in a penalty, so it's no wonder the first two games on the schedule of the four-team NHL in December 1917 ended in scores of 10–9 and 7–4.

Clint Benedict of the Ottawa Senators had already figured out a way around such an unfair ruling by faking injury or body contact, thus enabling him to go into a sprawl. On his knees so often, the six-foot-four Ottawa native was given the nickname "The Praying Goaltender," and his shenanigans became so popular, so fast, that league president Frank Calder had to act quickly. On January 9, 1918, he revised the rules to allow goaltenders freedom to flop.

"As far as I'm concerned, they can stand on their head if they want," Calder said, and the phrase was born.

On his knees so often, the six-foot-four Ottawa native was given the nickname "The Praying Goaltender."

The goalie position had already come a long way since the 19th century and hockey's earliest beginnings. Two curling rocks—or, failing that, cobblestones—had formed the net. In some places, poles with red flags on top, as far apart as eight feet, outlined a shooter's target.

The keeper used the same stick as his six mates (seven-man teams with a rover were the norm). "Umpires," and not referees or goal judges, would shout out, "Game ho!" when the puck went in—goals were known as "games" in some areas of Canada. Thin pads borrowed from the sport of cricket were the keeper's only form of protection.

Gradually, elbow pads came into use, and then crude wooden blockers, chest protectors from baseball, and the modified catcher's mitt.

But the head remained unguarded, and when players such as the "Big Bomber," Charlie Conacher, could reputedly fire a puck through the mesh, the risk of facial injury became a deep concern. Benedict was the first to fashion a leather mask in 1930, after a Howie Morenz drive broke his nose, but he found it harder to see the puck. Just under two months later he was again hit in the face and had to leave what turned out to be his last NHL game.

Almost 30 years would pass before Jacques Plante developed a fiberglass mask, debuting it under arduous circumstances when he, too, was badly injured. A hard backhand shot by Andy Bathgate in a game at Madison Square Garden made a mess of Plante's face. After a 20-minute delay while he was being stitched up, Plante was reluctantly given permission by coach Toe Blake to use a mask he'd experimented with during practice.

Plante was thankful the Canadiens won that game and then went on a bit of a roll, because it kept a skeptic such as Blake from blaming any poor performances on the mask. Previously, NHL coaches, players, and even goalies had seen facial protection as a sign of mental weakness.

While the face was a focus, other protective advancements were taking place. Goalies had fashioned leg padding from all manner of sources in the early days. The famously thick Eaton's department store catalogues were used by kids in pickup hockey, while Leaf great Johnny Bower recalls that in Depression-era Saskatchewan a discarded crib mattress, sliced in two and held to the legs with giant elastics, worked fine.

Pads were widened and strengthened, but horsehide and leather retained too much sweat and moisture from the ice and grew heavy as games wore on. In the 1980s, lighter materials were developed, while various other changes to the exterior angles of pads helped goalies take away lower corners from shooters. Many goalies designed optical illusions into the colouring of their pads to disorient shooters.

But when pads began to exceed a foot in width, around the same time that goalies were developing other tricks of the trade, such as extra-large sweaters that obscured the vulnerable five-hole, the league began to reduce equipment sizes to address a drop in scoring. They even brought in the "pad police" from the hockey operations office to make sure all equipment was standardized.

The commitment to improved fitness among goalies—no longer were they the misfit physical specimens on the team—led to better results and more daring play outside of the crease. Plante was the first to roam and help his team's defence move the puck, while before that, Chuck Rayner of the Rangers had begun using a poke check to disarm forwards on breakaways rather than sitting back in the net and giving the shooter a tactical advantage.

Goalies began to come out and clear pucks more often, curving their sticks for better control and passing. Ron Hextall of the Flyers was so accurate he scored a couple of empty-net goals.

In 2000, Boston University's Rick DiPietro was drafted No. 1 overall in part because he was as good as a third defenceman when the puck was in his zone. Again, in an attempt to inject more scoring, the league established the trapezoid, a set of lines that stopped a goalie from venturing into the corners of the defensive zone.

As recently as 2017, the league ordered goalies to streamline hockey pants that it judged to be getting too large. But where rules and equipment are concerned, goalies are likely to keep pushing the envelope. As they often say, "If you're not cheating, you're not trying."

Opposite: Rangers goalie Chuck Rayner's sprawling save would have been illegal in the NHL's inaugural season, when goaltenders had to remain on their feet. (Le Studio du Hockey/Hockey Hall of Fame)

THE FAMILY GAMES

On the very first opening night of NHL action, brothers Corb and Cy Denneny—from Cornwall, Ontario—scored for the Toronto Arenas and Ottawa Senators, respectively.

They beat siblings Sprague and Odie Cleghorn (of the Senators and Montreal Canadiens, respectively) to that honour, but fans would have to wait until 1932–33 for Charlie and Lionel Conacher to become the first brothers to be named to a postseason all-star team.

A long NHL tradition of familial connections had begun, one that produced any number of memorable moments on and off the ice. Soon enough it involved fathers and sons: Montreal Wanderers goalie Bert Lindsay and his kid Terrible Ted; Gordie and Mark Howe; Bobby and Brett Hull; and coaching legend Dick Irvin, whose son Dick Jr. would receive the Hall of Fame's Foster Hewitt Memorial Award for his broadcasting.

In between were grandfathers, uncles, nephews, cousins, brothers-in-law, and fathers- and sons-in-law, with even a brother-sister combo in Pascal and Manon Rheaume, the latter the first woman to play in an NHL

game, as goalie during an exhibition game for the Tampa Bay Lightning.

But at the top of the list of hockey clans are the Sutters, whose impact on NHL history began with six rink rats who went from savage ball-hockey games in a hayloft in Viking, Alberta, to careers spanning more than 5,500 regular-season and playoff games in the NHL, in which they racked up more than 8,000 penalty minutes.

The second generation—Brett, Brandon, and Brody, the sons of Darryl, Brent, and Duane, respectively—have pushed that game total past 6,000, while Darryl, most recently behind the bench in Los Angeles, has kept the lineage of Sutter coaches going into a fourth decade.

In 1923–24, more than one-third of the NHL's players— 14 out of 41—had or would have brothers in the NHL, and over 90 years later there were Sedins, Staals, Schenns, and Stromes populating the 30 teams. The Richards—Maurice and Henri—together won 19 Stanley Cups. Canadiens management was initially accused of letting Henri play for the team just because he was the Rocket's

> In 1923–24, more than one-third of the NHL's players— 14 out of 41—had or would have brothers in the NHL, and 90 years later there were Sedins, Staals, Schenns, and Stromes populating the 30 teams.

Max and Doug Bentley with Chicago coach Johnny Gottselig during the 1945–46 season. (Le Studio de Hockey/Hockey Hall of Fame)

Few brother acts in NHL history compare to twins and career teammates Henrik and Daniel Sedin of the Vancouver Canucks. (Mathew Manor/Hockey Hall of Fame)

brother, but he was very much an all-star in his own right. Frank and Peter Mahovlich also won Cups in Montreal.

Meanwhile, father-and-son ties eventually shifted to management: Scotty Bowman to Stan, Cliff Fletcher to Chuck. Two GMs, Ray Shero and Pierre Dorion, were sons of famous coaches and scouts, respectively. Kevin and Gord Dineen followed their pop, Bill, from playing to coaching.

Back on the ice, Paul Devorski devoured the rule books that his father, Bill, left around their house from his days as an official with the Ontario Hockey Association. Bill found out how much reading his son had done when he saw the local paper one day and found out Paul was quitting as a senior amateur player to become an official.

Paul worked his way through industrial-league hockey to work 1,594 NHL games before retiring in 2015, to be followed by younger brother Greg, who is still active as a linesman.

At some point, one of the Devorskis surely had to get between feuding siblings on opposing teams, hoping brotherly love would trump the desire to fight.

Decades earlier, Charlie and Lionel Conacher did fight once, Charlie coming to the aid of a young Leaf who Lionel was picking on. Keith and Wayne Primeau once came to blows as the former's career was coming to an end.

"Family is for the off-season," declared Brian Sutter, though Duane and Brent, who were the first in the family to win Cups, were careful never to wear their championship rings around their eldest brother, out of respect.

Many NHL brother combos haven't bothered with acts of mercy: Phil Esposito scoring regularly on young Tony in goal, for one, which irritated their mother back in Sault Ste. Marie, Ontario.

When Eric, Marc, Jordan, and Jared Staal were kids

growing up in Thunder Bay, Ontario, they spent hours together on a backyard rink at the family's sod farm. Never did Linda and Henry Staal imagine their four boys would one day all make it to the NHL.

"Not in a million years," said Henry, talking to reporters on April 26, 2013, the night Jared made his NHL debut with the Carolina Hurricanes and started on a line with Eric and Jordan.

That night the Hurricanes were playing the New York Rangers, for whom Marc played. But Marc had to sit out the game after suffering an eye injury on March 5.

Hurricanes coach Kirk Muller had a flair for the dramatic and started Jared with Eric and Jordan, though they didn't play the whole game together. Jared wore sweater no. 13 to go with Eric's 12 and Jordan's 11.

The Staals became the third set of at least four brothers to play in the NHL, joining the Sutters, as well as Georges, Billy, Bobby, and Frank Boucher from Ottawa, who played in the 1920s and '30s.

The Staals also became the fourth set of three brothers to play on the same team, along with the Bentleys and the Plagers.

Tough-as-nails defencemen Barclay, Bob, and Bill Plager, who were from Kirkland Lake, Ontario, played for the St. Louis Blues in the late 1960s and early '70s.

On March 1, 1969, in a game in Montreal, the Blues started Barclay at centre, Bob on left wing, and Billy on right wing.

Some brothers proved inseparable in the truest sense. When Sprague Cleghorn did not survive injuries he sustained in a car accident in Montreal in 1956, Odie died the day before his brother's funeral—of a heart condition that, it was speculated, had worsened because of Sprague's passing.

100

"NEXT GOAL WINS": EPIC OVERTIMES

t's a familiar refrain to anyone who has played hockey in the rinks, on the ponds, or even the streets. And especially among those who have ever played, or even watched, sudden-death overtime in the Stanley Cup playoffs.

Overtime in the playoffs is arguably the most exciting spectacle in sports. Two teams that have battled hard for 60 minutes need extra time to decide the winner. Suddenly, hockey joins baseball as a contest that is not decided by a clock.

The difference is that in baseball, the playing of complete innings allows each side an opportunity to win the game (or for the home team to at least tie the score and prolong the action). Not so in hockey, where it's "next goal wins."

Sometimes it happens quickly. Brian Skrudland's goal nine seconds into overtime evened the 1986 Stanley Cup Final between his Montreal Canadiens and the Calgary Flames at one game each. Skrudland is one of six players—along with Alex Burrows, J.P. Parise, Martin Havlat, Pit Martin, and John Tavares—who have scored within the first 15 seconds of overtime.

Sometimes it takes a while. The first game of the 1936 semifinal series between the Montreal Maroons and Detroit Red Wings took a very long while.

Back then, the quarter-finals were a two-game, total-goals series, while the winners of the league's two divisions received a bye into a best-of-five semifinal series.

Playing then in an eight-team NHL, Montreal won the Canadian Division while Detroit took the American Division title. The two teams finished first and second overall during the regular season, separated by just two points.

Game 1 of the series was played on March 24. Goaltenders Normie Smith of the Red Wings and Lorne Chabot of the Maroons held their opponents at bay through 60 minutes. The game extended into a sixth overtime period, in which 21-year-old rookie Modere "Mud" Bruneteau finally beat Chabot at 16:30. In all, the teams had played an extra 116:30. The Wings went on to beat the Maroons, 3–0 and 2–1—both in regulation time—to sweep the series.

Three years earlier, in the 1933 semifinal, Toronto and Boston had set the previous record for the longest game, one in which Ken Doraty of the Leafs broke the tie at 104:46 of overtime.

Detroit's Pete Babando became the first player in NHL history to score an overtime winner in Game 7 of the Stanley Cup Final. It happened on April 23, 1950.

Babando turned the trick when he beat New York's Chuck Rayner at 8:31 of the second overtime period to give the Red Wings a 4–3 win in the game, as well as the 1950 championship.

Tony Leswick accomplished the feat four years later to become the second Red Wing to score an overtime winner in Game 7 of the Final, this time against Montreal's Gerry McNeil.

It took more than three decades after Leswick's marker before there was another marathon game, this one also a Game 7. On April 18, 1987, the New York Islanders visited the Washington Capitals for the deciding game of their Patrick Division semifinal series. The game, which came to be known as the "Easter Epic," turned out to be one for the ages.

New York's Kelly Hrudey made 73 saves and teammate Pat LaFontaine beat Bob Mason at 8:47 of the fourth overtime period. With the goal, the Islanders defeated the Capitals, 3–2, and advanced to the division final.

The longest overtime in Stanley Cup Final history was played three years later between Boston and Edmonton. Game 1 at Boston Garden was tied at two after regulation time. During the third overtime period, part of the old building went dark as the result of a blown circuit breaker, which forced a 30-minute delay.

The situation echoed one that had occurred during the 1988 final—the same Bruins and Oilers were tied at three when the power went out, with no hope of it being restored. Game 4 therefore had to be thrown out. With the Garden booked and unavailable for a do-over, the scheduled Game 5 in Edmonton, two nights later, actually became a replay of Game 4.

This time, the lights came back on and, 15:13 into the third overtime, the little-used Petr Klima came off the Oilers bench to beat Andy Moog. Edmonton went on to win the series, four games to one, and their fifth Stanley Cup in seven years—their first without Wayne Gretzky.

The third-longest overtime of the NHL's first century occurred on May 4, 2000, in an Eastern Conference semifinal game between the Penguins and Flyers. Pittsburgh swept the first two games in Philadelphia, but the Flyers took Game 3 in Pittsburgh (in OT) to cut the Penguins' series lead to 2–1.

After 60 minutes, Game 4 was tied at one. Keith Primeau finally beat Ron Tugnutt at 12:01 in the fifth overtime period to give Philadelphia a victory that evened a series they eventually won in six games.

There are no words more exciting to a hockey fan than "next goal wins"!

Mike Lalor and Claude Lemieux pile on to celebrate Brian Skrudland's overtime goal in Game 2 of the 1986 Stanley Cup Final at the Olympic Saddledome in Calgary. (Paul Bereswill/Hockey Hall of Fame)

INDEX

Bodnar, Gus, 108, 261

Boivin, Leo, 35

Bonk, Radek, 159

Bossy, Mike, 84, 87, 122, 169, 197

Boston Bruins, **18–19,** 143, 316, 317
   acquisition of Phil Esposito, 136–37
   franchise granted, 16–17
   rivalry with Montreal, 202
   Stanley Cup championships, 43, 46,
      153–55, **154–55,** 160, 162
   trading of Phil Esposito, 175–77
   and WHA merger, 285, 286

Boston Celtics, 130

Boston Garden, 17, 129–30, **131,** 317

Bouchard, Emile "Butch," 96

Bouchard, Joe, **233**

Boucher, Frank, 203, 255

Boudreau, Bruce, 276, 277

Bourne, Bob, 87

Bourque, Claude, **53**

Bourque, Ray, 59, **142,** 143–44, **144,** 177, 235,
   270, 293

Bower, Johnny, 24, 267, 311

Bowman, Scotty, 104, 172, 231, **240, 241,**
      282, 314
   and 1970s Canadiens, 61, 148, 202, 240
   and Detroit Red Wings, 151, 239–42
   and the Russian Five, 55

Bowman, Stan, 242, 314

Bowman, Suella, 239

Boyes, Brad, 157

Bozak, Tyler, 157

Bozek, Steve, 134

Brackenborough, John, **18**

Brewer, Carl, 101, 115

Bridgman, Mel, 243

Briere, Danny, 127

Broda, Walter "Turk," **127,** 267

Brodeur, Denis, 265

Brodeur, Martin, 83, 264–65, **265**

Brooklyn, New York, 17

Brooklyn Americans, 52

Brooks, Arthur, 13–14

Brown, Andy, 231

Brown, Jeff, 213

Bruneteau, Modere "Mud," 316

Bryzgalov, Ilya, 91

Buffalo Sabres, 159, 172, 240, 305

Buller, Hy, 108

Burchmore, Bill, 230

Bure, Pavel, 211, 213–14

Burke, Brian, 91–92, 180

Burns, Pat, 165, 258

Burrows, Alex, 316

Busniuk, Mike, 243, 244

C

Cafone, Pete, 218

Cain, Herb, 203

Calder, Frank, 8, **9,** 11, 1, 54, 125, 129–30, 169,
   192, 309

Calgary Flames, 163–65, 316

California Golden Seals, **304.** *See also*
   Oakland Seals

Campbell, Brian, 227

Campbell, Clarence, **51,** 54, 62, **89,** 112,
      191–92, **192,** 261
   and amateur draft, 65
   and expansion, 302
   and power-play rule, 216
   replacement with Ziegler, 294
   and Richard Riot, 88–90, 130, 193, 202
   and television, 73

Campbell, Colin, 146

Canada Cup, 199, 236, 260, 270

Canadian Broadcasting Corp. (CBC), 73–76

Carlyle, Randy, 91–92

Carolina Hurricanes, 286

Carr, Lorne, 125

Carrier, Roch, 88

Carson, Jimmy, 26

Carter, Jeff, 128

Casey, Jon, 237

Cashman, Wayne, 136, 175, 219

Central Red Army, 199

Chabot, Lorne, 95, 316

Chadwick, Bill, 68

Charron, Guy, 102

Cheevers, Gerry, 38, 231

Chelios, Chris, 208

Cherry, Don, 38, 175, 177, 202

Chevalier, Jack, 218

Chiarelli, Peter, 153

Chicago Blackhawks, 17, 46, 81–83, 135–37,
      208, 242, 266, 269

Chicago Bulls, 208

Chicago Stadium, 207–10, **209**

Chimera, Jason, 190

Churchill, Winston, 267

Churla, Shane, 208

Chuvalo, George, 267

Cincinnati Stingers, 285

Clancy, Frank "King," 62, **94,** 95, 130

Clark, Wendel, 165, 260, 267

Clarke, Bobby, 218–21, 243, **244,** 246

Cleghorn, Odie, 312, 315

Cleghorn, Sprague, 312, 315

Cleveland Barons, 285, **303**

Cloutier, Real, 104

Coffey, Paul, 56, 188, 193–95, **194,** 224, 253,
      291–93, **292, 293**

Cogliano, Andrew, 277

Colletti, Ned, 276

Collins, Kevin, 213

Colorado Avalanche, 143–44, 278, 286, 290

Colorado Rockies, 285

Commonwealth Stadium, 188

Conacher, Charlie, 266, 267, 309, 312, 314

Conacher, Lionel, 208, 312, 314

Conklin, Ty, 227

Conn Smythe Trophy, 112–13, **113**

Cook, Bill, 255

Cook, Frederick "Bun," 255

Cooke, Jack Kent, 286, 301–2

Cooper, Carson, **19**

Cooper, Joe, 106

Cournoyer, Yvan, 59

Craig, Dan, 178

Crashley, Bart, 66

Crosby, Sidney, 157, 225–27, 296–300,
      297, 298

Crozier, Roger, 60, 113

Curran, Rick, 289

Cusimano, Jerry, 181

Cusimano, Peter, 181

goals scored by, 83, 265, 270–72
    pulling for extra skater, 81–83, 147
    rules governing, 11, 95, 147, 187, 309
Godfrey, Warren, 24
Godynyuk, Alex, 163
Goldham, Bob, 181, 261
Goldup, Hank, 125
Goodfellow, Ebbie, 108, 125
Goring, Robert "Butch," 85, 87, 123, 246
Gorman, Tommy, 29
Gosselin, Mario, 185
Goyette, Phil, 66, 135
Graham, Elizabeth, 228
Graves, Adam, 213, 308
Gray, Terry, 35
Green, Nick, 140
Gretzky, Janet, 26, 184, 186
Gretzky, Paulina, 186
Gretzky, Phyllis, 186
Gretzky, Walter, 26, 119, 121, 186, 260
Gretzky, Wayne, 71, 118–21, **119, 120, 185,**
    188, 236, 238, 291, 296
    in 1993 conference final, 258–60, **259**
    final NHL game, 118, 119, 254
    Hart Trophy wins, 50, 118
    and "Miracle on Manchester," 133–34
    and New York Islanders, 123–24, 151,
        197
    in NHL All-Star Games, 104, 208
    and outdoor games, 188, 276
    scoring records, 40–42, **41,** 118, 121,
        184–86, 222–24, **223**
    trade to Los Angeles, 26–27, **27,** 91, 293
    in the World Hockey Association,
        284, 285
Griffiths, Frank, 285, 286
Guelph Biltmore Mad Hatters, 182
Guidolin, Bep, 52

H

Hadfield, Vic, 255, **256–57**
Hainsworth, George, 187
Hall, "Bad" Joe, 14
Hall, Glenn, 43, 113, 135, 138–41, **139, 140,**
    141, 208, 210, 231

Halward, Doug, 193
Hamilton Tigers, 16–17, 169, 201, 255
Hammarstrom, Inge, 274
Hammond, Col. John, 16–17
Hanlon, Glen, 40, 118
Hannan, Dave, 293
Hardwick, Huntington "Tack," 129–30, 208
Hardy, Mark, 134
Harkness, Ned, 103
Harmon, Glen, **31**
Harmon, Paddy, 208
Harper, Stephen, 93
Harris, Billy, 85
Harris, Ted, 59
Hart, Cecil, 50
Hart, Dr. David A., 50
Hart, Gene, 221
Hart Memorial Trophy, 50–51, **51**
Hartford Whalers, 27, 40, 42, 103–4, 165, 174,
    250–53, 286, 294
Hartnell, Scott, 127–28
Harvey, Doug, 74, 96, 98, 169, 215
Harwood, Mel, 125
Hasek, Dominik, 51, 156, 242
Hassard, Bobby, 75
Havlat, Martin, 156, 316
Hawley, Sandy, 184
Hay, Bill, **53**
Hayes, George, 181
Heatley, Dany, 156
Hebert, Sammy, 13–14
Hedberg, Anders, 148
Heller, Ott, 160
Henderson, Paul, 101, 267, 283
Henning, Lorne, 84
Henry, "Sugar" Jim, 76
Herbert, Jimmy "Sailor," **19**
Heritage Classic, 188–90, 227
Herron, Denis, 105
Hewitt, Foster, 48, 75, **77**
Hextall, Bryan, 211, 270, 274
Hextall, Bryan Jr., 270
Hextall, Dennis, 270
Hextall, Ron, 83, 113, 270–72, **271, 272,**
    289, 311

Hill, Al, 244
Hiller, Jonas, 277
Hillman, Larry, 115
Hitchman, Lionel, **18**
Hockey Hall of Fame, 121
Hockey Night in Canada, 75–76
Hockey skates, 79–80
Hockey sticks, 79–80
Hodge, Charlie, 35
Hodge, Ken, 135, 136, 219
Holik, Bobby, 282
Horner, George "Red," 47, 95
Horton, Nathan, 153, 154
Horton, Tim, 43, 267
Housley, Phil, 252–53
Houston Aeros, 103, 285
Howard, Jimmy, 157
Howatt, Garry, 85
Howe, Gordie, **25,** 101, 115, 121, 162, 254,
    278, 312
    Hart Trophy wins, 50, **51**
    1000th point, 24–25
    return to the NHL, 103–5, **105**
    and Ted Lindsay, 70–71
    and Wayne Gretzky, 40–42, 184, 186
    and the WHA, 40–42, 103, **104,** 283
Howe, Mark, 103, **104,** 312
Howe, Marty, 103, **104,** 105
Howe, Syd, 127
Howell, Harry, 43, 255
Hrudey, Kelly, 317
Hubick, Greg, 172
Huddy, Charlie, **196**
Huffman, Kerry, 289
Hughes, Pat, 134
Hull, Bobby, 105, **113,** 135–36, **140,** 208,
    210, 312
    in the WHA, 148, 193, 283, **285**
Hull, Brett, 145, 224, 312
Hunter, Dave, 133, 293
Hunter, Tim, **194**
Hyland, Harry, 14
Hynes, Jim, 228

Williams, Dave "Tiger," 37, **39**

Williams, Justin, 128

Wilson, Doug, 208

Wilson, Johnny, 138, 141

Wilson, Ross "Lefty," 104

Winnipeg Jets, 148, 285, 286, 294

Winnipeg Victorias, 4

Winter Classic, 225–27

Wintz, Lester M., 159

Wirtz, Bill, 207, 208, 285, 294

World Hockey Association (WHA), 40–42, 283–86, 294

Worsley, Lorne "Gump," **34,** 66

Y

Yawney, Trent, 208

Young, Wendell, 193

The Young and the Restless, 222

Yoyogi arena, 178, **179**

Yzerman, Steve, 55, **57,** 71, 150, 151, 278, **279**

Z

Zamboni ice resurfacer, 199

Zanussi, Joe, 177

Zednik, Richard, 190

Ziegler, John, 71, 186, 205, 283, 294, **295**

Zucker, Jason, 249

Zucker, Stanford, 129

ABOUT THE AUTHOR

SCOTT MORRISON has provided cogent and colourful hockey analysis since his start in 1979, reporting on the Maple Leafs and the NHL for the *Toronto Sun*. Reporting and providing analysis for Sportsnet and CBC Television and Radio, and making regular appearances across the sports-radio dial, he brings a trusted and measured voice to the hockey media landscape, twice serving as president of the Professional Hockey Writers' Association. He has written numerous hockey books, including *Hockey Night in Canada: By the Numbers and Hockey Night in Canada: My Greatest Day*. In 2006 he received the Hockey Hall of Fame's Elmer Ferguson Memorial Award. He currently serves as a commentator and feature reporter with the NHL on Sportsnet and *Hockey Night in Canada*. He lives in Toronto with his son Mark.